# WHEN THE DEVIL DARES YOUR KIDS

# When the Devil Dares
# Your Kids

*Protecting Your Children from Satanism,
Witchcraft, and the Occult*

Bob and Gretchen Passantino

Servant Publications
Ann Arbor, Michigan

Passages from Scripture used in this work are taken from *The New King James Bible.* Copyright © 1979 by Thomas Nelson, Inc., Publishers. Used by permission.

Vine Books is an imprint of Servant Publications especially designed to serve Evangelical Christians.

Published by Servant Publications
P.O. Box 8617
Ann Arbor, Michigan 48107

Cover design by Steve Eames
Cover illustration by Earl Keleny
Interior illustrations by James Douglas Adams

91 92 93 94 95  10 9 8 7 6 5 4 3 2 1

Printed in the United States of America

ISBN 0-89283-721-7

**Library of Congress Cataloging-in-Publication Data**

Passantino, Robert.
   When the devil dares your kids / protecting your children from satanism, witchcraft, and the occult / Bob and Gretchen Passantino.
     p.  cm.
   Includes bibliographical references and index.
   ISBN 0-89283-721-7
1. Devil–Controversial literature.  2. Satanism–Controversial literature.  3. Witchcraft–Controversial literature.  4. Occultism–Religious aspects–Christianity.  5. Family–Religious life.  6. Teenagers–Religious life.  I. Passantino, Gretchen.  II. Title.
BT981.P37  1991
261.5'1—dc20
                                      91-21332

# Contents

## ACKNOWLEDGMENTS

SPECIAL THANKS TO our Answers In Action staff and Board of Directors; the pastors and congregation of our church, Christ Lutheran in Costa Mesa, California; also to Mike Borland, Ell Clounch, Judy Hanson, Tracy Schreiber, Jon Trott; and to *Cornerstone* magazine.

# Foreword

SATANISM IS A MUCH-DISCUSSED but little understood topic these days. The sensationalism and hysteria, on the one hand, have served to frighten people needlessly, obscuring the truth regarding the threat of devil worship. Blind skepticism, on the other hand, has become an understandably common reaction from those who have tired of warnings of demons at every turn.

The aphorism of the late Christian apologist C.S. Lewis regarding satanism is timely—there are two grand mistakes people make when dealing with the devil: one, to ascribe to him too much power; and two, to deny his existence entirely. Bob and Gretchen Passantino have reached that elusive balance Lewis implied was so important by dealing with the reality of Satan and his kingdom without falling for the extremes.

It is refreshing when a biblically balanced, well-researched presentation of satanism becomes available. The Passantinos' reputation for superior work in investigative journalism is confirmed to those who read *When the Devil Dares Your Kids*. Whether readers are pastors, counselors, teachers, or concerned parents, the practical application of the following material will enable them to understand the dangers of devil worship.

If occult crime and the threat of satanism were only passing fads, there would be little need to explore in detail the nether world of the Prince of Darkness. However, the Scripture seems to imply that demonic activity and satanic deception will increase in the last days (2 Thessalonians 2:7-12; 1 Timothy 4:1-3). As such, the best protection is to know what the Bible teaches about the Adversary and his minions and to see the patterns of how he attempts to terrorize both Christians and non-believers in this present age. It is this balanced perspective that is needed, and it is this balanced perspective that *When the Devil Dares Your Kids* has delivered.

I am thankful for the freedom Christians have in knowing the power of our God over the power of Satan; and I rejoice that Bob and Gretchen Passantino have illustrated so carefully the victory of the believer over the wiles of the devil. It is for us, then, to lay hold of this victory by understanding the biblical truth of both the horror of satanism and the hope we have in Jesus Christ. As the writer to the Hebrews reminds us, "Since then the children shared in flesh and blood, he himself likewise also partook of the same that through death he might render powerless him who had the power of death, that is, the devil, and might deliver those who through fear of death were subject to slavery all their lives" (Hebrews 2:14-15).

> John Stewart
> Attorney at Law
> Host "Live in L.A."
> KKLA 99.5 FM, Los Angeles

# ONE

# Satan Wants Your Child

J AMES IS EIGHTEEN YEARS OLD. He could be anybody's teenager, the order clerk at your local MacDonald's, your daughter's boyfriend, or the neighbor's son who waters your lawn when you go on vacation. But James is also a satanist: "What I like about satanism is the power that it gives me. The people at school know I'm into it, and they don't mess with me.... It also gives me the feeling that I can do anything I put my mind to.... Why should I love anyone else? All people want is to get as much as they can. That's the way life is. Satanism has taught me about life. It helps you grow up."[1]

Satanism, witchcraft, and a wide variety of occultic or psychic activities are bombarding American youth as we approach the end of this century. Forget the guy with the pointy ears and tail in red flannel underwear. Forget the threatening horror of Dante's *Inferno*. Today's Satan is more likely to represent self interests and indulgence, the individual's way to "get back at" those who cross him.

Today's witchcraft isn't about ugly old women with warts who entice poor little children with houses built of gingerbread and spun sugar. Today's witch more likely has a fertile imagination, works in a highly skilled, technically oriented field, and has a deep love and appreciation for the natural world.

You also don't have to go to the seamy little house with the neon flashing palm outside to get your fortune read anymore. Now party rental fortune tellers are in the phone book, listed right along with clowns, magicians, and caterers.

## THE OCCULT WANTS YOUR CHILD

The occult appeal to young people is especially strong, not only because adolescence is inherently a time of emotional vulnerability and turmoil, but also because the occult is ever-present in the teenager's world.

Comic books, once reserved for the early reader, now are full-blown epic stories of supranormal lust, power, violence, and occultic power. "Heroes," like DC Comics' Madame Xanadu and Marvel Comics' Mephisto and Wolverine, use magic spells, nudity, sex, and deceit to vanquish their foes and restore "justice" to the world. Even the venerable All-American Superman must fight voodoo curses and black magic in a never-ending struggle for truth, justice, and the American way.

Parents used to complain about rock music because it was loud and the musicians had long hair. Now groups like Niggers with an Attitude, Field of the Nephalam, Venom, Poison, Slayer, 2 Live Crew, King Diamond, and the DeadKennedys "entertain" our children with vivid songs of rape, sado-masochism, torture, satanic worship, sexual mutilation, patricide, and cannibalism.

Our new electronic world, where our kids often feel more comfortable than we do, provides a rich diet of occult and anti-Christian influence. Hand-held and television video games like Simon's Quest and Blaster Master challenge players to kill the vampire, break the evil spell, vanquish the demons, and win through white magic. Even the relatively innocuous Paper Boy gives extra points for destroying the personal property of non-subscribers. Computer bulletin boards, the contemporary equivalent of pen pals, not only enable our kids to meet and "talk" with new friends across the country by phone computerlink, they also provide information and instruction in a vast array of occult arts. Today there are almost two hundred boards dedicated to occult, metaphysical, or nonChristian religious issues. Board games like *Philosopher's Stone, Spellbook & Candle, Dial-a-Guru, Paradise Isle,* and *Wonderland* reflect the contemporary mystique of the occult. VCRs make horror instantly and immediately accessible to even young children on videos such as the *Friday the 13th* and *Nightmare on Elm Street* movie series.

It used to be that occult bookstores were tucked into grimy corners of rundown neighborhoods and did most of their business by discreet mail order. Today's "metaphysical" bookstore is more likely located next to your local college campus, supports environmental issues, and sells incense, herbs, magical oils and potions, candles, and charms as well as books and tarot cards. Young teenage girls devour books like *Modern Magick, Drawing Down the Moon,* and *Modern Ritual Magic,* eagerly looking for the mysterious path to beauty, romance, and harmony with the natural world. For reading enjoyment, they might try witch Cerridwen Fallingstar's "posthumous autobiography," *The Heart of the Fire,* which is the story of one of her "previous lives" as a martyred witch in medieval Scotland.

Occultism has come out of the shadows and into the marketplace of American consumerism. Old parodies of Christianity which marked the English Hell-Fire Clubs of the eighteenth century have given way to splashy stage extravaganzas exalting the self as God. Most contemporary satanists don't believe in a personal devil and certainly don't believe they worship the fallen angel described in the Bible. They worship themselves. Most contemporary witches hold to the basic philosophy that all of existence is a divine, organic unity, experienced through the natural heartbeat of ritual. Contemporary witchcraft and religious satanism, while not directly destructive, are essentially relativistic in their ethics and subjective in their testing of truth. Therefore, their worldviews provide the ethical and philosophical justification for the development of destructive occultism, the term John Cooper uses "to cover all cases of groups that seek to work evil or perform sacrifices of living creatures."[2]

Teenagers who become victims of destructive occultism[3] go far beyond these basic philosophies to an out-of-control world of depravity, hunger for power, drug-induced distortion, and deadly devastation. As we approach the end of this century, we must be aware not only of the threat, but also how to protect our young people from such destruction.

## THE DECADE OF TURMOIL

Most teenage experimentation with the occult is fleeting, more a reflection of their curiosity and frustration with adolescence than an indication of deliberate rebellion against parents and God. The teenage years are a decade of uncertainty and frustration for most: too old to be treated like children, too immature to be trusted as adults. Most young people and their parents survive the teenage years intact.

But for some young people the occult becomes a compelling, controlling force in their lives. Through its power, imagined or real, the practitioner delves ever deeper into the dark recesses of his or her soul until ethical values, family unity, and trust in authority are discarded in favor of the occult's maxim, "Do what thou wilt!" Some young people fall into deep drug or alcohol abuse or both. Some run away from home. Some former honor roll students flunk school and drop out. Some commit petty crimes to support drug habits or proclaim their disdain for authority. Some lash out violently against anyone or anything that stands in their way. But inside, these kids share a lot of the same feelings most adolescents feel. Arthur Lyons' description of Sean Sellers, who brutally murdered a convenience store clerk and his own parents "in the name of Satan" reflects this common feeling of alienation: "Sellers had difficulty making friends, felt alienated and inadequate, unable to 'fit in.' His attempts to look bizarre and to shock with his blood drinking were blatant cries for attention. But the attention he got was not the kind he really wanted; it only increased his alienation. An outcast, he sought out the King of the Outcasts, the Prince of Darkness, as his source of strength. Since nobody liked Sean Sellers, Sean Sellers would hate them back."[4]

Sean's murder of his parents while they slept in their bed is beyond comprehension to most of us as parents. Yet, the needs he had, the emotions he experienced, and the occultic world he turned to for power are shared by teenagers in our own communities, often in our own families.

## THE LURE OF THE OCCULT

Children grow up within a family context. Each family has its own values, rules, religious beliefs, traditions, and interpersonal dynamics. Young children mostly mimic their parents' worldviews. It is only as they mature, are exposed to other ideas, and begin to think abstractly that they test those views, modify some, and reject others. In adolescence almost any view is open to intense scrutiny and sometimes ruthless rejection. Contemporary satanism, witchcraft, and other forms of occultism, certainly minority viewpoints, are often attractive simply because they are different. Take Laurel[5] as an example.

Laurel was attracted to the occult because it seemed to have more answers and more excitement than what she had always believed. She came from a traditional family with a mother and father who believed in God and asked a blessing before every meal (the few times they all managed to be at the table at the same time). Laurel used to go to Sunday school, and it was important to her father that the whole family go to church on Easter. Her mother went almost every week. Laurel stopped saying bedtime prayers when, at the age of eleven, she realized she was praying to the left-hand corner of her bedroom ceiling instead of to God, whoever he was.

Like most teenage girls, Laurel was worried about her looks. She knew her mother only said she was pretty because that's what mothers were supposed to say. She worried about acne and getting a car for graduation.

Laurel also worried about "big things," whether the earth was going to be destroyed by pollution, whether war in the Middle East would encourage a terrorist to blow up her neighborhood mall, and whether God, if there really was one, cared about her. But she couldn't find anybody to talk to about these fears. Mom was too distracted with her little brothers and sisters, Dad was always tired, and her friends were just confused.

Then Laurel got a new English teacher. Miss Grant was awesome! She used their literature classes to talk about all kinds of exciting ideas and beliefs—many she said came from "the old ways," from people centuries ago who understood the spiritual unity of all life, who respected nature. Miss Grant was a witch (she preferred the term "pagan"[6]). Soon Laurel was devouring every resource she could find on "the goddess movement." She started calling herself "Diana."

Laurel didn't stop with the relatively innocuous, mystical neo-paganism she learned from Miss Grant. Laurel learned about destructive spells as well as rites of harmony. She soon shared her boyfriend's devotion to the music of Slayer and King Diamond. The shift in her beliefs was subtle at first, her actions not really out of the ordinary.

However, she ended up in a locked hospital ward, recovering from what was either an accidental massive overdose of drugs or a botched suicide attempt. Her parents were desperate to know where they had failed. Laurel refused to talk.

## KIDS AT RISK

The kids at risk for destructive occult involvement come from a variety of backgrounds and families. They may have been raised in a Christian home, or they may never before have been exposed to anything spiritual. They may be from poor neighborhoods, but more likely they come from middle class, suburban families. Wealth doesn't protect them. Frequently their vulnerability is enhanced if their parents have divorced, but the traditional nuclear family is not sure protection. Despite their variant backgrounds, kids involved in occultism also tend to have much in common. The typical kid at risk orients his life in a destructive way. He sees everything and everyone in terms of either "this is a threat to me" or "this will benefit me." Some of the strongest risk factors for occultic involvement include feelings of extreme alienation, a morbid fascination with destructiveness, continued use of drugs or alcohol or both, difficulty in excelling within "the system," a sense of powerlessness, a need to control people and events, an above average intelligence and creativity, and an attraction to the mysterious.[7] Many involved teenagers' lives reflect a combination of these risk factors. Many of the factors are closely intertwined and co-dependent. Some of them are not necessarily unusual or even negative in themselves but can provide fertile ground for a growing involvement in the occult.

**Extreme Alienation.** Many kids seem particularly and severely affected by alienation. What starts at twelve or thirteen as typical adolescent rebellion and moodiness escalates rapidly into hostile rebellion. Arthur Lyons describes this alienation as it affected adult members of the Church of Satan: "A common lament was the lack of control these people felt over their own lives. Often, feelings of inadequacy were turned inside out, and at social gatherings the Satanists would sneer disdainfully at 'outsiders.' 'Normal' people were chumps, moronic conformists; they, the Satanists, were different."[8]

Most parents expect their teenagers to exhibit some healthy pulling away from their absolute control. We remember how our own parents seemingly lost all of their wisdom when we turned into teenagers and miraculously regained it when we reached our twenties. We understand that the gangly six-footer doesn't like to be called "Baby" anymore and the fashion-savvy mall prowler doesn't want to be hugged in public. In fact, as parents we can even admit to being proud when our teenagers show the maturity to make their own decisions instead of always running to us for assurance.

But when assertiveness turns to aggression, independence becomes secretiveness, and youthful exuberance twists into destructiveness, then there is genuine basis for concern. The seriously alienated teen chronically rejects any adult authority, not just that of parents, teachers, or leaders. This rejection is consistent and habitual, not sporadic or occasional. He or she displays an open disdain for authority and is much less likely to try to justify his or her rebellion. Most teenagers greet rules they don't like with "But it's not fair!" The openly rebellious teenager is more likely to respond to rules with "I don't care what's fair. I'll do what I want and you can't stop me!"

The severely alienated young person views the world as the enemy. He trusts no one. He puts himself first because, "Nobody cares about me more than me."

Severe alienation doesn't always take an aggressive form, although it is always destructive. Sometimes a teenager's rebellion causes him to be withdrawn, to separate himself from family, school, and even friends. Debbie was a young teenager whose alienation accelerated into drug abuse and occultism. This alienation comes through clearly in author David St. Clair's description of how Debbie's mother tried to intervene:

She sat on the sofa, beside her daughter, trying to appear calm, trying to appear as if she had the situation under control. "Debbie," she said evenly, "you've been acting very strange lately. You haven't been eating. You've lost weight. You walk around chilled to the bone all the time. You don't take care of yourself. Just look at your hair. You haven't even combed it this morning." She put her hand on the girl's shoulder. "What's wrong? Tell me."

The girl shrugged. "Nothin'. I'm okay."

"I think you should tell me," the woman insisted softly in her best decorator-salesroom tone. "What seems to be the trouble? Is it school?"

"Why do you care?" the girl answered. "What's the big deal all of a sudden? You never cared before."

"That's not true. I've always cared. You know that."

"I don't know nothin' like that," the girl said.

"Your father and I have always loved you. We've always cared."

"You've always been gone, that's what you've always been," Debbie responded. "You guys are never here. You guys don't love me. You guys don't give a [expletive deleted]* what happens to me."[9]

**Morbid Fascination.** The popularity of horror movies clearly reveals our society's preoccupation with the macabre. A scan of the movie pages of your local newspaper or a quick survey of your local video store's shelves will confirm American fascination with horror themes. In fact, *Magill's Survey of Cinema*'s on-line service lists more than two hundred horror movies between 1980 and the first part of 1991, twenty-two in 1990 alone. Titles like *Holy Blood, The Terror Within, Hell High, 976-EVIL,* and *Dance of the Damned,* all movies from 1989 and 1990, reflect the commercial and entertainment appeal of horror. Books, comics, magazines, music, and

---

* Throughout this book we have not always chosen to delete inappropriate vocabulary from quotations. Our desire is not to shock or offend you but to give you a realistic picture of the language used by those involved in the occult.

underground videos also provide ready sources for gore entertainment.

Many teenagers who become involved in destructive occultism surpass the typical interest in horror. Most, but not all, are male. These kids don't just rent an occasional horror video or listen to a few sado-masochistic songs on CD. Instead, they become morbidly fascinated with a wide range of destructive, violent, bloody, occulticly characterized materials. A destructive obsession can manifest itself in many ways.

Sean Sellers, the drug user and self-styled satanist who brutally murdered a convenience store clerk, his mother, and his stepfather, liked horror films because they "fulfilled his longing for the excitement he could find nowhere else.... He identified with the more carefree characters— such as vampires—who, no matter how sadistic, never had to answer to anyone."[10]

One young man watched the movies *Hellraiser* and *Hellbound (Hellraiser II)* fifty times and continually drew pictures of the horror figures in those movies. He thought one graphic and bloody scene of a live human head being pulled apart by acupuncture pins was one of the funniest things he had ever seen.

Another teen memorized the lyrics to every Slayer song. He then recited "appropriate" Slayer lines rather than carry on normal conversation. He alternated between threatening to kill his mother or commit suicide. His favorite lyrics were "Spill your blood/ Let it run on to me/ Take my hand and let go of your life/... You spilt the blood/ I have your soul!"[11]

Some teenagers who become serious disciples of the occult have an unnatural fascination with animal torture, mutilation, or killing. While the vast majority of pet deaths are attributable to traffic accidents or natural predators, sometimes teenagers (singly or in small groups) kill neighborhood pets, or sometimes even their own pets. The most common of these practices is to slit the dog or cat's throat, drain and save some of the blood, and then disembowel the animal. Sometimes the head is severed.

Many teenagers occasionally wonder what it would be like to kill an animal, and most seem enthusiastic about an occasional gore film containing simulated animal torture. But the youth dedicated to occultic destruction often moves progressively toward actual animal sacrifice. This is especially so if the teenager is learning from someone who has already killed animals.

Kirsten first participated in an animal sacrifice by accident. She and her best friend were learning satanic rites from the friend's boyfriend. He had told them that nothing compared to the experience of drugs and ritual combined. Kirsten didn't believe in Satan, but her few experiences with drugs had been a good escape. It wasn't until the ritual was almost over that she realized Dave planned to kill the cat he had secured to the campsite's cement barbecue stand, which he used as an altar. She would have left, except she didn't want to be laughed at, and it wasn't really that bad since she was a little out of it from the drugs anyway. It was kind of like watching a TV show.

Kirsten didn't think about it much after that. But one night, as she watched a King Diamond video and petted her cat, stroking it softly under its neck, she cried.

**Drug and Alcohol Use.** More than half of American teenagers have experimented with illegal drug or alcohol use. Drug and alcohol use among high school dropouts is chronic and severe. Alcohol use, either in "bingeing" (drinking a lot of alcohol at one time) or daily use, has remained fairly constant even among teenagers who remain in school. In 1982, fully 66 percent of high school seniors admitted having used an illicit drug at least once, and although that percentage declined to 47.9 percent in 1990, it still indicates a rampant epidemic among American young people.[12] Chances are some of the young people you know have personally abused either drugs or alcohol at some time. Most young experimenters with drugs and alcohol cite peer pressure, a desire for emotional escape, a desire to feel a "thrill," and curiosity as the common reasons for trying drugs or abusing alcohol.

The kid at risk for occult involvement typically lists these reasons but adds others unique to his or her own vulnerabilities. Beyond the experimentation stage, such young people see drug and alcohol use as a way to express their alienation from others. It is a solitary experience conducive to absorption with oneself. The alteration of one's sensory perceptions and one's mental activity is closely identified with occultic, ritualistic practice. While the hippies of the sixties talked about the spiritual properties of drug experiences, today's teenage drug user is more likely to correlate his drug use with the spiritual power of ritualism. Solitary or self-styled occultists usually mix drug use and ritualism to enhance both experiences, increasing the mystery of each.[13] Those practicing occultism with friends or in some sort of group structure find that drug use increases the unity of the group. The symbolic defiance of authority associated with drug use is very important to young people at risk. Often drug and alcohol use is loosely justified by labeling parents as hypocrites, who condemn their children's drug use as they down martinis and pop pills at bedtime.

Continued drug and alcohol use can be an indicator of an extra vulnerability to destructive occult involvement. While continued drug use is in itself highly destructive physically, emotionally, and spiritually, it also negatively impacts daily living ability. The teenager who is an active user is more likely to get bad grades, to be a school discipline problem, to break the law (driving under the influence, breaking and entering, theft, as examples), to drop out of school, to suffer frequent illness and malnutrition, and is less likely to be able to hold a job. As the downward spiral accelerates, the teenager is more likely to look increasingly to his or her occult involvement as a possible way to arrest the disintegration of his life, or at least to make the disintegration more ritualized and less painful.

Tony thought his friend's preoccupation with ritual magick[14] was interesting but without much substance. He didn't think there was any genuine supernatural power in Greg's incantations, but they did impress their girlfriends, and if he really got into it, the goose bumps he experienced reminded him of a how a good suspense movie affected him. One night at a ritual Tony's girlfriend shared some acid her older sister had given her. Tony was not a big drug user, but he wasn't going to refuse in front of Heather. The acid and the ritual together provided the most exciting mind experience Tony ever had.

Over the next few months both his ritual practice and his drug use escalated together. He spent more and more time in his own private world of strange sensations and bizarre experiences.

By June he had flunked most of his classes, been dumped by Heather, and lost his car in a spectacular one-car collision with a tree that he could have sworn moved into his path without warning. Tony sat alone in the county jail, awaiting arraignment on charges stemming from a string of house burglaries—how else could he buy enough drugs? His magick had run out.

**Difficulty with "the System."** Closely related to the severe alienation some young people experience is extreme difficulty in excelling within standard social and academic structures. A vulnerable teenager may have one or more clearly diagnosed learning disabilities, or may be unsuccessful at learning within a traditional school setting. Many have been labeled as "problem" or "bad" kids from early grades.[15] Jimmy Troiano, who was heavily involved in drugs and occultism, was intelligent but couldn't perform in school. When he was a tenth grader his parents received a registered letter from the school board. "Their son was incorrigible. Their son wasn't doing himself any good at high school. Their son wasn't doing anybody else any good at high school either. It was the board's recommendation that Jimmy be sent to a special school."[16]

American primary and secondary education is structurally rigid, benefitting those who can learn in large group settings, from lectures and other auditory input, and with standardized testing methods. The student who learns best by doing, or by visual stimulation, or in individual tutorial settings is at a distinct disadvantage. The student with a thousand questions is more likely to be categorized as rebellious or insolent than curious. The student who has difficulty expressing himself in words, but who can build intricate scale models will flunk essay tests. The talkative student whose wit and imitative skill makes him the life of the party and a future successful high-power salesman is branded in the schoolroom as a disruptive clown. Most teenagers who learn differently conform enough to make it through the system, but some, for a variety of reasons, don't. These teenagers are at risk for destructive occult involvement. Perhaps they're tired of trying, or their parents aren't supportive, or they just can't cope, or they are fed up with always doing things somebody else's way. For whatever reason, they have given up on the system and become almost proud that they're labeled "bad kids."

**Sense of Powerlessness.** Every teenager experiences feelings of powerlessness. Frustration mounts for the teenager whose body is in awkward adolescence; whose expensive tastes are thwarted by a minimum wage, part-time job; whose time is controlled by parents and teachers; and who is faced, for the first time, with the immensity of the world and the insignificance of his or her own life.

Actually, this feeling can be normal and constructive. A

teenager is on the brink of adulthood and needs to trade the egocentrism of childhood for the extroversion of adulthood. Most of us remember (or have used on our own children) the mother's familiar refrain, "The world doesn't revolve around you!" Children need to be reminded of this frequently, and teenagers begin to believe and understand it as they mature.

Teenagers also need to learn that no individual outside of God is all-powerful. This is an important but scary dose of reality. Mommy can't fix all hurts with a kiss, Daddy's not always there for protection, and bad things sometimes happen even if you're good. Teenagers begin to learn, through the loss of a grandparent to old age, a neighbor to cancer, or a classmate to a car crash, that death is more than a plot device on television.

But a healthy perspective on one's place in the universe can be twisted into a destructive fear that can compel a teenager into destructive behavior. Very often the person who feels desperate for power over his own life lashes out at those he thinks are trying to control him. Barry is a good example: "Barry Braeseke and his father, Floyd, were not getting along. Quite often their arguments would escalate into physical confrontations. After one such fight, Barry decided to find a solution to his problem. He shared his frustration with his friends and explained that his life would be a lot simpler without his father around."[17] Barry killed his father, mother, and grandfather.

Destructive occultism can propel abnormally frustrated teenagers into the same kind of violence, an attack on those they believe are keeping them powerless. Sean Sellers was frustrated that his mother and stepfather tried to control his life, telling him when to be home, suspecting him of drug abuse (he happened to be guilty), and, worst of all, criticizing his girlfriend. "And the more Sean's mind toyed with the idea of life without family problems, without disapproval, the more vivid the idea became.... Sometimes he wished they weren't alive."[18] He shot them to death in their bed during a satanic blood ritual.

**The Need to Control.** The flip side of a sense of powerlessness is the need to control one's own life and the lives of others. Control is evidence that you are not powerless, that you are not subject to someone else's control. A desire to exert control over one's self is common to almost all teenagers, while only some seem to have a need to control others.

Healthy growth in this area leads to teenagers learning to make good decisions concerning how they spend their time, their commitment to education, their choice of mature, responsible friends, and their ability to resist peer pressure and stand up for their convictions. Any control they exert over others in this way encourages responsible behavior and healthy relationships.

A teenager with a destructive drive for control uses manipulation, deceit, physical intimidation, or violence, or a combination. This often manifests itself in occultic practices to enhance, illustrate, or increase one's power over himself and others. Remember James from the beginning of our chapter? He said, "What I like about satanism is the power it gives me. The people at school know I'm into it, and they don't mess with me.... It also gives me the feeling that I can do anything I put my mind to."[19]

*Power* and *control* are the two words we hear most often in connection with destructive occultism. Self-styled destructive witches and satanists tell us they like the power, or they need control, or they feel invincible because they have such power. Phil is a satanist who boldly admits to the power lure of satanism: "If you know anything about satanism, you know it's about one thing—power. Power over yourself, power over others, power over your surroundings. How many people take that power?"[20]

Ritualism and mystery heighten the sense of growing power occultists feel: they achieve "a satisfying sense of mastery over their own fates by the practice of ritual magic."[21] Richard Cavendish sees this need for control in those he calls "black magicians": "The driving force behind black magic is hunger for power.... Carried to its furthest extreme, the black magician's ambition is to wield supreme power over the entire universe, to make himself a god.... It is a titanic attempt to exalt the stature of man, to put man in the place which religious thought reserves for God."[22]

Occult mail order catalogs constantly advertise their merchandise's ability to enhance one's power over others or control of the future. From occult aphrodisiacs through wishing candles, prosperity charms, and potions to zodiac charts, the claim is the same: use this product, perform this ritual, and *get what you want. The Satanic Bible* commands "Hate your enemies with a whole heart, and if a man smite you on one cheek, SMASH him on the other!; smite him hip and thigh, for self-preservation is the highest law!"[23] The arrogance of an insatiable thirst for power is echoed when the same book urges satanists to "come forth in splendor proclaiming, 'I AM A SATANIST! BOW DOWN, FOR I AM THE HIGHEST EMBODIMENT OF HUMAN LIFE!'"[24]

**Intelligence and Creativity.** Remember how proud you were as a new parent when your baby sat up early, started walking at nine months, or said his first words at one year old? Remember the anxiety you felt as your child began kindergarten, and then your pride as you saw him excel in "reading readiness"? All parents want their children to develop their intellectual capacity, and pride over their academic accomplishments is natural.

But for some parents, the intelligence, creativity, and curiosity they encouraged when their children were young seem to be a curse as their clever, imaginative teenagers skillfully indulge in destructive occultism, drug and alcohol abuse, and lawlessness. Could there be some correlation?

"'You are out of your mind, Paul!' he shouted. 'Your great learning is driving you insane!'" Governor Festus' amateur misdiagnosis of the Apostle Paul is only one example of people who see a link between intelligence and mental or emotional instability. Actually, there is no statistical evidence to support a correlation between intelligence and mental illness.

One parent of a teen out of control struggled with this idea for months, and finally expressed his resolution to us: "Danny's being smart didn't make him into a bad kid, but it made him a *smart* bad kid!" On the other hand, lack of education or intelligence doesn't cause "bad" behavior either. White collar crime is just as criminal as blue collar crime.

However, enjoyment of an intricate system of ritual, a complex magical world view, and myth and mysticism can be enhanced by intelligence and creativity. Contemporary pagans, or witches, like Laurel's English teacher, typically display an intelligent facility with language, technology, and literature. Margot Adler, author of the most widely read and respected analysis of contemporary witchcraft, notes, "Most of those I talked to were highly imaginative, were avid readers of science fiction, and tended to put their ideals and fantasies in as many future settings as past ones."[25] Adler thinks they are often pegged as "oddballs" because, as they describe themselves, they tend to be "unenculturated, solitary, creative thinkers," "on the leading edge." One pagan explains why so many computer professionals are associated with paganism by stating that "the only correlation is intelligence."[26] Peter, an English magical practitioner, says that ritual magic "has improved his self-esteem, made his dreams more vivid and his spiritual and imaginative life more intense, and enhanced his creativity."[27] However, sometimes enhancement of one's creativity and intelligence can be used for violent, destructive, and antisocial ends by a teenager at risk.

Couple a troubled teenager's destructiveness with intelligence and creativity, and the power of his dysfunctional behavior can explode, harming himself, his family, and those around him. The horror becomes real, the violence shocking, and the teenager's cruelty sickening. Not every teenage occultic dabbler becomes a satanic killer like Sean Sellers; in fact most don't. "Occasionally, however, the symbolism of evil can become enmeshed with antisocial rage and psychotic impulses, and become a rationalization for violence."[28]

Eric had always had problems, and family members traced them back to when his father, a lifelong heroin addict, abandoned his family when Eric was in first grade. His family did everything they could to make up for it, but by junior high Eric was labeled "antisocial."

One day he put his creativity to use. Late that afternoon a teacher found Eric's victim, a kid who had called Eric a bad name. Eric had hanged him from the gym's skylight with an intricate system of ropes and knots. The tension in the rope around his neck was exactly calculated to keep him alive, but almost strangled.

**Attracted by the Mysterious.** It is important to remember that this factor is not exclusive to occult practitioners. Curiosity, inquisitiveness, and wonder are inherently human characteristics. The scientist, inventor, mystery writer, journalist, and stage magician all benefit from human curiosity about the unknown. Inquisitiveness fuels learning. It is the greatest motivator for the young student, and helps the high schooler commit to career goals.

Attraction to the mysterious is also an integral part of most religious practices throughout history and around the world. The use of masks or robes, ritualized vocabulary, liturgy, and initiation enhance an aura of religious mystery. In the Judeo-Christian heritage, mystery is one of the reminders that God is qualitatively different from his creation, that he is the one to be worshipped, we are the ones who worship. In fact, *mystery* is used frequently in the Bible, often in reference to teachings or ideas the natural man ordinarily would consider paradoxical or difficult to believe. Some theologians believe that an appreciation of the mysterious is part of the spiritual hunger of the natural human being for God.

Magic and ritual have a long association with the mysterious. Luhrmann says that people turn to ritual magic in a search "for powerful emotional and imaginative religious experience." This lure of the mysterious is a compelling force. Luhrmann argues, "The imaginative attraction of magic lies in its talk of ancient tradition, old ways, unknown powers buried in the earth, strange forces accessible to the gifted, and in the appeal of the forbidden, mysterious and beyond."[29]

The teenager propelled on a collision course with destructive ritualism has a heightened intensity regarding the mysterious. He or she will devour anything relating to the mysterious available on video, in books, magazines, comic books, and in music. Complicated magical runes will fascinate him for hours. Cryptic messages designed into heavy metal rock album covers will absorb her attention for hours. The small teenage group of self-styled witches will take increasingly large doses of drugs to sustain them through increasingly complex and bizarre rituals, their amateur attempt to pierce the cloak of mystery shrouding ultimate enlightenment. Curiosity metamorphizes into compulsion.

## KNOW THE RISK

Teenagers are at the most exciting and also the most dangerous time of their lives. Their futures are almost unrestricted, if they survive to adulthood. They are developing the maturity and knowledge to plan their careers, if they don't end up in prison. They have the strength and health of youth, if they don't destroy themselves through drug and alcohol use. They have the maturity to make religious commitments of their own, if they aren't destroyed by spiritual destructiveness. As John Cooper has observed so accurately: "Satanism blesses and encourages the expression of all that is natural to adolescent development—rebellion, defiance, and specialness—yet it lacks a positive, rational framework and totally disregards relational, social, and religious boundaries and values."[30]

As parents we have the bittersweet experience of letting go of our children as they approach adulthood. When our children seem propelled to self destruction, we need solid information, sound advice, and practical principles to rescue them, sometimes from themselves.

# TWO

# Satanism

JONATHAN CANTER, AT AGE NINETEEN, stabbed his mother forty times in the chest, stomach, and back and almost severed her left hand in honor of Satan. He prayed over her body, "Lord Satan, thou knowest I have stricken this woman from the earth, I have slain the womb from which I was born. I have ended her reign of desecration of my mind; she is no longer of me, but only a simple serpent on a lower plane."[1]

On the other hand, another satanist, rock singer King Diamond, is offended when people try to link such gore to his "religion": "Some people think that people who call themselves *satanists* are really like that, drinking the blood of babies and that sort of thing.... When I use the word *Satan,* it doesn't stand for a guy with horns. To me, that word means the powers of the unknown, the powers of darkness. It's not just power, it's *powers*—and there's a big difference. I don't believe in heaven, and I don't believe in hell as a place with flames where people are burning and having eternal pain. I don't believe in that at all. I believe in a place I call 'beyond.'"[2]

Contemporary satanists defy easy identification or classification. We have talked to some satanists who seemed rational, friendly, and polite, and who explained that to them satanism is a belief in the supremacy of the self, without, of course, violating anyone else's rights.

One former satanist explained to us that he and his friends had practiced satanism because it heightened their drug and sex experiences. He and his friends had spent more time thinking about sex and drugs than about Satan.

But Tommy Sullivan, fourteen, made a pact with Satan in order to obtain "the most extreme of all magical powers" in exchange for "killing many Christian followers who are serious in their beliefs."[3] Shortly after Christmas, 1987, Tommy repeatedly sang a song, his father said, "about blood and killing your mother."[4] On January 9, 1988 he stabbed his mother at least twelve times, killing her, and then set fire to his house in an unsuccessful attempt to kill his father and brother. He was found later, slumped on a bloody snowbank, dead from self-inflicted slashes to his wrists and neck.

Who are the real satanists? How dangerous is satanism? Where did it come from, where is it going, and how can we protect our loved ones from its insidious enticement?

## THE REAL SATANIST

Contemporary satanism is a form of religious belief and expression holding to the worship of Satan, whether Satan is defined as a supernatural person, a deity, a devil, a supernatural force, a natural force, an innate human force, or, most commonly, the self.

**Satanism through the Ages.** Satanism is a generic term covering a variety of beliefs and historical phenomena. Most people think of the Bible as the oldest source concerning satanism. However, the term satanism does not appear in the Bible.

*What the Bible Says.* Instead of using the term satanism, the Bible condemns occultism, particularly kinds of belief (idol worship), practice (witchcraft, divination, necromancy, and astrology), and persons (blasphemers, mediums, magicians, priests of pagan religions, and antichrists).

The Bible teaches that one of God's angels, Lucifer ("Light Bearer"),[5] rebelled against God and convinced some of the angels to join his rebellion.[6] The Bible associates many names with Lucifer after his fall, including Satan.[7] The Bible assumes that Satan and the other fallen angels, or demons, are persons possessing individual wills and intellect. Satan is not equal and opposite to God or to Jesus Christ. The Bible clearly teaches that God alone is all-powerful[8] and uncreated.[9] Satan is a creature, a spirit, with limited power and influence, and who eventually will be banished to eternal torment along with the other fallen angels and unrepentant humans.[10]

Occult activities are denounced by the Bible in the both the Old Testament[11] and the New Testament.[12] Many of these activities are found today in the New Age Movement and other psychic organizations, human potential movement groups, and older religious groups such as Theosophy, the Association for Research and Enlightenment, and the spiritualists. Individuals who reject the biblical God, worshipping and serving false gods or idols, are denounced by the Bible and loosely associated with Satan, the "father of lies."[13]

Today's typical teenage self-styled satanist, while certainly rejecting the biblical message, does not understand or consider himself or herself to be practicing ancient worship of the devil as described by the Bible.

*What History Says.* There is no unbroken chain of satanic worship through the centuries from biblical times to today. Rather, we can trace elements of contemporary satanism through two historical trends: rivalry with Christianity and anti-morality.

The Christian church always affirmed the biblical teaching that Satan was limited in his power and activity by the Almighty. However, throughout church history there have been sects and cults of Christianity whose teachings have been *dualistic* in nature. That is, they believed that all of existence is composed of equal and opposite characteristics: God and Satan, male and female, good and evil, light and dark. Satan was seen as an equal but opposite of God, and good could not exist without evil. Cavendish summarizes the importance of this view to the later development of contemporary satanism: "The early development of Satanist theory was influenced by widespread acceptance of dualism, the belief that opposing gods of good and evil exist independently of each other. By itself dualism does not imply devil-worship, but it creates a favourable background for it. There is more incentive to enlist in the Devil's ranks if he is on more or less equal terms with God than if he is subordinate to God and acts only on God's sufferance, as in orthodox Christian belief."[14] Often these sects and cults parodied the vocabulary, ceremonies, and teachings of orthodoxy.[15] They went beyond affirming dualism to rejecting orthodox Christianity.

Another kind of rivalry arose within folk groups reacting against the Christian church's intolerance of indigenous religions or folkways. Religious superstitions and nature religions abounded in the Western world of the Medieval and Renaissance Church. Examples of Church condemnation and persecution of those it considered "idolatrous" are scattered through the history and geography of the Western world.

A third kind of rivalry came from social classes that believed they were oppressed either directly by the Church, or by higher classes operating with the Church's power and blessing. It is from this kind of rivalry that the earliest traces of "Devil worship" are recorded. We probably will never know how much of what is recorded is historically accurate and how much was surmised or embellished by zealous clerics, but this genre is our source for the "Black Mass," the "unholy kiss," the holiday ceremonies of the sabbat and the esbat, and other features borrowed into contemporary satanism. This period of history marked the transformation of Satan from the serpent of Genesis to the lustful goat:

> Satan had begun to change in appearance by the time of the first mass executions for witchcraft in the fifteenth century. He had shed his snakeskin and had grown a coat of fur and horns. He had become hoofed and shaggy. He had become Pan and Priapus and Cernunnos and Loki and Odin and Thor and Dionysus and Isis and Diana. He had become the god of fertility and abundance and lust. He was the lascivious goat, the mysterious black ram. He was all of nature and indeed life itself to the peasant, who had often lived on the verge of starvation due to the crushing taxes of the feudal aristocracy. He was sex, and since to the peasant sex was identical to creation itself, and was one of the few pleasures not open to taxation, he was their god.[16]

Anti-morality is foundational to contemporary satanism and can be found among various groups in history. Geoffrey Ashe's definitive book on the subject, *Do What You Will: A History of Anti-Morality*, chronicles this history. "Do What You Will" is one of the most popular phrases borrowed by both satanist and witch, and often erroneously said to originate with Aleister Crowley.[17] It actually came from Francois Rabelais in 1535, as the motto for his imaginary community of sensual delight, Thélème. Rabelais was a French Franciscan priest and later Benedictine monk who threw off religious convention in his quest for earthly pleasures. Thélème was the counter-mirror of St. Augustine's City of God, and of the monasteries and convents of Rabelais' day: "All their life was regulated not by laws, statutes, or rules, but according to their free will and pleasure. They rose from bed when they pleased, and drank, ate, worked and slept when the fancy seized them. Nobody worked them; nobody compelled them either to eat or to drink, or to do anything else whatever.... In their rules was only one clause: DO WHAT YOU WILL."[18]

Thélème's escape from law did not include deliberate devil worship or satanic ritual. It did, however, both parody the Church and set the stage for later anti-morality developments, including the Monks of Medmenham, the Hell-Fire Clubs of the eighteenth and nineteenth centuries in England, and the various elitist pleasure clubs of Edmund Curll, Sir Francis Dashwood, and John Montague (the Earl of Sandwich). These clubs were open only to select aristocrats who had flung off their cloaks of religious ignorance and embraced the atheistic humanism of the Enlightenment. Primary to the clubs' functions was blasphemy of the old, out-moded religion of Christianity. The clubs also offered gambling, drinking, lavish banquets, and sexual orgies; "in other words, spitting in the eye of the Church and the official morality it stood for."[19] This attitude is parallel to that of contemporary satanists described below.

The two separate historical lines of a religious dualistic rivalry with Christianity and an anti-religious anti-morality were borrowed, combined, added to Aleister Crowley's own brand of occultism, and adopted in contemporary satanism.[20]

**Satanism Today.** Contrary to popular tabloid sensationalism, contemporary satanism is not a monolithic, rigid religious system with the far-reaching tentacles of a worldwide conspiracy. If satanism is the religion of the Self, then it is not surprising that it has almost as many varieties as practitioners. Arthur Lyons defines a satanist as "... anyone who sincerely describes himself as a worshiper of the Christian

Devil, *whatever he perceives that to mean....* What it does mean to the individual worshiper can vary drastically. Because many modern groups have picked up their practices from horror movies or fictional accounts of Black Masses, there is a great latitude among modern cults in both practice and belief."[21]

Detective Sandi Gallant notes the varieties of satanic beliefs, stating that organized satanic groups "... have set up their group to worship Satan in some particular form. The form is usually devised by the group itself, and it may differ from one group to another.... They may look upon Satan in different ways, too."[22]

While we cannot define contemporary satanism with one rigid system of dogma, we can observe some underlying beliefs held in common by *most* satanists.

*The God of Self.* First, most satanism is self-oriented. That is, the fulfillment, indulgence, satisfaction, or power of the individual is the ultimate goal of all belief, practice, and life. *The Nine Satanic Statements* of Anton LaVey's Church of Satan illustrate this absorption with the self:

1. Satan represents indulgence, instead of abstinence!
2. Satan represents vital existence, instead of spiritual pipe dreams!
3. Satan represents undefiled wisdom, instead of hypocritical self-deceit!
4. Satan represents kindness to those who deserve it, instead of love wasted on ingrates!
5. Satan represents vengeance, instead of turning the other cheek!
6. Satan represents responsibility to the responsible, instead of concern for psychic vampires!
7. Satan represents man as just another animal, sometimes better, more often worse than those that walk on all fours, who, because of his "divine spiritual and intel-

lectual development," has become the most vicious animal of all!

8. Satan represents all of the so-called sins, as they all lead to physical, mental, or emotional gratification!

9. Satan has been the best friend the church has ever had, as he has kept it in business all these years![23]

*The Unity of Good and Bad.* Second, most satanists agree that ethics are relative. That is, right and wrong are not absolute, but are determined by the individual. Some satanists, in fact, believe that right and wrong do not represent opposites, but instead a duality of reality. "Bad" and "good" are halves of one whole. Cavendish notes,

> There are a few convinced Satanists here and there in the world, but for most modern magicians the Enemy of Christendom cannot exist. According to occult theory, there are forces and intelligences, whether inside or outside the magician, which are conventionally condemned as evil, but a god who is entirely evil is as inconceivable as a god who is entirely good. The true God, the One, is the totality of everything, containing all good and all evil, and reconciling all opposites.... Where the churches, which brought the Devil to life in the first place, condemn his worship as the adoration of evil, magicians despise it as a failure to understand the true nature of the universe.[24]

Christian author John Cooper notes the logical relationship between moral relativism (ethics determined by culture, society, or personal inclination) and a rejection of ethics grounded in a just God: "A short and inevitable path leads from the belief in God's demise, as the arbiter of values, to the worship of sensual materialism represented by Satanism."[25]

Satanism so blurs the distinction between good and bad that right and wrong, good and bad, become meaningless terms. Nothing is all bad, nothing is all good. It is typical, then, when a contemporary teenage satanist seems to get a perverse pleasure out of destruction, torture, and death. The ancient biblical book of Isaiah gives warning that sounds directed at today's anti-moralist satanists: "Woe to those who call evil good, and good evil; Who put darkness for light, and light for darkness; Who put bitter for sweet, and sweet for bitter! Woe to those who are wise in their own eyes, And prudent in their own sight!"[26]

*Rejection of Christianity.* Remember when you were young and Sunday mornings you got dragged out of bed so the family could go to church? Today's typical teenager doesn't have that kind of memory. Most teenagers never or rarely go to church. In fact, the majority of Americans under thirty years old have had no regular church attendence at any time in their lives. They have little or no familiarity with Christianity or church worship.

Most teenagers learn about Christianity from the entertainment media. Television situation comedies teach them that pastors are buffoons, religious people are psychotic, and Christians hallucinate. Movies like *The Exorcist III* teach teenagers that religion is weak in the face of evil, faith is superstition, and Christians are fools. Contemporary music ignores religion, unless it perverts it with lyrics about masturbating with a crucifix, enjoying sex like a virgin (Mary), or drinking urine out of a communion chalice. No wonder most young people reject what they think is Christianity! Satanists project their rejection into the self-indulgent parodies of satanic ritual.

Contemporary American satanism rejects Christianity with all of its beliefs, practices, and commitments, but its rejection is not far removed from the basic rejection we find in the contemporary world in which we live. Most contemporary satanists don't believe in the Christian God or the biblical depiction of Satan. The idea of an all-evil Devil is as

ridiculous to a satanist as the idea of an all-good God. Cavendish notes, "People who worship the Devil do not regard
him as evil. To the satanist the supernatural being who is the
Enemy of Christendom is a good and benevolent god. But
the word 'good,' applied to the Devil by his followers, does
not carry its Christian or conventional meanings. Satanists
believe that what Christians call good is really evil, and vice
versa, though there is an ambivalence of attitude in satanism, as in black magic, a perverse pleasure in doing things
which are felt to be evil combined with a conviction that
doing these things is really virtuous."[27]

Christianity is often depicted as the religion of restriction,
denial of self, and law. Satanists' rejection of Christianity is
symbolic of their commitment to self-indulgence. Skeptical
occult investigators Shawn Carlson and Gerald Larue note,
"Satanists maintain that Christianity teaches abstinence
instead of indulgence, and therefore, in order to get close to
this force one must do many things that Christianity discour-
ages or even defines as sins."[28]

This analogous system runs through most satanic rituals,
artifacts, and symbols. The inverted cross is a well-known
satanic symbol and the Lord's Prayer is often recited backward in satanic rituals. To the typical satanist, Christianity is
oppressive and self-denying, satanism is freeing and self-
indulging.

*Power through Action.* Power is the ultimate promise and goal
of contemporary satanism. Linda Blood, a former member
of a satanic church, the Temple of Set, described satanism as
"a shortcut to power, and the only thing you have to do is
stick your neck out."[29] Cooper reminds us, "Participation in
deviant occultism becomes a path for dealing with life's
problems and expressing one's identity."[30] Satanic power
enables the satanist to achieve any personal goal through a
prescribed set of activities—rituals, magick, spells, or sacrifices.

*Rituals.* Rituals can be held alone, with a few other people, or in a large group. Many contemporary satanists learn satanism by themselves and improvise their activities as they go along, borrowing from movies, music, magazines, and books. Consequently, rituals vary widely from satanist to satanist, group to group.

Most rituals involve focusing power, identifying power, expressing a need, and accepting the power to meet that need. Often disparaging allusions to Christianity and Christian symbols are used, although "rituals today are more apt to be influenced by horror movies and Stephen King novels, and accompanied by the strains of heavy metal music rather than Church hymns sung backward."[31]

Rituals may appear relatively innocuous, almost like kids playing pretend, reciting strange words and making awkward motions in the hope that "something" will happen. Destructive occultists, on the other hand, may conduct openly sinister rituals including "homosexuality, promiscuous heterosexuality, alcohol and drug abuse, killing and mutilating animals, and... murder."[32]

*Magick.* Magick is defined, admittedly vaguely, by Anton LaVey in *The Satanic Bible* as "The change in situations or events in accordance with one's will, which would, using normally accepted methods, be unchangeable.... There is no difference between 'White' and 'Black' magic except in the smug hypocrisy, guilt-ridden righteousness and self-deceit of the 'White' magician himself."[33] LaVey goes on to classify magick in two categories, ritual (ceremonial) and manipulative. According to LaVey, ritual magick involves a formal ceremony, usually a particular site set apart for ritual magick and a specific time. He describes manipulative magic as "the wile and guile obtained through various devices and contrived situations, which when utilized can create 'change, in accordance with one's will.'"[34]

Most satanists, especially self-styled satanists who have

learned from *The Satanic Bible*, accept this understanding of magick and make it more specific by the way they individually use the satanic props and rituals to obtain their goals through means that are not normal.

Aleister Crowley, claimed by many satanists (and many witches) as an important forerunner, defined magick as the art of causing change in conformity with will. Crowley popularized spelling magic with a "k" to differentiate it from parlor tricks. Biographer Kenneth Grant explained that using the old English spelling "indicates the precise nature of the Current [power] which Therion (Crowley) embodied and transmitted."[35]

*Spells.* Spells, or incantations, are the particular words performed with the actions and props of rituals in order to practice magick. *An Encyclopaedia of Occultism* defines a spell as "a written or spoken formula of words supposed to be capable of magical effects.... The conception of *spells* appears to have arisen in the idea that there is some natural and intimate connection between words and the things signified by them."[36]

Most teenage satanists borrow spells from books on magic, *The Satanic Bible,* or from friends who are satanists. A typical spell contains repetitive vocabulary, magical words that are said to embody magical power, and a step-by-step system for moving from problem through to solution by magical power. A spell often uses common words or word pictures, especially those associated with life or sex, to stand for the intangible. For example, a young satanist may repeat a spell for power over an enemy using phallic imagery for himself and describing his opponent in terms of sexual impotency.

Immediately before Sean Sellers killed his parents he recited a spell to ensure his success, perhaps this one, found in his personal satanic diary, called a *Book of Shadows:*

O great desolate one, spawn of the abyss, enemy to the weak, send forth your most glorious blessing and heal the wounds of one of your children. Send forth the dire powers of darkness so that we may do your will. Send to us a burning flare of change so that we may place ourselves to help you.

Cast down the cowardly lies of suppression with a clap of earth-shattering thunder! Let your presence be known, for you are among your most talented. Upon this night, send the soul of mortality to your newfound child and grasp him/her as you would a lover.

We unite to strengthen through the true power of darkness an abandoned god, in all the black glory and richness of truth. Unite among us the powerful force of freedom, and through our power rise, to someday be free.

Allegiance to your power shall be sworn, as eternity revolves without end.[37]

*Sacrifices.* There are four basic kinds of satanic ritual sacrifices: the self, pain, parts of once living animals or humans, and live animals or humans. By far the most common sacrifice is the living sacrifice of oneself. The teenager gives himself symbolically and ritually to Satan in almost every ritual. This is a perverted analogy to the Christian's submission to God, expressed by St. Paul: "present your bodies a living sacrifice, holy, acceptable to God, which is your reasonable service."[38] Often the sacrifice of the individual life is symbolized or acted out in the ritual by sexual acts, including masturbation, mutual masturbation, homosexual practices, oral sex, and heterosexual intercourse. In harmony with the satanic creed of self-indulgence, the sexual participants should be willing, not forced. Their willing participation reinforces the satanic supremacy of self-interests and self-pleasure.

The sacrifice of pain is closely related to the sacrifice of the self. Anton LaVey and other satanists have noted that the physiological and emotional reactions to pain are very similar to those experienced in sexual ecstacy, which is symbolic of life. Pain symbolizes not only life, but also submission. Cooper explains,

Satanists are prone to offer Satan themselves, through slashing themselves with razors or sharp knives, generally on the arms (usually the tops of the forearms, to avoid striking an artery), the upper sides of the thighs, or the buttocks. Shallow slashes across the chest or breasts are not unknown, but care is taken not to cause dangerous bleeding; this rite aims not so much at shedding blood but at causing pain. Some criminally involved satanists, under the influence of alcohol or drugs, have reportedly cut off the joints of their fingers. The cultist starts with the first joint of the little finger at the first ritual and goes on to the second joint of the same finger at the next one. Satanists seek mutilation as an in-group sign, like tattoos in some cultures; but pain offered to Satan is the overarching point of this terrible practice.[39]

Satanists who use things other than themselves in ritual sacrifice usually use bones and/or body parts from dead animals or dead humans. Animal and human bones can be obtained legally. In fact, some mail order occult supply companies advertise animal or human bones. Animal bones also are obtained from carcasses found by the sides of roads or in the wild. Human bones often are obtained by digging up graves or breaking into mausoleums. The sale of animal or human body parts is illegal, and they cannot be obtained commercially.

Some satanists, usually working in small groups, actually sacrifice live animals during rituals. A live animal may not be used every time, but only when the "life energy" of the dying animal is considered necessary to empower the ritual.

In fact, many satanists refuse to take animal or human life. LaVey explains, "The fact of the matter is that if the 'magician' is worthy of his name, he will be uninhibited enough to release the necessary force *from his own body*, instead of from an unwilling and undeserving victim!"[40]

Satanists who sacrifice animals usually pick small animals or dogs. Suburban or urban satanists seem to favor cats and dogs, probably because they are so accessible. Rural satanists might kill rabbits, squirrels, or small farm animals. Most satanists who sacrifice small animals are teenagers. The thrill of the kill is akin to the chills they feel at a gory horror movie.

Satanists who practice the sacrifice of living animals could move to sacrificing living human beings. However, there is no evidence that such activity occurs with the vast majority of satanists. Satanic murders involve more than merely a ritual sacrificial victim.[41] Drug dealing, severe drug abuse, psychotic or sociopathic dysfunction, and emotional rage account for most satanically related murder. Sean Sellers killed the convenience store clerk because he would not sell him alcohol, and killed his parents after months of rebellion, tension, and conflict. Richard Ramirez, known as the "Night Stalker," killed and robbed and was characterized as emotionally dysfunctional. Ricky Kasso and Jimmy Troiano killed Gary Lauwers because Lauwers stole drugs from Ricky. Cooper notes, "While it is certainly possible that criminal cults have performed human sacrifices on drifters, hitchhikers, street people (the homeless), and recently born infants whose births are unrecorded, we cannot prove anything from silence.... Probably, therefore, human sacrifice forms little to no part of most satanic rituals. When it does occur, drug-intoxicated self-styled satanists or criminal occult groups enact the crime."[42]

But because satanic murder is rare does not mean that satanic practices are harmless. On the contrary, the self-centered drive for power inherent in all satanism allows for, and may even encourage, violence against those who stand between the satanist and his goals. Arthur Lyons notes this trend: "The escape into barbarity, as well as that into magical thinking, is an attempt by the individual to make himself feel powerful. When the two combine, it is not surprising to find religious cults that practice violence to be springing up in recent years. We should be concerned about the fact, but not panicked."[43]

There are many different kinds of satanists. There is no such thing as one test that will uncover satanic involvement or activity. However, if you are concerned about your teenager's possible involvement, the characteristics described here will help you to understand and identify the problem.

# THREE

# Witchcraft

G REG IS A SENIOR ENGINEER for a Southern California
defense contractor. He graduated *summa cum laude*
from M.I.T. and has been a member of the high IQ society,
Mensa, for most of his adult life. He works hard at his job,
and his coworkers turn to his creativity when they can't solve
engineering problems. On weekends he enjoys working in
his organic garden. He volunteers as director of a nonprofit
religious organization. The organization has an unusual
membership—all of them, including Greg, are witches.

Anne is also a witch. She's been on a spiritual odyssey for
most of her life. In the early 1960s she tried becoming a
Roman Catholic nun and then married a priest. In the later
1960s she tried chemical enlightenment with Timothy
Leary's LSD "experiments." The 1970s were devoted to eastern meditation and translation of Sanskrit holy writings.
Trance channeling occupied her time in the 1980s. Now she
has sacrificed everything, including her second husband
and her family, for true fulfillment and expression of her
womanhood with her lesbian lover in a witch's coven.

James Johnson is packing for vacation.

"Mostly A's, I think," the slender Pomona College fresh-
man says. "Maybe a couple of B's. Pretty good year."

Into the suitcase go T-shirts, socks, pants. Books, papers, a deck of cards, a razor. The dormitory detritus of a college boy.

In a separate valise, Johnson stows the rest of his gear: candles, mojo bags, painted rocks, incense. Then the amulets, talismans, charms and potions.

Johnson gives the room a final once-over. "Oh yeah," he says. Off a wall rack and into a side pocket of the suitcase goes the wand. Can't leave the wand behind, not with the summer solstice coming up.

Johnson hefts his bags into the hallway, then returns for a stout, gnarled branch easily as tall as he is.

To most of us, it's a stick. To Johnson, it's a "staff."

It figures.

James Johnson is a witch.[1]

Modern day witches[2] don't fit the cartoon stereotypes of the classic fairy tale. They don't have to be ugly or female. They characteristically oppose violence, hatred, and manipulation. They share a particular world view or way of understanding and relating to the world. There may be a few "bad apples," people who make up their own brand of witchcraft as a powerful magic means of getting their own way, but that does not describe the average contemporary Western witch. Modern Western witchcraft, often referred to as "the Craft," Wicca, paganism, or neo-paganism, is much more attractive to the average person than is satanism. One must dig below the surface to the belief system to find its discordance with traditional Christian values.

## THE NEW OLD WITCHCRAFT

The term *witchcraft* can refer to several different types of religious belief or practice. Witchcraft can refer to the religious rites of a minority religion within a society, a preliterate society's religious worldview, any of a number of ancient religious traditions outside the Judeo-Christian mold, or to a contemporary religious expression of unity with the divine cosmos.[3] Today's witchcraft bears little resemblance to the witchcraft of literature, the Bible, or church history.

**Witchcraft in Literature.** The witches familiar to us from classic fairy tales were archetypical representations of evil. These witches were ugly as in *Hansel and Gretel* or sinisterly beautiful as in Snow White, had magical powers, and were committed to destroying or controlling what was beautiful, innocent, and pure. Fairies, fairy godmothers, and handsome princes could thwart the witches' plans. Not until relatively contemporary literature, such as Frank L. Baum's *The Wizard of Oz*, do we find "good" witches as well as "wicked" witches.

**Witchcraft in the Bible.** The conflict between witchcraft and the Bible stems from the Bible's strict monotheism, or the belief in only one God, and the Bible's foundation of absolutism, that is, truth and morals are absolute, not relative or subjective. If there really is only one God, if truth is absolute and knowable, and if right and wrong come objectively from God rather than from within a subjective individual or society, then everything contrary to God is necessarily untrue and wrong. This absolutism is reflected in the biblical description of witchcraft.

Basic Hebrew and Greek terms translated "witchcraft" in most Bible translations usually refer to magical practices, often used to "enchant" or "bewitch," and are contrary to trust in and dependence on the sovereign will of the one true God.[4] Israel's theocratic (rule by God) government viewed the practice of witchcraft as treason, a capital offense, since to practice witchcraft one must turn from God, the Sovereign, to a rival power. The term used most often in the Hebrew Old Testament, *qesem*,[5] refers primarily to divination or sorcery, the practice of magic, especially to influence people or events for personal reasons, and is rejected from a biblical perspective.[6] *Magic* in the biblical world is a manipulative and deceptive imitation of God's miraculous power at work among men.[7] Sorcerers, magicians, priests of false gods, and witches are lumped together indiscriminately because they claim or exhibit powers that are counterfeits of God's power.[8] Acts of magic or sorcery are evil, not primarily because they are "superhuman," but because those who practice magic or sorcery deny the God of the Bible, who alone is divine, eternal, all-powerful, and infinite.[9]

Two common Greek terms used in the Greek version of the Old Testament or in the New Testament, *magos* and *pharmakos*, refer to sorcerers or those devoted to magical arts, paralleling the Hebrew concept.[10]

Most contemporary witches do not practice all of the occult arts denounced in the Bible and are understandably offended when well-meaning but misinformed Christians dismiss their beliefs with a few trite references to inapplicable Scriptures. Mediumship and astrology, for example, are more common among New Agers and psychics. Spells and incantations are, however, integral to most witchcraft. And, as we explore the worldview of the witch, we will see that contemporary witches' magic is also based on a non-biblical worldview and a concept of God contrary to the biblical God.

**Witchcraft in Church History.** Ecclesiastical (church) laws against witchcraft or the practice of magic, occurred in Christianized countries from the early centuries of Christianity. Most of these laws were devised to guard against worship of or belief in gods other than the Christian God. They opposed the pagan beliefs of the societies into which Christianity spread. Christians did not view God as one "God among many," or as a localized deity. According to the Bible, he was the only true God, the one supreme over all creation, societies, and people.[11] Therefore, individuals and communities with different gods were automatically wrong. They were considered idol worshippers.

During the early centuries of the church, witchcraft was seen as ignorant superstition. It was denounced, but the punishment for its practice was more often religious education than persecution.

By the fifteenth century the Church had incorporated from the Arabic world the study of some practices, such as alchemy and astrology (which later developed into astronomy), that once were viewed as sorcery but were reclassified as "natural" and "scientific." The Christian did not need to abandon the one true God to experiment with the natural laws assumed to allow the transformation of lead into gold.

In the fifteenth century ecclesiastical persecutions arose for the crime of "heresy," a term that was expanded to include almost anything those in power didn't like. In 1484 Heinrich Kraemer and Johann Sprenger, Dominican friars, were authorized by Pope Innocent VIII to stamp out witchcraft in Germany. They subsequently published *The Witches' Hammer* (in its original Latin, *Malleus Maleficarum*) which became the authoritative textbook on demonology and witchcraft used to expose and destroy occultism throughout the Western Christian Church.[12] Interestingly, the Church hierarchy never officially approved the text, so Kraemer and Sprenger forged their endorsement, a forgery not uncovered until 1898.[13] Information based on *The Witches' Hammer* directed European, English, and early American Church persecution against witchcraft for nearly three hundred years.

*The Witches' Hammer* institutionalized the stereotypical view of witches as evil, Devil-worshipping meddlers. It is from this source that we get the images of witches flying on brooms, of having magical, evil black cats, and of performing lewd sexual acts with Satan. Almost anything out of the ordinary, unrestricted by local feudal control or outside the traditionally understood biblical worldview, was considered witchcraft, evil, and deserving of destruction. Superstition became a synonym for magic, natural calamity and misfortune became symptoms of witchcraft at work. If you suspected your neighbor of stealing your cow, it was easier to convict him (or more likely, her) of witchcraft than robbery.

Unfortunately, this erroneous view of witchcraft and also an erroneous understanding of what biblical Christianity's response should have been to witchcraft, is how most people characterize both witchcraft and Christianity. We have had witches tell us, "You Christians would burn me at the stake today if you thought you could get away with it." Likewise Christians have said, "Witches have sex with demons and have sold their souls to Satan." Contemporary witchcraft and biblical Christianity are both very different from these caricatures.

**Witchcraft Today.** Contemporary witches often draw beliefs, practices, and tools from pre-Christian European traditions or from other nonJudeo-Christian traditions. But many also draw practices and tools from these Medieval witchcraft myths.

As contemporary witchcraft developed during the 1950s and 1960s, many self-styled witches attempted to "recover" the witchcraft tradition that had been "lost" or gone "underground" because of the Medieval persecutions. This claim to historical roots, although not valid, distinguished this witchcraft from the other "new" religions of the 1950s and 1960s. The *Encyclopaedia Britannica* explains the source fallacy:

> These practitioners usually turn out to be entirely sincere but misguided people who have been directly or indirectly influenced by Margaret Murray's article "Witchcraft" in the 14th edition of *Encyclopaedia Britannica*

(1929), which put forth in its most popular form her theory that the witches of western Europe were the lingering adherents of a once general pagan religion that has been displaced, though not completely, by Christianity. This highly imaginative but now discredited theory gave a new respectability to witchcraft and, along with the more practical influence of such modern satanists as Aleister Crowley and Gerald Gardner, contributed to the emergence of do-it-yourself prescriptions that have done much to encourage the unashamed emergence of the self-styled witches that are sometimes featured in the Sunday newspapers.[14]

Contemporary witchcraft has a little of the old, a lot of the new, and a lot of creative, imaginative additions by the many individual witches and witch groups, usually called covens. While the many kinds of witchcraft are natural reflections of witchcraft's pluralism, contemporary witchcraft can be described in general terms, and most witches share common foundational beliefs.

## WHAT IS A WITCH?

James Johnson, the collegiate witch from the beginning of this chapter, describes witchcraft by what it isn't: "Witches, real ones, don't believe in Satan, or practice black magic, or sacrifice furry little animals or any of that stuff."[15]

A teenage girl we interviewed in an occult bookstore explained that she was a pagan because "I love nature and living things. I want to be in harmony with the world and do my part to express the Goddess through my life." Her girlfriend, who clutched bottles of potions, incense, and candles as she waited at the cash register, had a clear goal in mind: "I think I have a good chance with this great guy at school. But I'm not leaving it to chance. When I get our life forces in sync, there's no way we won't be together."

A young English witch referred to her practices as "the art of producing results in a way that at first seems unnatural, for the witch has knowledge of how to deal with sickness and health, the past and the future."[16]

An informational sheet from Our Lady of the Woods in Wisconsin simply calls Wicca "an ancient religion of love for life and nature."[17]

A more useful definition of modern witchcraft, paganism, or neo-paganism comes from researcher Margot Adler, whose *Drawing Down the Moon* is considered the best introduction and survey on contemporary witchcraft. Adler recognizes the common beliefs of the divinity of all (pantheism), dualism or pluralism (including polytheism, belief in many gods and godesses), and relative morals.[18] She summarizes the basic beliefs shared by most pagans:

> The world is holy. Nature is holy. The body is holy. Sexuality is holy. The mind is holy. The imagination is holy. You are holy. A spiritual path that is not stagnant ultimately leads on to the understanding of one's own divine nature. Thou art Goddess. Thou art God. Divinity is imminent in all Nature. It is as much within you as without.
>
> In our culture which has for so long denied and denigrated the feminine as negative, evil or, at best, small and unimportant, women (and men too) will never understand their own creative strength and divine nature until they embrace the creative feminine, the source of inspiration, the Goddess within.
>
> While one can at times be cut off from experiencing the deep and ever-present connection between oneself and the universe, there is no such thing as sin (unless it is simply defined as that estrangement) and guilt is never very useful.
>
> The energy you put into the world comes back.[19]

Adler, herself a neo-pagan, says they understand "that the spiritual world is like the natural world—only diversity will save it."[20] She affirms that her book, like modern witchcraft, "espouses radical polytheism."[21]

The appeal of modern witchcraft to the typical disillusioned teenager is apparent in Adler's description of neo-pagans, who "... sense an aliveness or 'presence' in nature. They are usually polytheists or animists[22] or pantheists, or two or three of these things at once. They share the goal of living in harmony with nature, and they tend to view humanity's 'advancement' and separation from nature as the prime source of alienation. They see *ritual* as a tool to end that alienation."[23]

Wicca is one of the best-known branches of contemporary witchcraft,[24] with its own statement or creed contained in a one page document called the *Principles of Wiccan Belief.*[25] The unity and diversity of pagan pluralism is apparent in principle four: "We conceive of the Creative Power in the Universe as manifesting through polarity—as masculine and feminine—and that this same Creative Power lives in all people, and functions through the interaction of the masculine and feminine. We value neither above the other, knowing each to be supportive of the other. We value sexuality as pleasure, as the symbol and embodiment of Life, and as one of the sources of energies used in magical practice and religious worship."[26]

While it might seem contradictory to believe that all of reality is divinely one, and, paradoxically, that there are a God and a Goddess, most witches reconcile the two as does Buckland: "Ultimate Deity was equated with both masculine and feminine... broken down into a God and a Goddess. This would seem most natural since everywhere in nature is found this duality. With the development of the Craft, as we know it, there was also, as we have seen, this duality of a God and a Goddess."[27]

The plurality assumed in witchcraft makes it difficult to

define clearly and unambiguously. However, most witches agree with the following basic beliefs: 1.) all of reality is divine; 2.) there is dualism or plurality within the divine oneness; 3.) the spiritual world and the material world are one reality; 4.) the goal of human life is to live in harmony with Nature; 5.) ritual practice is the witches' path to harmony; and 6.) there is no "one true right and only way."

## IS WITCHCRAFT DANGEROUS?

Contemporary witches are generally positive, gentle, creative, and respectful of others and of nature. The contemporary witchcraft system, represented by the beliefs listed above, doesn't encourage violence, destruction, criminal behavior, or divisiveness within families. Many witches are positive assets to their communities, responsible citizens, good employees, and devoted family members. The average teenager who dabbles with the Goddess religion is at little risk for destructive occultism.

**Self-Styled Destruction Witchcraft.** There are a few loners or small groups calling themselves witches who engage in destructive or criminal acts or both. David Berkowitz, the infamous "Son of Sam" serial killer, is an example. These anomalous people may describe themselves as "witches" or describe their groups as "covens," or say they participate in "witchcraft."[28] However, they do not practice, believe, or participate in the contemporary witchcraft described in this book. Teenagers who become involved in destructive occultism, even if they use terms from witchcraft, are in the same danger of emotional, physical, and spiritual destruction as a self-styled satanist.

A teenager who is having serious problems in other areas of his or her life could take some of the vocabulary, rituals, or spells of witchcraft, add them to his or her own destructive activities, and end up in serious trouble. Don't take your teenager's interest in witchcraft lightly. Probe beneath his or her surface comments to be sure involvement isn't rapidly descending into criminal or other harmful activities.

**The Danger of Relativism.** Teenagers, like the girls we interviewed at the occult bookstore, are often interested in contemporary witchcraft because of its air of mystery, its dedication to the "natural" world, and its ability to intrigue one's imagination and creativity. Many people are attracted by the idea that all religious beliefs and ideas are equally good or true, just different paths to the same place. People are comfortable with witchcraft's enjoyment of unrestrained emotion and physical pleasure, exemplified in the witches' sexual freedom.

But if those ideas aren't actually true, if the witchcraft worldview leads witches to see the world as they would like it to be, rather than as it really is, then acceptance of the witchcraft worldview leaves one blind and unable to relate to reality. Pleasure based on illusion becomes disappointment, and peace based on fantasy turns to despair.[29]

*The witchcraft worldview is illogical, self-refuting.* If all religious beliefs and ideas are equally good and true, then why do witches say Christians are wrong to say witchcraft is wrong? Aren't Christians right, too? But if Christians are right, and Christians say witchcraft is wrong, then all religious beliefs and ideas are *not* equally good and true. But if all religious belief and ideas are not equally good and true, then witchcraft is wrong to assert that they are. Christians derive their sense of right and wrong, truth and error from the objective standard of God's revelation in the Bible, not from subjective standards like emotions, social consensus, might-makes-right, or cultural norms.

If all religious beliefs and ideas are equally good and true, then what if a religious nut had the religious idea that all who disagreed with him, including witches and Christians, should be tortured and killed? A Christian can protest, "God says murder is wrong, and God, as the divine judge, has the right to determine good and bad." The witch can either silently suffer, or inconsistently protest that the nut's religious idea isn't quite as good and true as the witch's.

Teenagers who accept self-refuting relativism possess no standard for judging ideas or beliefs. Open to all, they become subject to all. If nothing is objectively right or wrong, then how can your teenager argue against taking drugs? Does it harm the body? Who says? That's just your opinion. Maybe it helps the body on a level of reality you're not experiencing. How can your teenager argue against gang activity? What if the gang members are merely expressing their group exuberance with portions of the natural world the property owner only thinks are his. They believe everything is actually part of the god/goddess.

To be fair, the witches we know and talk with regularly do not advocate criminal activity, unethical personal relationships, deceit, or harm to anyone else, however "harm" is defined or determined. They have shown us we can trust them to tell the truth, deal fairly in business, and respect the rights of others. However, we believe their actions are inconsistent with their supposed allegience to relativism.

*The witchcraft worldview misunderstands the meaning of physical love and cheapens one of life's most important acts.* One neopagan publication describes the witchcraft view of sexual intimacy in this way: "The word is derived from *Eros*, the Greek God of Love. Love is the essence of Divinity, and is the 'creative action of the universe.' Eroticism in its religious reference venerates love play and the sexual act as divine, as creative physical expression of our union with Nature as we reconcile sexual opposites. Hence, love play and sex are natural and beautiful whenever shared in mutual consent."[30] In other words, as long as everyone involved consents and enjoys the act, you are expressing the unity of divine reality through sex.

The Judeo-Christian biblical understanding of sex, however, assumes that sex should be between a man and woman who have made a permanent, exclusive covenant between them before God and their government as a picture of the spiritual union between God and his people, Jesus Christ the bridegroom and the Church his bride.[31] The Bible makes it clear that there is only one true God,[32] and only one way to reconcile with God, through the sacrifice of Jesus Christ.[33] Marriage is meant to be permanent, monogamous, and heterosexual or it does not fairly represent that exclusive union of "as Christ also loved the church and gave Himself for it."[34] Contrary to how some caricaturize the Christian view of sex, it is not to be repressed, but expressed within the context created for it, marriage. Sex within marriage brings physical, emotional, and spiritual pleasure, can produce children, and is an expression of the mutual commitment, responsibility, respect, and love of the partners.

A Judeo-Christian biblical understanding of sex encourages responsible, committed behavior from teenagers. A witchcraft understanding of sex reinforces the false idea of the divinity within all and requires no commitment, responsibility, or love.

These are only a few of the concerns we have with contemporary witchcraft. Although the contemporary witchcraft worldview does not promote the same kinds of destructiveness inherent in contemporary satanism, it is inadequate and unfulfilling. A worldview that "feels good" but denies reality is useless. A worldview that will not admit objective standards of truth and error, good and bad, deteriorates into a relativistic gray where pleasure and pain, commitment and abandonment, sacrifice and selfishness are indistinguishable.

As Christians, we can share many values with contemporary witches, but the foundations for our values are completely opposed. Christians respect and care for nature because God has given us that responsibility as a moral obligation.[35] Witches respect and care for nature because they worship it. Christians care about others because we are made in the image of God, the one who cared so much that he gave his only Son for our reconciliation.[36] Witches "live wisely and well, without harm to others, and in harmony with Nature"[37] because they believe everyone and everything is divine. Christians are creative and imaginative, understanding reality and at the same time enjoying fiction, science fiction, and myth because creativeness is part of how we are in God's image.[38] Witches mistakenly tie their creativity and imagination to the underlying divinity of all.

If we are concerned that our teenagers reject destructive occultism, satanism, and even the attractive, but unfulfilling world of witchcraft, we must have something better to offer them. Reality, truth, and God are not nebulous substances we can run down to our local house of worship and purchase by the six-pack. To help our children, we must understand their own attempts to solve their problems and then offer them something better. The next chapter will help you to assess your child's vulnerabilities and involvement with the occult.

# FOUR

# Is Your Child Involved in the Occult?

K ATHI'S MOTHER WAS referred to our ministry by a local Christian radio station. She was close to tears as she described her problem to us over the phone. "I just don't know what's happened to my baby. She seemed like such a normal teenager, and she never missed her youth group meetings at church. How could she do this to us?"

Mrs. Brooks and Kathi had just finished a screaming argument about Kathi's newly revealed beliefs in witchcraft. Her mother had become aware of Kathi's witchcraft because she asked Kathi why she had incense and an intricately carved knife on her window sill. Mrs. Brooks couldn't understand how her daughter, raised in a Christian home and with plenty of Christian activities, could reject Christianity, worship Nature, invoke the power of the Goddess Diana, and perform magic rituals to bring harmony to her life.

Most Christian parents whose children become involved in the occult go through experiences like Mrs. Brooks. Certainly they are concerned and want to do everything they can to persuade their children to abandon their occultism and embrace the Christian faith. In fact, most teenagers and young adults who experiment with the occult end up returning to a worldview similar to what they were taught as children. However, parents can take positive steps to affirm the Christian faith and influence their children's religious choices gently and with respect. The first step is to recognize your children's vulnerabilities, curiosity, and initial involvement.

## THE DANGEROUS OCCULT FRINGE

George and Opal Gamble had a different kind of problem with their son. Philip, fifteen, was charged with killing his older brother, Lloyd, by shooting him twice in the head at point-blank range with a shotgun. He later said it had been a satanic execution, carried out on the holiday of Candlemas (February 2, also called the Feast of Ormelc).

Philip studied satanic literature, including *The Satanic Bible* with its chapter "On the Choice of a Human Sacrifice" (meant to be understood, according to LaVey, not as an actual sacrifice, but a "proxy" sacrifice). After Philip's arrest, his parents searched his bedroom and found hidden a variety of occult paraphernalia, including a hood, a long black robe, silver chalice, candle, red liquid, heavy metal music tapes, a sword, and a pentagram.[1] Philip's parents suffered with the double tragedies of the death of one son, allegedly at the hands of another son. How could it have been prevented?

Richard Chase had problems for much of his life, but even his psychiatrists didn't suspect that he would become a psychotic murderer, dubbed "the vampire of Sacramento" because he drank the blood of his victims.

Richard's childhood seemed normal. He was described as a passive or quiet child, and his family remembered him as "peaceful." He had a few problems as a child, wetting his bed until he was around eight, and setting a few small fires.

After his parents' divorce, Richard's mental and physical health seemed in permanent decline.

He became a heavy drug user and started killing small animals, eating them raw. He complained of constant physical problems. He shaved his head to see it change shape as the bones came through his skin. He complained to emergency room personnel that someone had stolen his pulmonary artery to stop his blood from circulating. He began drinking and injecting animal blood, he said, because his heart was weak and his body was falling apart. Finally he progressed to killing human beings, eating their blood and organs.[2] His parents, even though they knew of his mental problems, were shocked. Where had they gone wrong? What could they have done? How could they have predicted Richard's dangerous deterioration and, maybe, stop him before he turned to murder?

Most parents will never have to agonize like Richard's and Philip's. Most children who experiment with the occult are like Kathi. Even if they experiment with destructive occultism, few turn into satanic murderers or vampires. Contemporary witchcraft is strongly against any form of violence or destruction. Even contemporary satanism is, for most practitioners, mostly symbolic and rarely carried out destructively toward others. The majority of teenagers involved in the occult do so for the freedom, thrills, and easy sex and drugs. However, serious trouble develops when people who already have destructive tendencies find that destructive occultism is compatible, an observation made by Anton LaVey, who "recognized that many of those applying for membership did indeed have emotional and psychological problems and were attracted to his church *because* of their feelings of alienation from the rest of society."[3]

Even though your child might not be tempted to murder or violence, he or she might abandon the religious beliefs and morals you value and engage in beliefs and behavior that can be personally destructive, socially disruptive, or criminal. Drug use and sexual indulgence are rampant among teenage occultists.

Concerned parents can and should educate themselves about the ideas, symbols, words, tools, and practices of the occult as a constructive step toward protecting their children from occult destruction.

## RISK FACTORS

Most of the common problems of adolescence can be vulnerabilities for occult involvement. As you consider your teenager's life, keep in mind that the following problems characterize normal teenagers as well as teenagers who might be experimenting with or even committing themselves to destructive occultism. The difference is in the problem's degree or intensity and in the "solutions" the teenager chooses. Most teenagers feel alienated by their parents' beliefs, for example, but few respond to alienation by spray painting satanic symbols on the walls of their parents' church.

**Emotional Factors.** Teenagers who feel severe alienation from their parents and other adults can translate that alienation into active rejection of authority, status quo beliefs, and socially acceptable behavior. Severely alienated teenagers will withdraw almost completely from normal family and social interaction. Their lives become characterized by secrecy. What little interaction exists is usually combative, aggressive, and argumentative. When their role models act in similar ways, their behavior becomes even worse. Arthur Lyons notes, "An individual who feels alienated from society will gravitate toward those groups and pursuits that support his own self-image, and herein lies the danger; in an imitative society, the heroes who are worshiped are not great men, but celebrities. And the androgynous, black leather-clad, ghoulish stars of heavy metal are idols for misfits."[4]

Power is an important goal of the occultism. Paradoxically, teenagers involved in the occult feel both powerless and power. Teenagers at risk frequently act as though they are victims of others' power plays, and they are desperate to escape powerlessness. These same teenagers, as they practice their occult path to power, exhibit an increasing attitude of power over their own circumstances and often over others, especially their "enemies."

**Social Factors.** The teenager at risk can't seem to succeed very well in normal social settings. Instead, he or she fights the system, gets in trouble, and acts destructively.

This destructiveness is also characterized by the occult oriented teenager's morbid fascination with destruction, horror, torture, murder, and violence.

**Physical Factors.** Drug or alcohol use almost always accompanies contemporary satanism and is common to most destructive occultism. John Cooper goes so far as to say "satanism and drugs always go together."[5] He explains the sinister allure of drug use, saying:

The lure of drugs is probably the most potent recruiting tool Satanism has today. Experimenting, adventurous, and alienated young people do "try" drugs of every description, from alcohol to pot to the most dangerous street chemicals. The pleasures of the flesh represent the real values of many such youth's parents. They have grown up watching their parents drink alcohol at every opportunity, use tranquilizers, and in some cases, smoke marijuana or use cocaine. Such youngsters think older people are being hypocritical when they urge youth to "just say no," and they are not wrong in their assessment. Those parents may have been taught different values as children, although they do not live by them, but the youngsters may have had no such values conditioning. For them, the pleasure principle is the only standard of morality they know.[6]

Most teenagers involved in satanism and other forms of destructive occultism are usually very active sexually, showing little control over their physical desires. Involved teenagers might engage in group sex, self or mutual masturbation, homosexual activities, and other non-traditional sexual practices such as oral sex, bestiality, and anal sex. Sex magick is a very important element of many forms of magical practice.

**Religious Factors.** Teenagers who openly reject the religious values of their parents and yet seem extremely religious are at risk for occult involvement. A teenager consumed by non-traditional religious intensity immerses himself in alternate beliefs, especially those he believes will give him power over his own life. He can be drawn to magic, ritual, and the spiritually mysterious.

Teenagers attracted to the occult typically immerse themselves in mythology and the study of magic, ritual, and symbolism. A teenager may pick a particular mythological tradition from a particular country and/or time period, or she may study a variety of mythical traditions. Often an occultist will pick a particular mythical character or a god or goddess from the tradition he studies and pattern his own behavior, dress, actions, and symbolism after that figure.

In addition to the general risk factors for occult involvement, there are a number of specific clues and symptoms you can watch for to know if your teenager is at risk for involvement with destructive occultism. If you think your teenager might have a problem, check these factors carefully, but do not take action until you believe you understand the situation and know the best steps to take for successful intervention.

## SATANIC SYMPTOMS

The parents, teachers, and law enforcement personnel in Monroe County, Michigan, knew something strange was going on with local high school students. One boy, who lived with his grandmother, took all her religious pictures off the walls, turned her crucifixes upside down, and then beat her up. Two boys fought in the high school cafeteria and the winner jumped up on a table and flashed a strange hand salute, a clenched fist with his index and little fingers sticking up. The high school art teacher couldn't figure out why so many kids drew pictures of demonic-like men with goat's heads. The occult books were checked out more than any others from the school library. The adults knew something was wrong, but they didn't know what.

The teenagers were flirting with satanism. The power, the magic, the mystery—for most it was fun and exciting. For some, it was serious, deadly serious to Lloyd Gamble, who lost his life in a satanic sacrifice. After Lloyd's death, and his younger brother's arrest for the murder, the adults learned to understand the signs that had been so mysterious before: The "devil's sign" hand signal, the two fingers representing the horns of the "goat" image of Satan; the goat's head baphomet pictures symbolizing the dark lord; and the books that fed the teenagers' imaginations, rituals, and spells. Knowledge became the adults' first step toward positive intervention for the involved kids.

**Ideas.** Power, destruction, anarchy, self-interest, indulgence, and vengeance are central ideas in satanism. Cooper describes contemporary satanism as "utter selfishness, pure egotism in action, and a quest for personal power and unlimited sensual pleasure."[7] *The Satanic Bible* affirms the importance of these ideas, and most teenage self-styled satanists use *The Satanic Bible* as their main information resource. We have paired these ideas with supporting quotes from *The Satanic Bible*.

*Power.* The teenager who seems preoccupied with gaining power for himself and freeing himself from the power of others may be involved in satanism. If your teenager is involved in satanism, he either may exert power over others, or may subject himself to a powerful satanic leader. Be concerned if your teenager either instills fear in his friends, or is afraid of one of his own friends. Members of a satanic group often serve their leader almost slavishly, showering him with expensive presents and taking care of all his needs.

"Blessed are the strong, for they shall possess the earth— Cursed are the weak, for they shall inherit the yoke! Blessed are the powerful, for they shall be reverenced among men— Cursed are the feeble, for they shall be blotted out!"[8]

*Destruction.* The anger typically exhibited by a teenage satanist is destructive. He shows no respect for others' property, and almost a delight in destroying things. He might trash his room, overturn headstones in a graveyard, crash a car and laugh at the damage, or destroy the boys' locker room at school.

"Behold! The mighty voices of my vengeance smash the stillness of the air and stand as monoliths of wrath upon a plain of writhing serpents. I am become as a monstrous machine of annihilation to the festering fragments of the body of he who would detain me."[9]

*Anarchy.* The satanist is not just rebellious, he is committed to fighting any restrictions, rules, or laws. Teenage satanists manifest this lawlessness, called *anarchy,* through refusal to obey parents, breaking rules at school simply to break rules, and flagrant violation of laws, especially those regarding drugs and alcohol. Teenagers typically break rules to get what they want. Teenage satanists not only break rules to get what they want, they break rules as a religious rite.

"Before none of your printed idols do I bend in acquiescence, and he who saith 'thou shalt' to me is my mortal foe!"[10]

*Self-interest.* The satanist is supremely self-absorbed. The typical teen looks at the world in a self-centered way, but the teenage satanist openly proclaims and asserts his self-absorption. A teenage satanist might repeatedly declare, "What's in it for me? I don't care about anything that doesn't benefit me."

"I break away from all conventions that do not lead to my earthly success and happiness."[11]

"The Satanist believes in complete gratification of his ego."[12]

"Satan represents all of the so-called sins, as they all lead to physical, mental, or emotional gratification!"[13]

"Satanism represents a form of controlled selfishness."[14]

*Indulgence.* A satanist in New York told a journalist, "Satanism represents indulgence."[15] The teenage satanist, even though he tries to keep his satanic involvement secret from his parents, will have a life characterized by sensual indulgence. Teenage satanism and drug use go hand-in-hand. Drugs are the quickest and easiest way to achieve physical and emotional pleasure. It's a safe bet that if your teenager is involved in satanism, he or she will also use drugs or alcohol or both. Drug use can cause severe mood swings, sleep and diet disruption, loss of weight, poor skin condition, loss of coordination and dexterity, and general deterioration of health, including many opportunistic infections. Theft and sale of stolen items and/or intermediary drug dealing finance this expensive and destructive indulgence.

Sex is probably the second most used indulgence technique. Promiscuity is rampant in our society and among our teenagers, and one of the lures of satanism is its emphasis on sensual indulgence. Teenage satanists who fill their lives with varieties of sexual indulgence suffer the consequences of emotional and spiritual destruction as well as the all-too-common physical consequences, including sexually transmitted diseases (STDs) and pregnancy. Ultimately, indulgence does not represent freedom, but the bondage of self-destruction.

"Satan represents indulgence, instead of abstinence!"[16]

"Life is the great indulgence—death, the great abstinence. Therefore, make the most of life—HERE AND NOW!"[17]

*Vengeance.* "Vengeance is mine," declares the satanist in mock echo of God.[18] The satanist's motto is to get back at others before they can get back at you, and this is evidenced in the teenage satanist's actions at home and school. The teenage satanist takes everything personally. No one gets away with wronging him, even if the wrong was inadvertent or thoughtless. This vengeance may take physical form, such as lashing out and slapping Mom when she forbids the teenager to go out at night. It might be stealing a classmate's CD player to retaliate for the classmate cutting in line. Certainly some teenagers practice vengeance and have no connection to satanism, but satanists pride themselves on taking vengeance against their "enemies."

"Satan represents vengeance, instead of turning the other cheek!"[19]

*Hate.* What parent *hasn't* heard "I hate you!" from his or her child? Childish anger develops in the teenage satanist into an ugly, destructive rage against anyone or anything that stands in his way. Teenage destructive occultists often resort to physical assaults to express their anger and achieve vengeance. Their hatred, although certainly emotionally involved, includes cold, long-term calculation and produces specifically directed destruction.

"Hate your enemies with a whole heart, and if a man smite you on one cheek, SMASH him on the other!; smite him hip and thigh, for self-preservation is the highest law!"[20]

**Symbols.** There are hundreds, perhaps thousands, of symbols associated with satanism. Satanism has taken many common symbols and given them new, satanic meanings. Other symbols are unique to satanism, whether historical or contemporary. Many more symbols are difficult to identify because they are made up by individual satanists and independent satanic groups. The most common symbols include the inverted pentacle, or five pointed star inscribed on a circle; the baphomet, or goat-headed hermaphrodite deity; and the number or mark of the Beast, 666. If your teenager is involved with satanism, you may see some of the following symbols on his school papers, art work, notebooks, on his or her bedroom walls, clothing, or jewelry. Often these symbols are inscribed on furniture, walls, floors, or trees. They are commonly found at or near ritual sites. Sometimes the symbols are tattooed on the satanist, especially on the web of skin between the thumb and index finger, usually on the left hand. The symbols here are only a few of the many used by satanic groups and solitary satanists.

It is *very* important to remember that many teenagers copy these symbols from their friends or favorite heavy metal musicians and are not actual satanists. It is also vital to remember that sometimes these symbols or ones like them are used in nonsatanic ways. These are common, but *not exclusive* to satanism.

*The Baphomet.* This symbol consists of a ram's head with horns inside an upside-down, five pointed star, and often within a circle or ring (sometimes containing runic symbols). It is one of the most common satanic symbols. In satanism, the goat represents Satan, especially symbolic of lust. The star is upside-down, with the two points up representing the universal duality of good and evil and the single point down toward hell, to represent the contrary nature of satanism. Presenting things backward or upside down is common imagery in satanism. The circle or ring represents power, both concentrating power within the circle and protecting the individual in the circle from outside forces. In fact, the circle is the fundamental symbol of satanism and witchcraft. No ritual can be performed without a ritual circle of power and protection. The ritual circle is usually nine feet across and may be drawn with chalk (easy to clean from carpets) or paint, or made of small stones or other material.

*The Goat of Mendes.* Another name for the baphomet, or goat's head, this symbol was used commonly in witchcraft until it became a favorite of the satanists. Many witches don't use it today because of its close association with satanism. The pattern for this picture is a famous print by the magician Eliphas Levi in the Middle Ages. Sometimes satanists turn the pentagram on the goat's forehead upside down to make it a satanic pentagram. Note that the goat head is on a human body with both male and female physical characteristics, symbolizing the occult idea of the polarity of existence— male/female, good/evil, God/Satan. The right hand points upward, symbolizing "white" or "positive" power; the left hand points downward, symbolizing "black" or "negative" power. The black and white snakes entwined around the phallic symbol echo the black/white polarity again. The Goat of Mendes also often appears within a double circle or ring.

*The Devil's Sign, Horn, or Salute.* This gesture is used by satanists and copied by many people, especially teenagers who copy the gestures of popular heavy metal bands whose songs have occult or satanic lyrics. The *left* hand is fisted, with the thumb clasping the middle two fingers. The index finger and little finger are thrust up, symbolizing the horns of the satanic goat. The left hand is used because black magic has long been called "the left-handed path." The left hand has been associated with evil, destruction, and treachery since ancient times. One theory about its origin as a negative symbol is that ancient warriors, mostly right-handed, would offer their left hands in a mock gesture of peace so they could keep their fighting (right) arms free. The Bible uses common idioms like "the right hand of fellowship" and "the right hand of God" to refer to what is good and related to God's power. Some satanic dabblers don't know much about the gesture and perform it with either hand, or clasp the thumb inside the two middle fingers. The traditional satanic salute should not be confused with the "Horned God" gesture of the witches.

*The Sign of the Beast, 666.* The satanists borrowed this symbol from the biblical passage in Revelation 13:18: "Here is wisdom. Let him who has understanding calculate the number of the beast, for it is the number of a man: And his number is six hundred and sixty-six."[21] The passage is part of a description by the Apostle John of the spiritual warfare in the last days. The beast is against God and his faithful followers. The literature of Revelation is apocalyptic, a literary form whose message is specifically designed to be enigmatic or hidden. Christians and others have speculated about the meaning of this passage for almost two thousand years and a host of evil men have been nominated to the position of "the Beast." Very likely John had in mind the Emperor Nero. Others nominated more recently have included Mussolini, Hitler, Anwar Sadat, Henry Kissinger, Saddam Hussein, or even Ronald Reagan. Aleister Crowley called himself the Beast and inscribed 666 on his clothing, books, furniture, and walls. Since the beast, whoever or whatever is meant by the biblical passage, is against Christianity, it is natural that satanists would appropriate the beast's number to their own use. Often 666 is further encoded and presented in a wheel shape as FFF (F is the sixth letter of the alphabet), or as multiples or divisors of itself. 333 could represent 666, as could 18 (6 x 3), or 216 [(6 x 6) x 6].

*Number, Letter, Word, or Symbol Reversal.* If satanism is "anti" God and everything normal, then it is easy to see how reversals can be appropriated as satanic symbols. Some satanic sects use dogs in sacrifices because dog is God spelled backward. How appropriate, they reason, to kill God by sacrificing a dog! Reversal of letters or words is also a good way to code one's messages. Magical numbers like 13, 6, and 9 are often written upside down or coded. A teenager's notebook may be covered with the scribbled words "red rum." It doesn't refer to a rose tinged alcoholic beverage, but to "murder." "NEMA NATAS" is often spray painted on a church wall or in a cemetery. Backward it spells "Amen,

Satan!" The satanist who scrawls "live" on his artwork isn't protesting suicide, he's secretly promoting "evil."

NEMA NATAS

LIVE-EVIL

RED RUM

*The Infinite Double Cross.* Everyone is familiar with the idiom to "double-cross" someone, to deceive or betray by acting in contradiction to what was expected or promised. This idiom has been adopted by satanism, symbolized by a cross with an extra horizontal bar, and combined with the symbol for infinity, what looks like a horizontal figure eight. This symbol can represent the satanist's infinite or never-ending hatred of God, Christianity, and anyone or anything standing in his way. It can also stand for satanism's infinite antagonism to the cross of Jesus Christ. This symbol appears in *The Satanic Bible* above the listing of the "Nine Satanic Statements."[22]

*The Cross of Nero.* This symbol was drafted by the anti-nuclear power protesters and was referred to as the "peace sign" in the 1960s. However, to the satanist it symbolizes the destruction of Christianity. The cross is upside-down, has broken arms, and is circled by satanic power. It is named after one of the most horrible murderers of Christians during the early years of the Church, Emperor Nero, who hated Christianity and lighted his courtyard with Christians dipped in oil and set afire.

*Double Lightning Bolts, Anarchy, The Upside-Down Cross, The Cross of Confusion, and No Christianity Practiced Here.* The last symbols included in this section are also common to many satanists, although they may not be as familiar as those above. The Double Lightning Bolts [A] were used by Hitler's dreaded Shützstaffel, or SS; and for the Nazi occult Thule Society. This is especially popular among neo-Nazi "skinheads." The Anarchy symbol [B] of a stylized uppercase letter A with a long crosspiece spanning the diameter of a circle, represents lawlessness or the destruction of all authority and government. The Upside-Down Cross [C] has been common to satanism since the time of the anti-morality Hell-Fire Clubs of the eighteenth century. It graphically represents Christianity's opposite, overthrow, and rejection. The Cross of Confusion [D] is an ancient Roman symbol adapted by satanism to symbolize that the cross, or Christianity, ends in confusion (the incomplete left-handed circle). The No Christianity Practiced Here symbol [E] is of recent origin, imitative of No Parking Here or No Swimming Here signs by combining the Christian cross with the slashed circle, the international symbol for "No," or "Forbidden."

There are countless other symbols designed or appropriated by satanists, including Black Mass indicators, the symbol for a satanic traitor, the anti-justice sign, the blood ritual symbol, varieties of arrows to direct power and mark locations, and the many complex figures used in black magic and satanic pledges. However, if your teenager is involved with satanism, some or all of the symbols presented here will probably be found along with others, including ones he or she has self-designed.

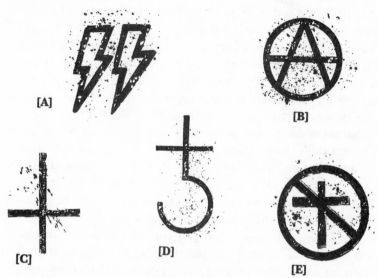

[A]

[B]

[C]

[D]

[E]

**Words.** Satanism gives cryptic or coded meaning to many common words. Not only does this allow satanists to communicate with secrecy, the very encoding is supposed to focus power and negative energy to be used by the satanist. We have already discussed the practice of inverting words or spelling them backward. The two most common reversed terms are "Natas Nema" (Satan, Amen) and "Live" (Evil). Often a satanist will have a secret satanic name which may be his own name backward, or a special name that is always said and written backward.

Opposites are very important in satanic communication. An innocent looking note that says "I love my mom" actually may mean the opposite, "I hate my mom." "Good luck" may mean "God damn you." Usually the teenager's actions and attitude telegraph his or her real feelings clearly, in spite of the innocuous words. We certainly don't mean to imply that every teenager who writes or says nice things is a secret satanist!

Often satanists believe that words and especially names have magical power. That is one reason a satanist keeps his satanic name secret. The person who possesses and uses his name can possess and use his power. Writing an enemy's name in blood on parchment and then burning it during a ritual is said to possess strong destruction magic. Sometimes a satanist will ritually name a doll or small animal after an enemy and then sacrifice this representation of his enemy to release destructive power against him.

Satanists use names of animals to symbolize different powers and skills they possess and use. They may call themselves by a particular animal's name and recite that animal's skills and actions as they ritually call on the power to accomplish a deed. The drug dealer may pattern himself after the coyote, who is silent, cunning, and almost invisible as he glides through the shadows. The disgruntled employee may pattern his ritual around the panther, who is able to stalk his enemy, destroy him with a swift lunge, and then feast on his carcass.

Figures, terms, and names from mythology are adopted by satanists to describe the members of their group, their goals, and their powers. They may gather these names from comic books, role-playing games, video games, or even school books.

**Books.** By far the most popular book used in satanism is *The Satanic Bible*. It is available in most secular bookstores and in almost every occult, metaphysical, or New Age bookstore. Most public libraries have multiple copies, and many public school libraries also carry the book. *The Satanic Bible* contains both the philosophy and the introductory practices of Anton Szandor LaVey's brand of satanism. Another book by LaVey, *The Satanic Rituals*,[23] is also popular. It contains a variety of rituals, including destructive rituals for harming enemies.

Other books often consulted by those studying satanism include *Malleus Maleficarum*,[24] *The Witches' Hammer*, available in many translations and editions; several books by Aleister

Crowley, including *777*,[25] *Gems from the Equinox;*[26] *The Magical Record of the Beast 666;*[27] and *The Book of the Law;*[28] *The Black Arts;*[29] various occult dictionaries; and *The Satanic Mass.*[30]

There are many self-published, photocopied, and mimeographed booklets and handbooks on satanism, mostly circulated from one satanist to another or within small satanic groups. Philip Gamble had a pamphlet like this called *The Power of Satan,* evidently distributed by a small group called the Continental Association of Satan's Hope.[31]

Song lyrics, like books, from groups such as Slayer and King Diamond that specialize in occultic images provide ideas for novice satanists.

Most satanists treasure their *Book of Shadows* more than any other book. *Book of Shadows* is the satanist's private diary, occultic journal, record of rituals and spells, and collection of important documents.

Each *Book of Shadows* is unique to its owner. Most are handwritten. Some are written in blood. Some are beautifully decorated and include intricate, macabre drawings. Some are scribbled in loose leaf or spiral bound notebooks. Often all or portions are written backward or in the satanist's own code.

*Book of Shadows* is not only the satanist's private collection of magic, the satanist believes it has a magical power of its own. He carefully guards it and keeps it secret from everyone else.

**Tools.** A novice teenage satanist may use nothing more than some drugs or alcohol, a candle and some black and red stage make-up for his first rituals. Some sophisticated satanic groups have developed elaborate ritual sites, altars, costumes, and ritual tools. Sado-masochistic satanic groups also use a collection of sex and bondage devices, many available from underground mail order sources.

Typical satanic tools are described in *The Satanic Bible.* Participants in satanic rituals wear black robes, preferably hooded or cowled, and are either naked underneath or wear black underwear. Most satanists believe that their robes have more power if they are handmade by each participant. Women who participate in satanic rituals often disrobe, wear sexually suggestive clothing, or are completely nude. The woman who becomes the living altar is always naked. The only jewelry worn by men or women should contain satanic symbolism, such as a baphomet necklace or a ring with an inverted pentagram insignia.

The satanic altar is most commonly a naked woman lying on her back on a table or bench. Solitary satanists usually use a consecrated table, most commonly rectangular but a special trapezoid shaped top is preferred. The baphomet, or Goat of Mendes, is always exhibited during rituals. It may be on a poster on a teenager's bedroom wall, in a picture frame on an altar, or even woven into a hanging tapestry.

Candles represent the light of Lucifer, Satan's name before his fall. Lucifer means "Light-Bearer." LaVey states that only all black candles and one white candle should be used. Black candles are especially significant because darkness, the candle, produces light, the flame. Some satanists also use red candles, and candles of other or mixed colors often signify particular magical powers.

A bell, from a simple small dinner bell to an elaborate, engraved silver bell, is used to mark the beginning and end of the satanic ritual. The bell is usually rung nine times or in some other multiple of three.

A chalice, or wine goblet, preferably made out of silver (symbolic of night, the time of the silver moon), is used for the unholy communion of the Black Mass. The chalice may be made out of any material except gold, which is representative of God. Some satanists steal their chalices from churches. A variety of liquids are drunk from the chalice according to the ritual performed. Wine is the most common, although other kinds of alcohol, Kool-Aid, soda pop, blood, urine, and semen, sometimes in combination, are also used.

The sword of power symbolizes force, as does the wand or

staff of power. A satanist may have either the sword or the staff, or both. Sometimes the sword's hilt is intricately designed with satanic symbols. Sometimes it is nothing more than a hunting knife or butcher knife. A small dagger or knife also is often used, and some satanists call it by its witchcraft name, athamé.

Parchment or parchmentlike paper is inscribed with the satanist's written message and then burned in the candle flame to release the power of the written words and accomplish the magic of the ritual. The most sought after parchment is handmade by the satanist from the skin of a dead animal, preferably a sheep. Parchment also can be purchased readily, or paper can be substituted.

Other tools can include oil, incense, candles shaped like people or animals, a mortar and pestle for grinding and mixing potions, human skulls (available by mail order) on which candles are burned, effigies or dolls for focusing destructive spells, and communion wafers (available from religious supply companies), sometimes stolen from churches.

Remember, many teenagers experiment with satanism for a new thrill, and their understanding and use of these tools is often inexact and inaccurate. Also remember that some of these items have innocent uses, too. Your teenager's parchment may be part of a school art project and her incense may be used to combat sweat sock odor. If you look carefully and thoughtfully evaluate your teenager's emotions and relationship with you and other adults, you will probably be able to discern teenage occult involvement from flirtation.

**Practices.** The Black Mass is the key ceremony of contemporary satanism. Certain elements of the Black Mass, a perversion of a Catholic High Mass, are described in *The Witches' Hammer* from the fifteenth century, although the Mass was not central to the sabbat until the eighteenth century. Black Masses were often performed in Hell-Fire Clubs of the eighteenth century, mostly as a theatrical setting for sexual orgies.

One famous and deadly practitioner of the Black Mass was Gilles de Rais, marshal of France in the fifteenth century. He was burned at the stake for performing the Black Mass on his estate in a special chapel with inverted crosses and black candles. Here he sodomized young boys, then sacrificed them, saving their blood for his unholy "sacrament."

Another famous case involved King Louis XIV's mistress, the Marquise de Montespan. She hired Catherine Deshayes to perform sex magic so she wouldn't be abandoned by the king. Deshayes and two priests, Abbe Mariette and Abbe Guibourg, engineered Black Masses to Astaroth and Asmodeus, demons of love and lust. In the mass a child's throat was cut and its blood drained into a chalice. The blood was mixed with flour to form a wafer slipped into the king's food by Madame de Montespan. The plot was uncovered in 1679, and several hundred people were implicated.

There are several varieties of Black Masses used by contemporary satanists. LaVey describes the Black Mass in *The Satanic Bible* and in *The Satanic Rituals*. However, many individual satanists make up their own Black Mass, borrowing elements from various occult sources and adding opposite practices from their own experiences or knowledge of Christianity. Most Black Masses include an individual role-playing a priest; upside-down crucifixes; Christian prayers such as the Lord's Prayer recited backward or prayers to Satan; some mockery of Christian Communion or the Eucharist, such as using communion wafers stolen from a church, or made out of feces or flour mixed with urine, and sometimes drinking blood or urine from the chalice. The Black Mass represents rebellion against the Christian God, his church, his laws, and his morals.

Satanic festival meeting rituals are usually called sabbats (religious rites) and esbats (magical rites). Many satanists use the two terms interchangeably or prefer one term over the other to refer to all group meetings. Satanic rituals are used to accompany drug use or sex or as a setting for practicing magic, including magic to benefit the member(s), to harm enemies, or to invoke demons or Satan. These rituals vary widely according to type and practitioner, with the one constant being inconsistency. As the pre-eminent anti-rule religion, satanism naturally spawns as many different rituals as there are satanists and occasions.

Most rituals contain a few common elements. All use a ritual circle of power, candles, and usually incense. All rituals begin with bell ringing and a prayer to Satan. Almost all rituals involve drug or alcohol use. Most rituals have one purpose. That is, the ritual may involve magic for increasing one's wealth *or* cursing an enemy, but probably not both goals in the same ritual.

Contemporary individual satanists, especially teenagers, often make up their rituals as they go along. Time, imagination, materials, and location are about the only restrictions. Because most teenagers have little experience with Christianity, they are less likely to pattern their rituals in parody of Christianity. Most teenagers also have little belief in the actual existence or power of demons, and enjoy their rituals more for the internal power they feel than to invoke supernatural power:

> The "Satanism" of the "stoners," like that found in most adolescent diabolist groups, seems to be more a way of venting aggressive, antisocial feelings than for the purposes of trying to raise demons in any literal sense. From all available evidence, their "rituals," whether involving the desecration of a church or graveyard, the ritualistic disemboweling of a cat, self-mutilation or blood drinking, are made-up-as-you-go affairs, inspired more by the use of narcotics or the deviant attraction of the acts themselves than by any real commitment to or knowledge of Satanism.[32]

Satanic rituals can occur at any time. The timing of teenage satanists' rituals usually coincides with times of stress and need in the individual's life, and only secondarily to a calendar of "unholy" days they may have copied from a book or learned from another satanist. According to LaVey, the most important satanic holiday is the individual satanist's own birthday: "Every man is a god if he chooses to recognize himself as one. So, the Satanist celebrates his own birthday as the most important holiday of the year. After all, aren't you happier about the fact that you were born than you are about the birth of someone you have never even met?"[33]

The other two major holidays listed by LaVey are Walpurgisnacht, also called Beltane, (April 30 or May 1) and Halloween (October 31). The Christian holiday of Walpurgisnacht (German for the night of St. Walpurgis) replaced the pagan celebration of the spring equinox. Traditionally the spring equinox marked when life was renewed and spirits, both good and bad, celebrated with wild revelry. Halloween (All Hallow's Eve, the day before All Saints' Day) was a designated Christian holiday to replace a pagan fire festival from the time of the Druids in Great Britain. The spirits of all who had died during the previous year were either placated and went to their eternal reward, or not, in which case they became evil spirits bent on causing mischief and promoting evil.

Other holidays described by LaVey include the summer and winter solstices and the spring and fall equinoxes, the first days of the four seasons. Some satanists celebrate on the actual day, others within five or six weeks after the solstice or equinox.

Holidays listed by others include Candlemas, also called the Feast of Ormelc (February 2) and Lammas Day (August 1). While these are the important satanic holidays, a satanist can perform on any day, and especially those days when he needs extra power—the day before final exams, the day he is fired, and so on.

## SIGNS OF WITCHCRAFT

The debauchery, destruction, and cruelty of satanism contrasts strongly with the nature-loving, harmonious, and self-affirming world of contemporary witchcraft. The teenage satanist may disembowel a neighbor's cat. The teenage witch may affirm belief in the divinity of all life and turn to vegetarianism. Police reports may include the finding of satanic symbols at the scene of a grisly sado-masochistic homosexual murder. Police may be amused when they discover "skyclad" (naked) witches celebrating spring, discretely hidden in a remote forest glen.

Yet when a teenager's turn to witchcraft is a rejection of the religious, spiritual, and moral values he or she learned in childhood, parents understandably are concerned. The typical witchcraft or pagan worldview is contrary to Christianity and based on relativism. For parents to communicate effectively with and rationally persuade the teenage witch, they must first learn to recognize probable witchcraft involvement.

**Ideas.** Teenagers attracted to witchcraft are usually imaginative, creative, enjoy nature, appreciate beauty, and are intrigued with the mysterious. Through witchcraft they develop the common ideas or beliefs characteristic of witchcraft, including pantheism, limited polytheism, dualism, relativism, and the power of magic.

*Pantheism.* If your teenager is learning a witchcraft worldview, he or she will make comments like, "Everything is one," "My God is Nature," "God is in everything," or "We're all part of the divine." Pantheism is the belief that all of reality is divine. God is all and all is God.

This is clearly contrary to the Christian or biblical worldview that God is separate from the universe, created it, sustains it, and acts in it.[34] The biblical worldview allows for communication and relationship between a person and God, while pantheism recognizes only one ultimate personality.

*Polytheism.* Tom Williams came home unexpectedly early one evening and walked through his house toward the back yard. Imagine his shock when he looked through the kitchen window and saw his sixteen-year-old daughter and eight of her friends dancing naked in a ritual circle, raising their arms in praise of the Goddess Diana.

Witches believe that all of reality is divine, but they also practice worship of many lesser personifications, or gods and goddesses. The Goddess Diana is the favorite among witchcraft groups, Pan is a favorite god. There are many gods and goddesses of witchcraft, often different names for the same deity, but all representative of different aspects of the natural world—including seasons, times of life, types of life, and basic life activities such as hunting, growing, harvesting, and procreation. It is not important whether or not the witch believes that any or all of these gods and goddesses have any objective existence, because the purpose of their worship is to bring the worshiper into a greater experience of the oneness of reality: "The multiplicity of Goddess and God individualities are aspects of the infinite variety of creation stemming from Goddess and God.... The omnipotence of Divinity is merely another word for Its polytheistic unity."[35]

Unlike satanism or traditional Judeo-Christian or Muslim worship, worship in witchcraft is not from subject (worshiper) to object (God), but is instead an exercise in experiencing unity with the divine All: "Through religious practice we, as individuals, strive to intensify and expand our experience of Divinity and our sense of dynamically harmonious relation with Great Nature."[36]

*Dualism.* "Polytheism begins with the Female and Male principles, the Goddess and God, or Divine Lovers, from Whose love all creation is derived."[37] Witchcraft sees an eternal and equal dualism within Divine Nature. Everything is seen in relationship to the God and Goddess polarity. This leads, inexorably, to a celebration and indulgence of sexual love, "the symbol and embodiment of Life."[38] The Great Rite, the most important witchcraft ritual, acts out in ritual the eternal male/female sexual union of the God and Goddess. In the Judeo-Christian tradition, on the other hand, the sexual union is necessarily monogamous, exclusive, heterosexual, and permanently committed as a representation of the interpersonal commitment between God and those who love him.

*Relativism.* The subjectivity of witchcraft's worldview is expressed in the assertion that there are many ways to truth and many understandings of the Divine. However, this relativism seems contradicted by witchcraft's rejection of absolutist religious views such as those of Christianity: "Our only animosity toward Christianity, or toward any other religion or philosophy-of-life, is to the extent that its institutions have claimed to be 'the one true and right and only way....'"[39] If all ways are equally true, then isn't the exclusive Christian way also true? But if it's exclusively true, then other ways are false, and all ways are therefore not equally true. Relativism ultimately is self-contradictory. It is illogical.

*The Power of Magic.* Different witches describe the power of magic in different ways. Some sound as though they believe there are elemental powers within the unseen universe that can be used or captured by the witch to perform acts or accomplish ends. Other witches stress the power of magic as the ritualized ability to harmonize oneself with the life pulse of the universe. Some witches link the power of magic primarily to its emotional and spiritual effect within the practitioner. All witches, however, describe the power of magic as natural, not supernatural: "We acknowledge a depth of power far greater than is apparent to the average person. Because it is far greater than ordinary, it is sometimes called 'supernatural,' but we see it as lying within that which is naturally potential to all."[40]

Teenagers who understand and practice contemporary witchcraft are attracted not only to its positive, environmentally sensitive, harmonious commitments, but also to the witches' apparent ability to live creatively, powerfully, and magically. The beliefs described above are fundamental to contemporary witchcraft, but teenagers may call witchcraft what is instead superstitious magic more akin to the satanic.

**Symbols.** There are many symbols associated with contemporary witchcraft. As in satanism, the individual freedom of the practitioner allows for a wide variety of symbols, some borrowed from other disciplines, some almost exclusive to witchcraft, and many from the common world given special witchcraft significance. Since witchcraft draws actively from many of the historical and international myth traditions, many of the symbols of those myths and religions are also used. Some witches stick to one particular magical tradition (Celtic, Greek, Roman, Native American, or Hindu) while many pagans, especially teenage dabblers, take a little from a variety of traditions.

*The Pentagram.* The five-pointed star, called a pentacle when encircled, is one of the basic witchcraft symbols. Each point represents one of the elements of the universe, clockwise from the top: spirit, water, fire, earth, and air. The star also symbolizes humanity, the top point being humanity reaching toward the heavens, the bottom two points being humanity straddling the natural world.

*The Circle.* The circle is fundamental to almost all kinds of magic ritual and witchcraft. In witchcraft the circle represents eternity. It is also used to represent both the focusing of power and the protection afforded participants within the circle. For ritual purposes the circle is nine feet across. Most witches draw or inscribe a circle on the ground or floor, and then also "draw" a corresponding circle in the air with their ritual knife. No one is allowed to cross either circle during a ritual without the high priest(ess) or assistant ceremonially "cutting" the invisible circle and then resealing it.

*The Elements.* Witchcraft describes five basic elements of the universe: spirit (like a spoked wheel), water (an upside-down triangle), fire (a triangle), earth (an upside-down triangle with a horizontal line spanning the tip), and air (an upright triangle with a horizontal line spanning the tip). These figures can be found together or individually. They often are placed on a tool or item of ritual significance. Each is associated with different purposes or goals of magic. They may be inscribed on jewelry or sewn on clothing.

| Spirit | Water | Fire | Earth | Air |
|--------|-------|------|-------|-----|

*The Sabbatic Goat.* The Goat of Mendes represents completely different ideas in witchcraft than in satanism. Witches do not believe in Satan or satan worship. In witchcraft, the goat's horns represent the waxing and waning moon. The horn represents the light of universal knowledge available to anyone who learns how to access it. The goat is reminiscent of the sacrificial goat of the Old Testament, and reminds the witch that self-sacrifice or self-discipline is necessary for an individual to achieve true enlightenment. The male and female physical characteristics remind the witch of the god/goddess polarity of the universe. Of course, many teenage occult dabblers are unaware of the distinctive interpretations of the figure in witchcraft as opposed to satanism, and consequently both teenage satanists and witches may use and understand the figure indiscriminately.

*The Hexagram.* Some occultists believe this figure, composed of two interlocking triangles, one upside-down, is one of the most powerful symbols in the practice of magick. The hexagram is often encircled, increasing its power and significance. It is also referred to as the "Seal of Solomon" in kabalic mysticism, and became a common symbol among some groups of Jews during the Middle Ages, but was not distinctively identified with Judaism until the 1700s. The hexagram symbolizes the masculine (right-side-up or piercing triangle) and feminine (upside-down or receptive triangle) principles united, essential to the propagation and continuation of life. The two triangles are also the elemental symbols of water and fire.

*The Moon.* The moon, most commonly in crescent shape, is symbolic of the universal feminine principle, in distinction from the male symbolism of the sun. The moon goddess is Diana, and many witches who are dedicated to Diana use the moon as their symbol of recognition. The waxing, growing larger, moon's points are to the left; while the waning, or diminishing, moon's points are to the right.

*The Ankh (Onk).* This Egyptian symbol for life or fertility combines the straight line phallic symbol of the male with the open curve of the female symbol. The union of male and female produces life and is representative of universal polarity. The ankh may also represent immortality, the never-ending regeneration of life through birth. In contemporary witchcraft, this is often a symbol representing reincarnation.

*The Gods and Goddesses.* Polytheism is integral to the contemporary witchcraft point of view. However, it is not important whether or not the gods and goddesses actually exist. Instead, they are mythological representations of all the nuances of the divine bios: the elements, seasons, or stages of life, for example. Witches commonly pick one or several gods or goddesses as primary in their own worship. The gods or goddesses they pick represent their vital interests and personify their goals. Often traditional depictions of these gods and goddesses are inscribed on jewelry, woven into clothing, or pictured. The goddess representing the totality of earth's divine life is the Greek goddess *Gaea,* sometimes spelled Gaia. Gaea is the primary deity of many contemporary neo-pagans. Other common gods and goddesses include Diana, the Roman goddess of the moon and the hunt; Pan, the Greek god of nature and sensual pleasure, natural indulgence; and Cernunnos, the Celtic "horned god," identified with the spirit of wild animals.

Gaea

Diana

Pan

Cernunnos

*Yin and Yang.* This ancient Chinese symbol represents the eternal duality of all reality. A circle is divided in two by a backward "S" curved line. The left half is black with a small white circle in the larger section, the right half is white with a corresponding small black circle. In Taoist philosophy, black represents the female (Yin), passive aspects of reality while white represents the male (Yang), dominant aspects of reality. Contemporary pagans or witches have adopted this eastern symbol to represent the god/goddess polarity of their worldview. Frequently this symbol adorns bumper stickers and posters.

*Medicine Wheel.* This symbol, a black circle divided into fourths, with a black dot in each of the quarters, is a common Native American symbol. It has been adopted by the contemporary Native American Church to symbolize magical power. Many use this symbol not only to represent the magic circle, but also as a focusing point for a ritual or spell.

*The Sun.* The sun, commonly represented by a circle with a black center or a quartered circle, is considered masculine in the pagan world view. This figure often appears in conjunction with a moon symbol, representing the feminine aspect of life, both symbols indicating the duality of existence, the god/goddess motif of witchcraft mythology.

*The Kabalah.* This medieval Jewish mystical symbol, also called "The Tree of Life," has a wide variety of meaning and use. The word means "doctrines received from tradition."[41] At one time it referred to the entire body of Jewish theological and religious tradition, but by the Middle Ages it referred primarily to a Jewish mystical occult tradition of interpretation. The symbol of ten stylistically arranged circles, each connected to the other by three solid bars, is used for many different kinds of magic for a variety of purposes. By renaming the circles and bars, the figure can represent the names of God, the destiny of man, the visible and invisible paths of wisdom, the zodiac, the tarot, even the archangels and planetary spirits. Many kabalah symbols are intricately colored and embellished, each color and stroke carrying a magical connotation.

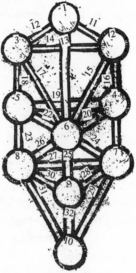

*The Moon Sign.* This hand sign is often confused with the satanic salute. The thumb and little finger are extended, the other fingers folded into the palm. The two extended fingers shape the hand similar to a crescent, the feminine principle, the goddess. Surfers make an identical sign, but twist their wrists back and forth to signal "Hang ten," or "good luck" in surfing.

Teenagers who are dabbling in witchcraft are likely to use many witchcraft symbols. Contemporary witchcraft is philosophical and complex, and many teenagers don't have the patience or long-term commitment to study it deeply. Symbols are an easy way to identify with a movement that is more appealing to a teenager's emotions and curiosity than intellect.

**Words.** Contemporary witchcraft's vocabulary is not as deeply cryptic or coded as that of satanism. Words are considered as possessing magical power, although that magical power may be defined differently by different pagans. Some pagans believe the spiritual world actually exists and exerts a real magical influence on the material world. Some believe that mind and emotions arise from the material world and are its "after-effects." Magic to this kind of witch arises from the material world and is natural, not supernatural. Still others don't care whether or not anything immaterial exists, or if magic is real, natural or supernatural. These neo-pagans practice magic because it works and makes them feel better.

Following magical tradition, witches associate magic with words and the use of words in ritual. Proper word usage focuses the attention and emotions of the practitioner, attracts and focuses magical forces, and organizes and directs the purpose of the magic.

Many witches take new names at their initiation to symbolize their new "birth" into the divinity of all life. Often the new name is the name of a god or goddess whom they want to imitate. Common witchcraft terminology is quickly adopted, even by teenagers.

An *adept* means one who is expert or skilled in magic.

*Alchemy,* which once referred to the "art" of transforming base metal into gold, in today's witchcraft is a metaphor for personal enlightenment.

*Arcane,* from the Latin meaning chest or depository, refers to knowledge which is secret or esoteric.

*Astral* refers to the world or reality between the material and that of pure spirit, or divinity. It is most commonly used in the term *astral projection,* the magical practice of extending one's consciousness beyond the confines of the body. Such "out-of-body" experiences are explained variously by different witches, some believing the spirit actually leaves the body and others explaining it by elevated mental states.

A *cantrip* is a recorded spell that reads the same forward

or backward. It is said to be powerful magic.

The *cone of power* is said to come from the combined psychic energy of a group focused through ritual within a magic circle, organized and used for a particular purpose, directed by the priestess or priest of the group.

*Coven* is still the most common term to describe a witch-craft group committed in ritual to each other. However, some witches avoid the term with outsiders since some satanists also use the term. Many witches restrict the number in a coven to thirteen.

*Empathy* is given special significance in witchcraft. It means more than to identify with someone, or to share someone's emotion. In witchcraft empathy includes a mystical or magical sensitivity to another's psychic state.

A *familiar* is in special mutual psychic empathy with a witch. The familiar is not human, and is usually a small animal, especially one sharing natural characteristics such as bravery or cunning with the witch.

A *grimoire* is a collection of magical spells, charms, recipes, and herblore consulted by witches to determine the best magic for any given situation.

*Runes* are an important letter symbolism of witchcraft. Any alphabet used in a magical way is runic. The ordinary meaning of the letters masks the magical meaning given by the witch who uses them.

A magical sign or coded symbol that stands for an individual, human or otherwise, is called a *sigil.*

*Thaumaturgy* and *sorcery* are interchangeable terms for the use of magic to affect a situation or person outside of the magician himself or herself.

*The Web* is a term used in witchcraft to refer to the matrix of all matter and energy, intertwined, together the divine reality.

If your teenager is involved in witchcraft, it is likely that he or she will use a variety of special terms, including many of the terms and symbols listed here. If you occasionally hear one or two terms used off-handedly, don't be too alarmed. Many teenagers pick up witchcraft terms from television cartoons, popular songs, and movies. However, if your teenager's vocabulary becomes peppered with witchcraft terminology, especially if he or she seems secretive about the words or avoids their use around you, then be concerned that your teenager may be studying witchcraft seriously.

**Books.** The number of books on witchcraft and paganism has exploded over the last five years. Today many secular bookstores have an entire section dedicated to "Gaia," "the Goddess," "Paganism," or "Magick." Llewellyn Publications specializes in publishing witchcraft and pagan books. There are dozens of books that tell about witchcraft, and there are also many witchcraft books that instruct in the art of witchcraft as well as providing information. There are even novels utilizing a witchcraft motif.

Most teenagers learn their first witchcraft from books. The most popular book by far is *The Spiral Dance*[42] by a witch who uses the name Starhawk. Starhawk has written a number of books since then, including the popular *Dreaming in the Dark.*[43]

The most comprehensive survey of contemporary witchcraft is by journalist-pagan Margot Adler, *Drawing Down the Moon.*[44] Other popular books are *Modern Magick: Eleven Lessons in the High Magickal Arts,*[45] Stewart Farrar's books, including *What Witches Do*[46] and a book he co-authored with his wife and high priestess, Janet, *A Witches Bible Compleat,*[47] *Modern Ritual Magic,*[48] and *Buckland's Complete Book of Witchcraft.*[49]

The most important book to a witch or a witches' coven is *The Black Book,* or *Book of Shadows.* This book, usually handwritten and beautifully decorated, contains all of the rituals, spells, records and rules of the individual coven, invocations, notes, and traditions of the witch or coven. There are no two exactly alike. A teenager's Black Book may be in a notebook, a bound diary, or one of the popular fabric covered blank books available in most stationery and gift stores.

**Tools.** The most important tool to a witch is his or her own body, attuned to the divinity of life through careful attenuation, ritual, and magical practices. Next to the body, the *athamé*, or witch's knife is the most important. This consecrated ceremonial knife usually has a black, intricately carved hilt. It is used in every witchcraft ritual, but never to draw blood. Some witches call the knife by its Scottish name, *yag-dirk*, or its Saxon name, *se-ax*. Athamés are available in most occult stores and by mail order, although the best one is made individually by the witch who will use it.

Solitary witches often do not use a sword, but most covens possess a *coven sword*, used for drawing the magic circle for a ritual. Circles are not only drawn on the ground or floor, but also in the air. The invisible circle and other signs drawn in the air are usually drawn with the athamé or a specially consecrated *air dagger.*

The *bell* is used to signal the beginning or ending of a ritual or ritual segment. The vibration of the bell represents the unseen natural powers and also increases the magical power of the ritual.

Every witch wears a *cord* or *cingulum* at the waist, used ritually for binding, loosing, and measuring. Knot magic is said to be especially powerful as a "storage" place for power. The cords are nine feet long (nine is three times three, the magic number) and can be various colors. They should be made of a natural fiber, and the best are hand braided by the one who is to wear them.

*Candles* are used to light the ritual circle, to represent the basic element of fire, to purify, and for several other reasons. Usually four candles are used, and are placed at the compass points. The candle corresponding to north is lighted first.

Different colored candles can be used for different purposes. The colors correspond to astral colors, symbolic significance, or days of the week.

*Salt* is used ritually for consecrating, purifying, and protecting from evil.

*Bowls and chalices* are used for various ritual purposes. The chalice filled with water and consecrated symbolizes the basic element of water. The chalice is also used for the ceremonial liquid used in blessing. Water in the bowl can be used for *scrying*, or "seeing through" a clear or reflective surface to obtain magical discernment, or clairvoyance.

Many witches engage in ritual *sky clad*, or naked. Alternatively, the witch or coven may cover the naked body with a *robe.* The robe should be made of a natural fiber and should be handmade or at least decorated by the witch who will be wearing it. Until fairly recently most witches wore white robes. Over the last few years colored robes have become popular. The robe may be a solid color or a combination of colors.

The *altar* is the central focus of the ritual. It is placed in the ritual circle and holds the other ritual tools such as the athamé, chalice, salt, and pentacle. Almost any flat, elevated surface can be used as an altar, although a handmade one permanently consecrated is preferred. Such an altar should be made of natural materials and no metal. Often witches use a circular altar, but rectangular ones are the most common. A teenage witch may use the nightstand, desk, or a small table in his or her bedroom.

The ritual *wand* and the optional wizard's *staff* are used by most witches. There are many different kinds of wands, some nothing more than a bare willow or ash branch, some highly decorated and colored, and specially crafted. The wand is an emblem of the basic elements of fire or air, and is used for consecration or direction of energy in rituals where the athamé or other blade cannot be used. The wand is short while the staff is as long as its owner is tall. Both the wand and the staff are consecrated to their individual owner, and no one else is supposed to handle or use them. A teenager will hide his wand or staff, or at least try to keep anyone else from touching it.

There are many other tools, some used only in certain witchcraft traditions. Others are common, but are also easily available to teenagers who have only a passing interest in the occult. *Incense,* for example, is used in every witchcraft ritual, but many teenagers use it in conjunction with drug use, while they are listening to music, or just for fun. *Herbs, roots,* and *potions* are used ritually for healing and magical purposes. Witchcraft, based on the assumption of the unity of all life, is "into" organic, naturopathic health techniques. *Wortcunning,* or herbal lore, combines various ancient folk remedy traditions and witchcraft. Herbs and roots are used not only medicinally, but also magically. Other witchcraft tools include the *pentacle, talismans, amulets,* and *deity statues* or representations.

**Practices.** The primary practice of today's witch or pagan is not the ritual. Because of the pantheistic witchcraft worldview, the witch sees himself as an integral part of the divine organism. Consequently, the witch's primary practice is his daily living. Life is the greatest ritual of all.

Still, practicing rituals is very important in witchcraft. Some rituals can be performed alone, and some witches never practice with others. However, the longer someone practices witchcraft, the more they seek contact and experience with other witches.

Contemporary witchcraft or satanism has become very social. Today there are dozens of witchcraft traditions and associations that meet several times a year for pagan festivals. The festivals include rituals, socializing, crafts, entertainment, workshops and seminars, food, and herb/root and potion booths. Many contemporary festivals draw entire families of witches. This added attraction of friendship and a sense of belonging draws many disaffected or alienated teenagers. Concerned parents need to consider this social need and find an acceptable alternative for their children.

There are many different kinds of witchcraft rituals. The Great Ritual or Rite is one of the most important and is symbolic of the unity in duality of the universe. The Great Ritual involves actual or symbolized sex as a picture of the creative unity of the god and goddess, often referred to as the goddess and her consort. Another well-known ritual is called drawing down the moon, where the presence of the goddess is invoked through ritual, the high priestess personifying or embodying the goddess.

Other rituals include special rites for particular holidays. The four great festivals are February 2 (Candlemas), April 30 (May Eve), July 31 (August Eve), and October 31 (Halloween). Lesser festivals are held on the solstices (June 22 and December 22) and the two equinoxes (March 21 and September 21). Rituals are often held at full moon and/or dark moon. Other holidays are associated with particular witchcraft traditions and the mythology from which they draw.

Rituals are held for specific purposes of celebration, healing, rites of passage, and initiation. A witch may perform a ritual individually or with a group at almost any time for a variety of purposes. The tools used in rituals were described previously. Witchcraft rituals are much less rigid and uniform than those of satanism.

> Rituals of magic and worship may be simple or complex. They may include invocations, chanting, meditation, sacred drama, poetry, music, dancing, and other acts of celebration, and spell working. Magic is worked for various goals, including prosperity, healing, and spiritual growth. Divination is often practiced by various methods, such as Tarot reading. There may be a shared meal and socializing. Covens... meet at Full Moon, some at Dark Moon, and the Solstices, Equinoxes, and the four Celtic fire festivals of Imbolc (February Eve), Beltane (May Eve), Lughnasadh (August Eve), and Samhain (November Eve).[50]

## IS YOUR CHILD INVOLVED IN THE OCCULT?

This chapter gives you a wealth of information to help you understand the vulnerabilities your child may have for occultic involvement. Clearly satanism is a destructive influence on teenagers and can combine with dysfunctional behavior and alienation to create a teenager in crisis.

Witchcraft is much more attractive to teenagers searching for the meaning of life and for personal control over themselves and the world around them. However, with its contradictory dogmatic relativism it provides a worldview unable to evaluate moral options.

Carefully evaluate your concerns for your teenager. If you have good cause to believe your teenager is involved in satanism or witchcraft, there are constructive steps you can take to help.

The first step is to recognize the signs of involvement. That is what you have learned in this chapter. The second step is to understand the most important peer influences reinforcing your teenager's occult involvement. The following chapter will help you understand the enormous influence music, videos, movies, and other media sources exert on teenagers.

# FIVE

# The Media Connection

ROGER COULD HEAR Tad's stereo blasting through the wall of the garage as he pulled in from work. It irritated him, especially after a hard day, but he tried to remember not to get on his kid's case like his parents had hassled him when he had been a teenager. What was it about being a teenager that made loud, obnoxious music absolutely mandatory?

Roger remembered how his father turned bright red as he shouted at his hippie son about the moral decadence and hearing loss that would certainly result from Roger's steady audio diet of the Beatles, the Rolling Stones, and the Doors. Roger knew Dad's anger had turned to rage when his flush spread across his balding head and his eyes started to bulge. Roger chuckled at the memory as he opened the inside door and stepped into the kitchen.

"What are you in such a good mood about?" Roger's wife looked relieved that tonight his mood didn't reflect the freeway frustration he endured daily on the way home.

"Just thinking about how funny Dad looked when he used to scream at me about my music when I was a teenager. Remember how parents predicted social anarchy if kids started wearing their hair as long as the Beatles?"

Alyce laughed, "I remember my mother lecturing me about the Rolling Stones' bad grammar in 'Satisfaction.'"

"And Ed Sullivan made them change 'Let's Spend the Night Together' to 'Let's Spend Some Time Together' on his show." Roger shook his head ruefully. "Well, I guess we survived okay. Tad will, too. Kids will be kids!"

Tad, surrounded by quadraphonic CD sound in his bedroom, didn't hear his parents. He lay on his bed, staring at the poster of his favorite metal band, Motorhead. As he stared intently, he sketchily copied a twisted figure on a stylized cross. The man—if it was a man—had the body of Jesus Christ but the head of a snarling wolf. Tad was copying it from the poster. "That Jesus guy," Tad muttered to himself, "He should have bit those m****r f****r's heads off, 'stead of just hangin' there." Tad didn't believe in any of that wimpy sacrificial lamb stuff. He'd rather be the wolf and enjoy a nice lamb dinner! Frustrated with his crude sketch, Tad threw his pencil at the wall. He was always amazed at the artistic vision he possessed when he was loaded, but the vision never quite made it onto his paper. Tad fingered the satanic pentacle dangling from his left ear and started to chant as he dug into his backpack for more drugs.

A young Texan named Ricky was also into metal music. His favorite band was AC/DC, his favorite album their *Highway to Hell.* His favorite song on the album was "Night Prowler," a creepy metal ballad about a murderous prowler stealing into a terrified victim's bedroom, death his only companion. Ricky was convicted of thirteen counts of murder and thirty other felonies, including robbery, sodomy, oral copulation, attempted murder, and burglary as the infamous Night Stalker, Richard Ramirez, the man who held Southern California hostage for the summer of 1985.[1]

Tad and Ricky are very different. Tad is part of a close, upper middle class nuclear family, his worst offenses were recreational drug use, mouthing off to adults, and dabbling in satanic ritualism alone in his bedroom. Ricky's barrio childhood was anything but secure, he immersed himself in destructive occultism, and he seemed to get his biggest sense of accomplishment from brutally torturing and then killing his victims.

But Tad and Ricky have three important things in common: drugs, satanism, and metal music.[2] In fact, contemporary teenage satanic practice occurs, almost without fail, in conjunction with drugs and metal music. Researcher John Charles Cooper recognizes the connection and even says "satanism and drugs always go together," explaining,

> It is fanatical to believe that every youth who plays fantasy games or enjoys heavy-metal rock music is into occultism, but young people found engaged in destructive occultism usually are hyperinvolved in thrash metal, like Ozzy Osborne, Slayer, Venom, and Poison. The lyrics, dress, symbols, and lifestyles of these heavy-metal singers and performers make Satanism attractive to many young people from a very early age. Join the sadistic lyrics and blatantly perverse sexuality of these rock bands to the intoxication of alcohol, pot or hard drugs, and you have very heavy conditioning that might well tip a teenger into antisocial behavior.[3]

Never before has destructive occultism been hawked so crassly directly to teenagers through metal music, movies and videos, books, and even comic books and magazines.

Until the last three decades, the primary source of information on occult subjects was word of mouth, secondarily through books. A typical teenager's closest brush with the occult was playing with an Ouija board or giggling through a mock seance at a slumber party.

Today's teenagers are confronted on every side with the commercialized occult. Their favorite bands recite satanic lyrics; tee shirts are emblazoned with satanic pentacles; top grossing movies feature immortal demonic murderers; corner bookstores are dedicated to the Goddess; comic super heroes call on demonic powers to vanquish the enemy; and the most popular mail order jewelry includes inverted cross earrings, human skull charm bracelets, and goat's head necklaces.

The satanic connection to teenage media is inexorably entwined with drugs, sex, and rebellion. Take the common upheavals and uncertainties of adolescence, intensify them through constant loud repetition, and utter lawlessness and senseless violence is the common result. This out of control self-indulgence can become a dangerous, compelling bondage drawing a teenager into eventual self-destruction. Rebellion becomes suicide, "Satanism blesses and encourages the expression of all that is natural to adolescent development—rebellion, defiance, and specialness—yet it lacks a positive, rational framework and totally disregards relational, social, and religious boundaries and values."[4]

Teenage destructive occultism is a symptom or result of a lack of values in the teenager's life. If nothing matters, then nothing matters; values don't conflict because *there are no values*. Life becomes nothing but a constant battle of mutual exploitation, ending only in destruction. While much of popular media is not overtly occultic, the constant message preached to our teens is self-centered destructiveness, a message in perfect harmony with the sermons of contemporary satanism.

## MUSIC AND MUSIC VIDEOS

Nowhere is this mutual exploitive destruction more obvious than in contemporary metal music, described by metal rocker Alice Cooper as, "nothing but a fist in your face."[5] The entire purpose of metal music is to rejoice in destruction. Bands and fans alike are out to get whatever they can from each other—almost always including sex and drugs, often within an occult setting.

Tad's metal music represents the ultimate destructive end of his father's late 1960s acid rock. While acid rock *preached* self-indulgence and moral relativism, metal music *is* self-indulgence and active defiance of all morals.

Head banging is one of the favorite pastimes of metal music fans. It's exactly what it sounds like: fans bang their heads repeatedly against the wall, floor, stage, or door while they listen to their favorite band. Why? Because it hurts and it's outrageous, that's why. As metal master Ozzy Osborne explains, "I like death and destruction, frenzy and hatred."[6]

Bands' names reflect the anti-morality of the metal scene, among them: Annihilator, Atrocity, Beggars and Thieves, Death, Death Angel, Faith No More, Heathen, Field of the Nephalam, Helloween,[7] Here Comes Trouble, Lizzie Borden, Lynch Mob, Malevolent Creation, Megadeth,[8] N.W.A. (Niggers with an Attitude), Pestilence, Poison, Sacrifice, Seduce, Slaughter, Slayer, Suicidal Tendencies, Trixter, Trouble Tribe, Venom, and Violence.

Album and song titles reinforce the violence, destruction, and sexual depravity of the worst metal messages, among them: Appetite for Destruction; Cowboys from Hell; Dirty Deeds; Eternal Nightmare; Headless Children; Highway to Hell; Kill to Survive; Killers; Mob Rules; No Rest for the Wicked; The Number of the Beast; Screaming for Vengeance; Screwed, Blued, and Tattooed; Souls of Black; Stick It Live; Ultimate Sin; and Welcome to Hell.

These are not fringe, underground local bands strictly off limits to impressionable teenagers. Each of the groups and titles above are in ordinary strip mall record stores and are advertised in popular teenage fan magazines available at local grocery stores.

The lyrics to most metal pieces are crude, shocking, and bluntly violent. Favorite themes are animal mutilation and sacrifice, bestiality, bisexuality, grave robbing, human sacrifice, incest, incubus[9] and succubus[10] activity, looting, matricide, masturbation, murder, necrophilia,[11] patricide, property destruction, sado-masochism, self-mutilation, sexual perversion, suicide, and torture.

Sex and drugs pervade the metal scene. Drugs of choice are present everywhere at concerts, and dares to see who can get the most loaded are common. Sex, especially perverted sex, is rampant. Fans with fans, fans with band members and roadies,[12] males with males, females with females, and group sex are the norm rather than the exception.

One teenage girl we interviewed protested, "I don't do drugs or sex—I'm totally straight, but metal's my favorite music and I go to clubs at least once a week."

Questioned further, Lori explained, "Well, sure, the sex and drugs are there, all around. I could buy anything I wanted within a couple minutes of getting to the club. And guys and girls are always hitting on me to put out. But I just don't do that. I'm there for the music. I guess I do kinda stick out from the crowd."

We asked Lori what her parents thought about her choice of music. "They don't know too much about it. They don't listen to it except to yell at me to turn it down."

Would she be bothered if they listened to the lyrics or went to a club to see what it was like? "Are you kidding? I'd be dead, totally dead! They have no idea what goes on there. My mom thinks it's like going to a school dance or something. I don't think they could handle it. No way."

It didn't seem to bother Lori that she felt compelled to conceal what she said was "just for fun" from her admittedly open-minded parents.

Metal music may be the most decadent contemporary music, but it's not the only kind that promotes lifestyles contrary to most Americans' values. Rap music's combative lyrics have made the news recently, and critics cite rap's heavy emphasis on sex and violence. *The Los Angeles Times,* in a review of female rap group BWP (Bytches With Problems), observed,

> Of the 46 groups that rap kingpin Russell Simmons either manages or has signed to one of his record labels, he says his absolute favorite is the female New York rap duo Bytches With Problems. He can even recite their lyrics from memory.
>
> There's just one problem—the lyrics are so filthy you couldn't print any of them in a family newspaper. But that hasn't stopped Simmons' RAL Records label and his distributor, Columbia Records, from releasing the BWP album, "The Bytches." In fact, the foul-mouthed group's first single, "Two Minute Brother," is already at No. 6 on the rap chart.[13]

At the end of 1990 pop singer Madonna's new video single, "Justify My Love," was rejected by cable's MTV because of its obvious depictions of sexual intercourse between Madonna and her boyfriend and suggestions of lesbian sex. The video was replete with suggestive religious imagery, confusing sexual indulgence with religous ritual through the use of crucifixes and other religious symbolism.

The most obvious influence of contemporary destructive music is its effect on followers' morals or values. One's ethics are usually reflective of the society around him, and when a teenager surrounds himself with self-indulgent, cruel, and violent attitudes and ideas, it is no wonder that he or she will gradually begin to reflect that worldview in his or her own life.

Teenagers who immerse themselves in these kinds of lyrics and ideas soon begin adopting the attitudes reflected in the songs. Whether or not the bands believe what they sing (or scream), a steady diet of death and thrash metal perverts the way the listener thinks and relates to those around him or her. Assault, rape, swearing, and robbery become initial reactions rather than extreme responses to the daily frustrations of adolescence.

Parents concerned about their teenager's possible involvement with destructive occultism should watch MTV with them and listen to the lyrics from their favorite songs. If your child is turning into "an attitude," listen to the attitudes he's copying. Don't assume that the school system, grocery store managers, music stores, or the entertainment industry will ensure a healthy diet for your child. The ultimate responsibility is yours.

**Role Models.** When radio, television, and movies blanketed the nation, our heroes changed drastically. Heroes of other generations were generals, mayors, saints, hard workers whose lives profoundly impacted their local communities or the larger society. Today's heroes are rock stars, actresses, and TV sitcom cartoon characters. Looking for heroes is a human habit, and today's teenagers are no different from those of other generations. They will have role models, they will look up to others, and they will imitate those they admire. What has happened is that they use foul-mouthed, loaded egomaniacs as role models, look up to singers who spit on them and call them "mother f****rs," and imitate bands whose life motto is "Get sex and get wasted."

Most bands don't want to accept the responsibility of being role models. They try to say they're not trying to influence anyone, they just want to play and have fun. But it takes serious commitment for a teenager to spend three months of his part-time income for studs, spikes, and leather to look just like his favorite Judas Priest musician. Of course, adulation and imitation (the sincerest form of flattery?) result in greater record sales and higher concert takes. Consequently, bands inconsistently deny being role models when censors and parents accuse them of corrupting youth, but swell with pride when those same youth buy their records, imitate their costumes, and spit and swear right back at them. This inconsistency is apparent in comments by Mike Muir of the metal band Suicidal Tendencies:

> I don't think that I have any major influence over anybody, but I think the most effective thing about Suicidal Tendencies is the fact that when we play live people see us as a very believable thing, and it's very believable because it's the truth. There are certain people that can tell stories and they can act and this and that, and you are impressed by what they are doing, and you can see certain plays and what a person says brings tears to your eyes, but they are acting and they do it night after night. I think the thing is that people realize what Suicidal is, and it's not an act, and they realize that the success that we have had... it's because we have always stood up for what we believed....[14]

**Mutual Exploitation.** A second serious problem with contemporary destructive music is the mutual exploitation rampant throughout the industry and between industry and consumer. Destructive rock is big business.

Metal bands use backers' money for hair stylists, makeup artists, poster designers, sound equipment, studio rental, clothing designers, and a host of other essential services, without which they couldn't be nearly as spontaneous and natural.

The clubs operate pay-for-play programs where bands guarantee to purchase a minimum of tickets for their show and then must turn around and sell them to their fans. The club is guaranteed a full house, good publicity, and attractive profits on drinks and food.

The band gets an audience, publicity, profit (if they sell enough tickets), sex with however many females, males, or both they want, free drinks and food from their fans, and that ever-elusive recording contract with a major label. They are all convinced they'll make it.

The fans get to buy records, outrage their parents, and

drown their teenage sorrows in a cesspool of drugs, alcohol, noise, and head banging, celebrating youth by sharing sex with a "star" who can't remember their names and then shoves them off the bed so he can grab his next "lover." One metal musician described girls as "the fleas and ticks of rock and roll."[15] Another band member recalled his band's early years of struggle, when "chicks didn't get in our room without a sack of groceries."[16] A metal singer expressed the sentiments of both band and fan, saying, "You can take advantage of them as much as they can take advantage of you."[17]

Many parents are unaware of how much financial and emotional exploitation their teenagers may experience from the contemporary music scene.

Lori, the club hopper we interviewed, estimated at first that she spent maybe twenty dollars a week or so on club tickets. That was easily covered by her part-time income from the boutique where she worked. As we talked, she remembered that she also spent twenty dollars a week on drinks and snacks at the clubs. "Actually," she added, "I don't really get much money from my job because I'm always using my pay for clothes, jewelry, and shoes. Even with my employee discount I spend most of my check on clothes. But it's worth it. I love to be the most outrageously dressed girl in our group." When she added CD purchases, posters, and related expenses, she estimated her weekly costs at an even $100. "But that's not bad!" Lori pointed out, "Friends that do drugs or drink can spend a hundred in five minutes."

**Drugs, Alcohol, and Sex.** Drugs, alcohol, and sex go with metal music as naturally as peanut butter and jelly with Wonder bread. Metal bands typically project the image that drugs and alcohol are a kick and sex keeps them going. The number of metal players and singers who have ruined their bands or died from drug and alcohol use rises steadily. Sexually transmitted diseases are rampant among the club crowds, band members, and fans alike. This rampant chemical destruction and sexual debauchery perhaps partly explains the popularity among teenagers of the film biography[18] of Doors' singer Jim Morrison, whose decadent onstage behavior was legendary and who died of heart failure at age twenty-seven at the height of his career.

Heavy metal musician Chris Holmes bragged that he drank five bottles of vodka, straight, every day. He predicted he would be dead in ten years, but that was all right because life would be meaningless in ten years anyway. He called himself "the happiest s.o.b. and m****r f****r there ever was," and yet in the same breath said, "Drinking is the only thing that lets me be free. I don't dig being the person I am."[19]

This ambivalence is a common result of a relativistic world view. Nothing is bad, nothing is good, nothing matters. Even those metal musicians who swear off drugs and alcohol do so by personal inclination, not because they believe in absolute moral values. Ex-drugger Dave Mustaine of Megadeth expresses this ambivalence. At first he says drugs and alcohol are not for him, but he certainly wouldn't want to push *his* values on someone else. That is, of course, unless someone wants to do drugs or alcohol around him. Then he calls them selfish and has them removed from his presence:

> A lot of it has to do with the fact that I'm off of drugs and alcohol. I hate to be a preacher or anything like that, I mean if it still works for someone else that's cool. I wish it still worked for me but it doesn't. It's kinda hard to come out here and play when you see someone that you wanna hang out with, some friends or something and they come up and they're out of it. Just for my own safety and for my dedication to our following, I cordially and gracefully excuse myself, and I ask them to be removed because I'm not gonna sit around and let some other selfish pig f**k up my attitude and make me slip and go get loaded

and ruin it for all these other kids who wanna see Dave now that he's back on track.[20]

The only difference between relative values and selfish values is that selfish values are relative to the person with the most power.

**Violence.** Little wonder, then, that relative values quickly degenerate into a self-centered "do unto others before they do unto you." The destructive themes of metal band names and song lyrics mirror the basic attitudes of many band members and fans. Bruce Dickinson of Iron Maiden explained how exploited kids could get revenge through their own exploitation:

> ... personally speaking, there's something you can do which is infinitely more satisfying in the long term, more wonderfully subversive than anything that they can ever do to you. And that's to read books. And that's to figure out your own philosophies on life and that's to decide that when you become an adult you are going to make sure that that philosophy runs through as much as possible, everything you do. So if you get to be an employer, if you get to be the boss at your local bank and you find out that some religious fundamentalist has come to apply for a job, you don't give it to him. In the same way you have reverse discrimination, then you f**k the people that are f*****g you. That's how you do it, because they will f**k you, they plan it.[21]

What a fitting companion to Anton LaVey's satanic pledge: "Give blow for blow, scorn for scorn, doom for doom—with compound interest liberally added thereunto! Eye for eye, tooth for tooth, aye four-fold, a hundred-fold! Make yourself a Terror to your adversary..."[22]

**Satanism.** Most metal bands, even those with overtly satanic song themes and lyrics, deny they are serious satanists. Most embrace satanic symbolism because of its anti-morality stance rather than as a positive commitment to a satanic being or religion. In fact, most satanic themes in metal music come from the same kind of self-indulgent disdain for traditional religion that characterized the Hell-Fire Clubs of eighteenth-century Britain.

Motley Crue's once popular "Shout at the Devil" was not a Satan worshiping song, they said, but represented the teenage urge to "shout at," or defy, anything or anyone who stood in their way—parents, teachers, police, or employers. Parents took slight comfort in the idea that their kids weren't worshiping Satan, but merely calling Mom and Dad Satan.

Metal band import Sepultura played "death metal" for a while, but then abandoned the explicitly satanic lyrics for broader themes. Band member Max Cavalera explains, "The main thing that made us decide to change was lyrics. Lyrically I was not happy with death metal. We have more to say, mainly from where we come from you know, from all the s**t we have to live every day, we have something more serious to say than just 'SATAN' or something like that."[23]

Yet Sepultura, like most metal bands, sees nothing wrong with satanic lyrics, and their current lyrics still reflect the decadence inherent in contemporary satanism. Even if the satanic lyrics were nothing more than symbolism, what they symbolize is the core of contemporary self-indulgent, self-centeredness unique to satanism.

In fact, even the most explicitly satanic band, Slayer, denies its members actually practice satanism or believe in the demonically supernatural their lyrics celebrate. King Diamond is the only widely popular metal musician to consider himself a serious, dedicated satanist, and Diamond carefully explains that he doesn't believe in the supernatural—only in natural forces beyond most humans' knowledge or control.

Most fans understand the symbolic nature of the satanism they see and hear from their favorite metal bands, but their absorption of these ideas is still dangerous. Whether the fan studies satanism seriously or not, he or she continually reinforces the selfish destructiveness that characterizes both metal music and satanism.

**Suicide.** Raymond Belknap killed himself after drinking all afternoon and listening to Judas Priest. His buddy, Jay Vance, tried to kill himself but survived, not succeeding until almost three years later with an overdose of methadone.

Randy Duncan killed himself while listening to rocker Ozzy Osborne's "Suicide Solution."

Harold Hamilton killed himself while listening to the same song.

Ricky Kasso, self-described satanist and fan of AC/DC, Black Sabbath, and Judas Priest, hanged himself in his cell, awaiting arraignment on charges of ritually murdering a friend over a bad drug deal.

Michele Kimball killed herself after writing the words to a heavy metal song in her journal.

John McCollum killed himself while listening to "Suicide Solution."

Philip Morton hanged himself while listening to a Pink Floyd album containing "Goodbye Cruel World."

David Olive and Phillip Gomiser carried out their suicide pact listening to Led Zeppelin.

Michael Jeffrey Waller killed himself, his father said, after he listened to "Suicide Solution."

Did the music cause these and dozens of other teenagers to commit suicide? No court has supported that contention, in spite of the fact that several suits have been lodged against bands and their record companies by distraught parents. The bands steadfastly refuse to take any blame for teenage suicide, claiming they have a right to free speech and that their influence over fans cannot cause a fan to kill himself or commit crimes or acts of violence. So far the courts haven't been convinced otherwise by the parents.

Despite the fact that metal music is often important to kids who also commit suicide, that does not prove that the music is a cause of the suicide. More accurately, teenagers at risk for suicide often betray their vulnerabilities by antisocial, destructive activities, including listening to destructive music. The vast majority of metal fans don't end up killing themselves, committing crimes, or acting violent. But teens who do commit suicide often also listen to destructive music.

Arthur Lyons describes the correlation: "An individual who feels alienated from society will gravitate toward those groups and pursuits that support his own self-image, and herein lies the danger; in an imitative society, the heroes who are worshiped and imitated are not great men, but celebrities. And the androgynous, black leather-clad, ghoulish stars of heavy metal are natural idols for misfits."[24] Cooper points out that the satanic trappings of metal music, while not explicitly causing violence or suicide, "all contribute to the conditioning of already alienated young people into antisocial acts."[25]

Music and music videos probably have a bigger impact on teenagers' values and their fascination with destructive occultism than anything else. The blatant anti-social, selfish, rebellious, and violent themes of some contemporary music are identical to the values of contemporary satanism. Backward masking and subliminal messages are hardly necessary to subvert our children's morals when the blatant message of the music exalts the satanic creed. Comedian Jay Leno once remarked jokingly, "You know what you get when you play Twisted Sister's 'Burn in Hell' backwards? 'Go to church and pray on Sunday.'"[26]

## MOVIES AND TELEVISION

Movies and Satan? Most parents remember *Rosemary's Baby, The Exorcist,* and *Damien.* Most would probably add to the group the shock-shlock of the *Halloween* and *Nightmare on Elm Street* series. Of course we can throw in the B-movie horror flicks shown on local stations on sleepy Saturday nights.

But the movie invasion of the occult goes far beyond these slick presentations. More than two hundred horror movies from mainline producers and distributors littered the theater landscape between 1980 and 1990.[27] Many were comedic in intent, such as 1989's *Beetlejuice,* but many took occult powers for granted and seriously presented a world-view of occult victimization.

Spiritual and moral relativism pervades even the comedy occult movies. Almost all assume that good and evil are equal opposite forces, that Satan has as much power as God, and that anyone can "tap into" occult forces for good or evil. In *Beetlejuice* the demonic ghost is more fun, intelligent, and likeable (in a raunchy sort of way) than the straight, uptight yuppie parents. The two *Ghostbusters* movies didn't mention God at all except in a few expletives. The religious figures, both Christian and Jewish, were totally useless in combatting the forces of evil, leaving the viewer with the message that traditional religion is a nice story, but powerless. What succeeded against the threatening ghosts, carnivorous gargoyles, and hot-dog-stuffing spirits? In the first movie it was the combined power of the techno-magic ghost buster guns. The second movie was a little more sophisticated. Happy thoughts and patriotic symbols, most notably the Statue of Liberty, vanquished the pagan warrior demon and caused the city of New York to laugh and love again.

The *Halloween* and *Nightmare on Elm Street* movies are the best known of the terror occult movies. The sole purpose of these movies is to scare the viewer. The more mental, emotional, and physical terror the movie can induce, the better. The movie makers are not concerned with whether or not occult powers exist or work, they are concerned with affecting the viewer. The viewer, for the time he or she is watching the movie, suspends critical evaluation and lets the terror-inducing drama and special effects elevate blood pressure, increase adrenaline flow, start perspiration, and thrill the emotions. The experience is what matters, not the reality.

The underlying cause of terror in most of these movies is that evil is *never* destroyed. Like Freddy, evil always comes back. This is a fundamental shift in perspective from movies before the 1960s. *The Wizard of Oz*, for example, had elements of terror, especially for children. The wicked witch had power, was scary, and struck at a child's most important securities—mother, friends, home, and life. But imagine if *The Wizard of Oz* were remade today. The wicked witch wouldn't melt away, the water would metamorphose her into some hideous monster that would snatch the ruby slippers just as Dorothy got ready to click her heels together to go back home to Kansas. The credits would roll with Aunt Em hugging Dorothy. Over Aunt Em's shoulder we would see Dorothy, hugging her back with apparent love, her eyes revealing the wicked witch's possession of her.

A subgroup of the occult movie genre is the gore movie, like *Hellraiser* or *Hellbound (Hellraiser II)*. Through the magic of special effects and close-up camera work, the viewer experiences complete revulsion and disgust. You can watch in slow motion a human head exploding like a ripe watermelon, blood and brain matter flying toward the screen. See the demon-possessed amputee use his shiny hook hand to eviscerate a child with a few bloody strokes. Gasp as special effects make you think you're actually watching maggots crawl out of a decomposing human head. The descriptions could go on almost endlessly.

Not many people enjoy this kind of movie, but the genre has a hardcore following of fans whose greatest experience is watching gore on wide screen. Most of the gore fans are young males, teenagers whose faces are still soft with peach fuzz but who laugh at almost unspeakable human depravity.

Is it all fun and games? What kinds of values are reinforced by repeated exposure to scenes of murder, torture, dismemberment, and occult depravity? Long ago the Apostle Paul said that people who enjoy even just watching such depravity develop a seared or dead conscience.[28] They become unable to respond emotionally or morally against depravity. The voyeurs of cinematic torture may become the silent witnesses to real life debauchery.

A five-year-old boy used a kitchen knife to stab a two-year-old girl because he wanted to see what it was like, just like in the Freddy and Jason movies he'd watched on television the week before.[29]

A Southern California prosecutor told of a teenager who shot his mother and then threw things at her "to see if she would jerk, to see if she was still alive."[30]

Gore movies didn't cause either of these two events, but the children involved appeared to be completely self-absorbed and unable to comprehend the reality of pain and suffering. These children are not far removed from the recent *Closetland*,[31] a movie with only two characters: a young female victim and a sadistic torturer who pulls out her toenails with pliers, anally rapes her with a red hot poker, electrically shocks her genitals, and then reveals he's the same fiend who raped her repeatedly when she was five.

If *The Wizard of Oz* were remade as a gore movie, the witch's monkeys would tear Dorothy, instead of the scarecrow, limb from limb, and feast on her raw and bloody flesh.

Action used to mean cops chasing robbers, and suspense used to mean would boy get girl. Today action more typically means bad cops chasing likeable robbers, and suspense means will there be anyone left alive by the end of the movie?

Contemporary action and suspense movies reflect the

moral decay glorified in the entertainment world, but we don't usually think of it in an occult context. However, a significant portion of today's movies in this genre also contain implicit or explicit occult overtones.

*First Power* starred likeable young Lou Diamond Philips as a detective (cops and robbers action) attempting to solve a murder (which rapidly multiplies to many murders—will anyone survive?). The occult twist is that the main suspect has been executed in the gas chamber but has been resurrected by Satan to continue his gruesome killing. A mentally bizarre nun explains to the detective that there are three powers or forces: the third power is possession, the second, prophecy, and the first, resurrection. The power appears to be neutral, open to use by either demon or angel. Philips' antagonist is demonic.

*The Believers* starred actor Martin Sheen and delved into the frightening occult world of Santeria[32] and its destructive companion, Palo Mayombe.[33] Sheen's character, representing the typical white American—assumed to be "Christian," at least by heritage if not conviction—is confused, terrorized, and almost powerless in the face of the immense power of the black magic.

*Marked for Death* starred martial arts action actor Steven Segal. While nominally a cops-chase-drug-dealers movie, the power and suspense of the film came from the undercurrent of Palo Mayombe and Voodun, commonly called voodoo, magic that empowered the drug dealers to almost triumph through supernatural terror.

The underlying current through these and other occult-tinged action suspense movies is that evil has all the power, and the "good guys" win only by luck or happenstance.

If *The Wizard of Oz* were filmed in this genre today, Dorothy and her friends would die from the witch's curse in the poppy field before they ever reached the Emerald City.

Don't think that today's "mainstream" movies reflect our contemporary society. These movies may be mainstream by comparison to wilder films, but they do not reflect the majority values of our society. Film critic Michael Medved, co-host of television's "Sneak Previews," asserts that millions of ordinary Americans find their basic values ignored or ridiculed in today's movies.[34] Medved cites this as one of the reasons for the drastic decline in movie attendence, from 90 million in 1948 to barely 19 million today. He comments, "Tens of millions of ordinary Americans therefore find their basic values ignored or assaulted by movies. The assault comes in three areas: an underlying hostility to marriage and family; a pervasive glorification of ugliness; and finally, a contempt for America's most cherished institutions and traditions."[35]

Think of some of the most popular recent movies. *Good - fellas* and *The Godfather III* esteemed murderous organized crime bosses as role models for loyalty. *Rambo* and all of its sequels reminded us that the American military is crooked, inept, and criminal—in need of saving by a mentally unbalanced Vietnam War veteran. *Three Men and a Baby* showed us we could have all the fun of parenthood without any of the commitment of marriage.

The spiritual degeneration of today's movies not only opens the door to the more virile-appearing occult, but also denigrates traditional Judeo-Christian values. Medved summarizes this spiritual decay: "Instead of spirituality, Hollywood today offers only spiritualism—with heavy overtones of the occult—particularly in the form of the sorry recent series of 'sex after death' love stories, including: *Chances Are*, the reincarnation comedy with Cybill Shepherd and Robert Downey Jr.; Steven Spielberg's *Always*; *Made in Heaven*; and, of course, *Ghost*, with Demi Moore and Partick Swayze. At least *Ghost* suggested that immoral behavior in this world might have dire consequences in the afterlife—and this brief nod to traditional religious sensibilities helped to make it the No. 1 box-office hit of 1990."[36]

*Ghost*'s fortune teller (played by Oscar winner Whoopi

Goldberg), although a charlatan, still provides the psychic key to the movie. Think of recent children's "mainstream" movies. Bill Cosby's *Ghost Dad* mocked traditional Christianity and made the occult fun. The two *Teenage Mutant Ninja Turtle* movies taught children that evil is never really vanquished, and eastern meditation works better than prayer.

If *The Wizard of Oz* were a contemporary mainstream movie, Dorothy and the scarecrow would have some meaningful intimacy in the corn field, and the Wizard would explain that the wicked witch wasn't really wicked, but came from a dysfunctional family.

With the proliferation of cable and video, television has become a melting pot of movies, plays, movies that would never make it on the big screen, and small, independent experiments. It is impossible to provide a thumbnail sketch that does justice to the varied impact of today's television.

One of the biggest impacts is that the gore, terror, occultism, and horror once accessible only with a paid ticket is as close to your toddler or teenager as the remote control on your living room coffee table. Cooper notes, "Even very young children routinely rent horror and occult films. The video store and VCR provide all the conditioning into occultism the most devout Satanist could wish."[37] Not only is the occult in the middle of the living room, it can be replayed as often as your child can push "Rewind."

Alternative programming on cable offers instruction in tarot reading, psychic predictions, witchcraft lessons, panel discussions on past life experiences, trance channeling exhibitions, and yoga exercises. Traditional values are undermined with made-for-cable homosexual soap operas and public television "documentaries" on how Christianity is only a myth and Jesus a clown.

Television series and specials are no friend to traditional family values. Religion seems to play no part in most television characters' lives, even though three quarters of Americans say religion is very important to them and that they consider themselves "born-again." If traditional religion has any part in a typical television program, it is presented as unusual, not for ordinary people. *Growing Pains'* Seaver family doesn't go to church. Roseanne and her family don't talk about God or faith. The religious people most likely to appear on television are caricatures: 1.) the simple-minded, naive, inept, and ignorant religious "fundamentalist;" 2.) the narrow-minded, bigoted, hypocritical, wolf-in-sheep's-clothing evangelist; 3.) the priest or nun who falls from office through the irresistible lure of sex; or 4.) the maniacal, psychotic criminal with a religious delusion. Futuristic technology has become the magic of today's television. *Mork and Mindy* replaced God with a head alien to whom Mork reported every week; *Alf's* title character was an alien; *Quantum Leap* combined out-of-body experiences with possession, fate, a wise-cracking hologram, and an omniscient computer; and *Star Trek: The Next Generation's* gods and goddesses were super space technician charlatans.

Children's programming stuffs cartoons and commercials with occult references and practices, including spells, magic, pantheism, polytheism, reincarnation, psychic powers, and supernatural forces. Often the occult references are offhand plot devices that substitute for good story telling, but they still accustom children to a magical worldview. They differ qualitatively from the supernaturalism of classic fairy tales, where good and evil are distinguishable, morality is rewarded, and evil ultimately is vanquished by good. Instead, the typical supernaturalism of children's programming promotes relativism, a neutral force or power that can be used either for good or evil, and eternal dualism; evil is a necessary complement to good.

Overt occult themes are scattered across television, too. Psychics are always good for a movie of the week, especially if the psychic helps the police capture a crazed religious fanatic killer. Shirley MacLaine's reincarnation and trance channeling dominated the ratings the week *Out on a Limb* aired. Precognition, seances, and fortune tellers all help boost ratings for otherwise lackluster shows.

The occult influence in contemporary television and movies is far more subtle and pervasive than blatant. While parents may be able to successfully warn teenagers against blatant occultism, it is much more difficult to identify the subtle worldview shifts and magical assumptions common in movies and television.

## THE PRINTED WORD

The occult is a favorite theme in books, magazines, and comic books. In addition to the occult texts discussed in Chapter Four, psychic mysteries, monthly horoscopes, and devilish comic anti-heroes reinforce for teenagers the magical worldview. Teenagers today do not read very much, but when they do, girls gravitate toward novels and teen magazines, boys toward specialty magazines and comic books.

Novels for teenagers run to romance, mystery, and relationship problems. Judy Blume, the most prolific and popular writer for teens, sometimes includes ideas about reincarnation, psychic phenomena, pantheism, witchcraft, and fortune telling. There is little overt support for traditional religious values such as fidelity in marriage, no sex outside of marriage, respect for parents and authority, and other absolute morals. Religion has almost no place in contemporary teenage novels. Magic is acceptable, prayer is not.

Popular teen magazines undermine a Judeo-Christian worldview on two levels. First, most magazines indiscriminately publish astrology charts, horoscopes, classified ads for psychic activities, and stories of the supernatural. Second, and more subtly, they appear to give lip service to traditional values. For example, a small article may assert that physical beauty is unimportant compared to inner beauty, but most of the magazine focuses on physical beauty—hair, figure, style, and make-up.

Specialty teen magazines often overturn traditional values and may present explicit occult views. *Mad* magazine makes you laugh, but it does so by undermining authority, poking fun at religion, and mocking moral conservatives. Several metal music magazines, including *Metal Edge* and *Metal Maniacs,* feature bands that use occult symbolism and terminology, and offer mail order occult jewelry and supplies.

Supermarkets abound with small pocket books on I Ching (Chinese divination), tarot, astrology, psychic predictions, occult phenomena, and UFOs. Tabloid magazines blare headlines about priests who explode during exorcisms, witches whose curses kill people, and extra-terrestrials that are kept in cages by the United States Air Force.

Comic books provide teenagers with exciting stories and larger-than-life role models. Unfortunately, many of the new comics, some labeled "for mature readers," also provide readers with graphic images of infidelity, sexual perversion, including necrophilia and oral sex, black magic, destructive occultism, rape, murder, mutilation, homosexuality, sado-masochism, and foul language. Some comics even include full page, illustrated mail order forms for sex toys, sado-masochism devices, and sex tools. Former comic book store owner John Fulce notes the strong anti-Judeo-Christian worldview of many comics: "Indeed, entire comic books are devoted to the 'new gods' with their new values and morals. These new gods, incidentally, are not Love and Peace, but Lust and Violence. They are gods requiring little in the way of self-restraint or self-sacrifice, and they promise everything a self-centered reader could want. Like Baal of the Bible, comic-book gods are hard to resist."[38]

Even some school textbooks have been tainted with the occult. Public school districts and textbook publishers have been scrupulously vigilant about erasing any trace of traditional Judeo-Christian religion from the schoolroom, going so far as removing Bibles from school libraries and changing history books to say the first Thanksgiving was not for the pilgrims to thank God, but to thank the Indians for showing them how to survive in the New World.

However, such censorship does not extend to new age and occult beliefs and practices. Teachers instruct students to find their own inner spirit guides, literature readings include incantations and spells, and social studies curricula sometimes suggest having a contemporary witch or satanist address the class on social awareness days.

The bombardment of occult material on teenagers today is vast. Do not think your teenager doesn't have to deal with the lure of the occult. Unless you keep them in solitary confinement throughout their teenage years, your teenagers will have been confronted by the occult many times in many ways. You cannot eliminate the exposure, but you can control it and help your teenager to react constructively and intelligently about his or her religious choices.

Most teenagers flirt with the occult, attracted by the mystery, power, and promises of ability to know or control their own futures. Teenagers who are the most vulnerable to destructive occultism are those whose deep personal needs are not being met. Their problems will be manifest in more ways than simply through interest in the occult, usually through drugs and sex. If the teenager's problems are not addressed seriously and dealt with constructively, he or she can slide easily into a more serious involvement in destructive occultism and more serious criminal behavior.

# SIX

# Occult Crime

[Warning: This chapter contains accurate descriptions of actual crimes that are brief but explicit. This is necessary to provide readers with a realistic understanding of the criminal element of destructive occultism. If you think you may be upset by the crimes reviewed here, skip to Chapter Seven. Do not give this book to your teenager to read unless you have reviewed this chapter and believe it is appropriate.]

R AGE. REVENGE. HATRED. The forces of destruction coursing through teenagers embittered by the demons of self-pity and overwhelming despair compel some teenagers to devastating acts of criminal ruin. Drugs are the essential prerequisite, suicide the most popular choice for violent rebellion, and vandalism the tacky residue of teenage mockery. Occult crime is symptomatic of teenage rage, not the cause.

If you and your teenager are in crisis regarding his or her occult involvement, then you probably know firsthand the excruciating pain of defiance, abandonment, and isolation. If your teenager is an occult "dabbler," enjoying the mystery of the occult but not yet sucked into the vortex of occult destruction, then your fear for your child's safety compels you to seek solutions that will grab your child from the edge of the calamitous precipice. If your teenager has shown no signs of occult dabbling or involvement, your commitment to protecting your child from the occult places you in the best position possible to ensure that your teenager finds his or her answers within the dynamics of your own beliefs and family values.

For the teenager who is already out of control, occult crime becomes the almost unavoidable culmination of escalating self-destruction. Vandalism and religious desecration are added to sex and drugs, accompanied by dealing to provide capital for the drugs. Soon such activity is not enough: animal mutilation and sacrifice prove the teenager's commitment to the left-handed path. For a few teenagers, the commitment is a commitment to their own death, suicide. For another few teenagers the carnage of human destruction is directed toward others, not themselves.

## OCCULT CRIME EXPOSED

This chapter focuses on the crimes associated with occult involvement. Occult crime is not a special classification of crime unlike any other illegal behavior. Rather, occult crime is ordinary, everyday crime committed by teenagers and adults who by and large fit the common profile of offenders. Occult crime is distinguished from ordinary crime because the perpetrator is committed to an occult worldview.

The mother of a teenage suicide victim is no less devastated if her child wrote a prayer to Satan before he pulled the trigger. The father of an adolescent rapist is not consoled if his son's crime took place in a ritual setting. Occult activity and behavior associated with criminality is more an indicator of the perpetrator's serious social and moral problems than it is a primary motivator for illegal activity. As expert John Charles Cooper notes,

People attracted to the dark lord of evil tend to have problems relating to others and to the "real" world of social obligations. Such people choose Satanism as an arena in which to act out their personal fantasies in unbridled hedonism, utter materialism ("going for the gold"), and in rituals and behaviors that inflate their very damaged egos. Becoming Satanists leads many of these inadequate or antisocial personalities into self-abuse (slashing their arms as sacrifices to Satan) and to suicidal behavior. Other, perhaps more damaged personalities, act out their hostilities and gain a sense of superiority by harming others.[1]

This survey of occult crime is divided into two general sections: adult occult crime and teenage occult crime. We also mention some of the more sensationalistic reports of occult crime that actually have no reasonable evidentiary support. Adults often commit the same crimes as teenagers, and teenage occult crimes are not exclusive to adolescent perpetrators, but there are tendencies which characterize each group. Our survey of occult crime will prepare you to search for the answers to the problems your teenager faces, and to adopt principles of recovery from destructive occultism.

**The Occult Cult Tangent.** This book is a practical handbook for parents of teenagers. There are other aspects of the occult with which typical American teenagers have little or no contact. Ethnic magical systems with little American teenage involvement include the Caribbean Santeria and Palo Mayombe; Haitian Voodun (popularly called Voodoo); Mexican Brujeria; and Brazilian systems, Macumba (and its sects, Lucumi and Umbanda), Quimbanda, Pajelanca, and Candomblé. In addition, Hoodo is a Southern Afro-American derivative of Voodun.

These magical systems are definitely occult, but ethnic identification is the greatest risk factor for involvement rather than typical adolescent vulnerabilities. Therefore, these systems are not dealt with in this book.[2]

**The Witchcraft Connection.** Chapter Three carefully outlined the typical contemporary witchcraft worldview. It is a magical worldview, and thus properly is part of the occult. We believe it has serious shortcomings as an adequate foundation for dealing with life. However, by the definition of contemporary witchcraft given here, criminal activity would be inconsistent with this kind of witchcraft. There may be contemporary witches who break the law, but such action is inconsistent with the second half of the wiccan rede "and it harm none."

Witchcraft is often confused with destructive occultism, and some occultists attempt to divide witchcraft into "white" and "black" forms. Some criminal activity is done by people claiming to be witches or claiming to practice "black witchcraft." This is especially likely to occur when a youngster studies, learns, and practices on his own, making up his own terminology and confusing the distinctions between witchcraft and satanism. Such practitioners do not follow the contemporary witchcraft/pagan/neo-pagan belief system and there is no qualitative difference between them and destructive or satanic occultists. Anton Szandor LaVey, founder of the Church of Satan, asserts that from his perspective there is no distinction between "white" and "black" magic: "White magic is supposedly utilized only for good or unselfish purposes, and black magic, we are told, is used only for selfish or 'evil' reasons. Satanism draws no such dividing line. Magic is magic, be it used to help or hinder. The Satanist, being the magician, should have the ability to decide what is just, and then apply the powers of magic to attain his goals."[3]

We disagree with the witchcraft worldview. Its relativism makes teenagers vulnerable to destructive occultism. Some teenagers who begin dabbling in witchcraft quickly turn to destructive occultism for its perceived greater power. However, this chapter on occult crime has little to do with the witchcraft described in Chapter Three. The perpetrators of occult crime are destructive occultists.

## WHAT IS OCCULT CRIME?

Robbery, drug dealing, vandalism, animal killing, suicide, and murder are crimes against persons and society whether they are perpetrated by destructive occultists or atheists. What distinguishes occult crime from other crimes is not the crime itself, but the perpetrator's occult worldview. The perpetrator's commitment to magical power and destructive occultism turns simple vandalism into anti-religious vandalism, rape into ritual rape, murder into sacrifice.

In one sense, there is no such thing as "occult crime." Crime is crime regardless of the perpetrator's religious persuasions. However, a person's religious persuasion may affect how the crime is carried out and may condone the criminal act. Many occultists do not engage in illegal activity, although drug use is an almost universal common denominator. Nonoccultists commit suicide, murder, and vandalism and deal in drugs. Occultists can commit the same acts, consistent with their destructive worldview and in a magically prescribed manner. Crimes are committed by persons, not religions, but the same problems that render a person vulnerable to destructive occultism also render him or her vulnerable to criminal activity. Ultimately, the individual is responsible for his actions and his beliefs. "The devil *made* me do it" sounds like a plausible excuse, but is more often an attempt to escape personal moral responsibility.

A satanist who begins to participate in illegal activity tends to perfect his skill and increase the severity of his crimes unless he is given a good reason to stop. Unchecked, a destructive teenage occultist can easily turn into an antisocial adult criminal. A survey of adult occult crime will help us understand the severity of the threat to our vulnerable teenagers.

## PROBLEMS WITH PROSECUTION

While the incidence rate of occult crime is certainly nowhere near the gigantic proportions carelessly reported by sensationalists, tabloid magazines, and afternoon television talk shows, it is probably significantly higher than court records show.

The primary reason for this discrepancy is that the ritual or satanic accoutrements do not add materially to the evidence. That is, the presence of occult signs at a crime scene or in a suspect's home or belongings are not are not considered integral to the criminal act itself, any more than finding a Catholic saint's medal dropped by a bank robber would implicate the Catholic Church as motivating robbery.

For example, Tuan A. Tran, father of two-year-old Purdy Tran, sued for custody in a divorce case, protesting that his daughter was not safe in a house with her mother, a lesbian witch.[4] Tran introduced evidence that Purdy was kept in a rundown Southern California mansion, home to a coven of thirteen lesbian witches, five pit bulldogs, an occult library, an "Indian lady" mummy, a Medusa-headed "lizard lady" tapestry, and numerous pentagram symbols. In a sworn declaration Purdy's babysitter reported that she had "an evil feeling about it." Superior Court Commissioner Robert A. Schnider granted temporary custody to Tran, specifically noting, however, that he didn't want to "judge anyone's lifestyle" and based his decision entirely on the presence of the pit bulldogs: "The court finds that living in a residence containing pit bulldogs poses a significant danger to the minor child and expressly bases its order on that finding and not on the various other allegations."[5] Without clear evidence that the occult connection was *in itself* harmful to the child, the commissioner could not fairly consider it in determining custody.

A secondary reason is that some law enforcement and district attorney personnel, aware of the media hysteria concerning occultism, see occult elements of a criminal case to be liabilities for their cases' credibility rather than assets. One prosecutor told us, "I don't want a perfectly good drug dealing case to go down the drain because I present occult elements that the jury laughs at. I can get a conviction on the evidence without having to throw in the suspect's weird ritual mumbo-jumbo."

A third reason occult aspects to particular crimes are often not introduced in criminal cases is the incredulity of law enforcement and courts. Many people do not believe "devil worship" or "black magic" exist or can be taken seriously even by their practitioners. One person we interviewed said, "If the guy spray painted graffitti on the wall, he's guilty of vandalism. Whether he sprayed 'I love Mom' or 'I love Satan' doesn't matter to me. Don't try to tell me the devil made him do it. He's just a punk."

A fourth reason occult crimes are a smaller part of the crime picture than sensationalists would have us believe is because there are many spurious reports, rumors that aren't true, false stories, and incidents so muddled by outside interference that it may never be possible to discern what actually happened.

In the latter category lies the McMartin Preschool case, the most expensive criminal trial in California. After two trials and more than five years, none of the defendants were found guilty in the most notorious ritual child abuse case ever. Nearly everyone associated with the case, including jury members, parents, and court figures agreed that the amount of contamination of testimony effectively and fatally diminished the weight of the children's testimonies.[6]

Spurious reports often sound intriguing at first report, but then later turn out to be nothing of significance. For example, in February 1987 police in Florida arrested two well-dressed young men with six young, dirty children. In a search of their van, police found what they called satanic cult photographs. The police told the press the young men were members of the "Finders, a bizarre Satanic cult" head-quartered in Washington, D.C. Lyons summarizes the initial police press release: "The children, the police claimed, had been given up by their parents to the cult, which was part of an international child-pornography network. 'As far as we're concerned,' a spokesman told reporters, 'this goes from coast to coast and from Canada to Mexico.... Adults are encouraged to join this group and one of the stipulations... is that they give up the rights to their children.'"[7]

However, careful, thorough subsequent investigation found no evidence of satanic involvement, no evidence of criminal activity on the part of the Finders, and no evidence of child abuse. In fact, the Finders was a community of fol-lowers of the Chinese philosopher Lao-tse.[8]

Another interesting "noncase" concerned murderer Henry Lee Lucas, who at one time had admitted to Texas law enforcement that he had sexually abused and murdered between 360 and 600 people as part of his membership in an international satanic cult called the Hands of Death. No evidence was found to support Lucas's often inconsistent "confessions," which he has since recanted, and he was con-victed of three murders in Texas, for which he was sen-tenced to death.[9]

In some cases there is no evidence to back up a particular story of satanic crime. Such is the case with Michelle Smith's story of childhood ritual abuse, human sacrifice, and sexual exploitation. Michelle told her story with her psychiatrist, who later became her husband, Lawrence Pazder, in *Michelle*

*Remembers.*[10] Through hypnotic therapy Michelle supposedly remembered a childhood of satanic horror. However, in the more than a decade since publication of the book, no objective or corroborating evidence has been located to verify her subjective memory experiences.

Of the reported stories that simply are not true, the most well-known is the ritual abuse survivor story told in *Satan's Underground.*[11]

Because of these kinds of problems related to verifying occult influences in crime, bizarre occultism is mostly linked only to more bizarre crimes such as murder. The lack of significant statistics in lesser crime reports should not be misunderstood to signify that murder is the "crime of choice" for destructive occultists. The occult connection is simply reported more in connection with murders than lesser crimes.

## CRIMES WITH OCCULT CONNECTIONS

However, there are documented crimes with occult connections. Many involve drug use. Cooper believes "the lure of drugs is probably the most potent recruiting tool Satanism has today"[12] and "Satanism and drugs always go together."[13] Expert Arthur Lyons notes the long association between drugs and magic: "Narcotics have always played a role in Western ceremonial magic. Hemlock, henbane, opium, and belladonna were traditional sorcerer's drugs, and in the traditional Black Mass, hashish was often burned instead of incense. It is much easier to materialize a demon from the depth of one's own mind than all the way from Hell."[14]

In fact, most of the satanists we know or have interviewed had a history of drug abuse before they started practicing satanism, continue to use drugs, and attribute their enhanced drug experiences to their satanism. One ex-satanist told us, "I didn't believe in any demons or devils or anything. I liked the feelings of power and self-indulgence, the ritualizing of my drug use. Satanism without drugs? What's the point?"

A satanist runs the same risks of arrest for drug use and/or dealing as a nonsatanist. Again, because the drug use is not specifically *caused* by the satanism, such crimes are not usually cataloged as "occult crimes." The only time occultism may slip into a case like this is if the satanist or a group of satanists are arrested for drug abuse or dealing while they are in the midst of a ritual. From a criminal justice perspective, the ritualism is incidental, not primary, to the drug offense.

Concerned parents should be aware that a teenager's involvement with satanism is almost a guarantee that he or she is also involved with drug use and often drug dealing to pay for his or her own supply. Drug use has devastating effects on users' physical, mental/emotional, and spiritual health as well as making the users vulnerable to criminal charges.

Violent sexual crimes also sometimes have an occult connection. Northern Californian Cameron Hooker abducted a hitchhiker and kept her as a sex slave for seven years. He was sentenced to 104 years in prison. In trial testimony Hooker was described as "a man obssessed with bondage, sexual slavery and witchcraft who finally kidnapped a woman on whom he could practice his bizarre interests."[15] Hooker obtained his wife's aid in the kidnapping by telling her she would burn in hell if she didn't help him. She was finally able to break free from his domination with the help of a Christian pastor.

The first child abuse conviction where elements of ritual abuse were entered into court testimony involved a Cuban ex-convict, Francisco Fuster. Fuster, convicted and sentenced to 165 years in prison, had run a babysitting service. According to his wife, he raped her with a crucifix and sexually assaulted children in his care. The abuse allegedly took place within a ritualistic context, including chanting and animal sacrifices.[16]

Quite often accusations of child abuse involving the occult do not result in court convictions. There are a variety of reasons for this: 1.) sometimes the accusations, most commonly made by noncustodial parents in bitter custody disputes, are unfounded, 2.) sometimes the case is pursued, but the occult aspects of the case are considered irrelevant to central concern for the child, 3.) sometimes the perpetrator is unknown, and 4.) sometimes there is insufficient evidence to convict.

Innocent children who are victimized by child abuse deserve every protection their loved ones and society can give them, and it is horrendous to think that even one perpetrator should escape punishment for his or her crime. But in order to protect the innocent we must have standards of justice and evidence that are objective and conclusive. Consequently, some cases are not prosecutable, despite our private feelings. Were our society to relax our standards of proof, subjective feelings, coincidence, and conjecture could convict the innocent as well as the guilty.

The Lauren Stratford story is the most well-known example of occult criminal charges that are unfounded. Lauren Stratford claimed to be an adult survivor of satanic ritual abuse that began when she was a young child and continued into her twenties. She wrote her story, the bestselling *Satan's Underground*, telling of child sexual abuse, rape, kiddie porn, ritualistic abuse, prostitution, torture, brainwashing, and child sacrifice by an interstate group of satanists. She recounted her personal experiences, including being forced to participate in the sacrifice of her own six-month-old baby, Joey, during a blood ritual. The book sold more than 130,000 copies and Stratford maintained a high media profile, appearing on most of the afternoon television talk shows and radio programs across the country, teaching at law enforcement and therapy seminars, and speaking before Christian congregations and groups. Stratford and her most visible supporters, including Harvest House Publishers, end-times speaker and author Hal Lindsey, and Hal's sister-in-law occult "expert," Johanna Michaelsen, claimed that her story was true and documentable, supportable by evidence.

However, there was *no* documentation and *no* evidence. In fact, the evidence showed that her story was *not* true. In a lengthy, thorough background investigation we and our associate, Jon Trott of *Cornerstone* magazine, uncovered Stratford's true name, Laurel Willson, and her true story, one of emotional instability and myriad conflicting fantasies, but by no means a true story of satanic involvement or abuse.[17]

After our story broke and was covered nationally[18] Harvest House Publishers withdrew from publication both *Satan's Underground* and Stratford's second book, *I Know You're Hurting.* Neither Stratford nor any of her supporters has been able to produce any evidence either countering our article or affirming her published story. Stratford continues to maintain that the story is true, but offers as support only nonproofs: 1.) no one would make up a story like this; 2.) people have been spiritually helped by the books; 3.) others around the country tell similar stories; 4.) some therapists believe her; and 5.) the reason her family members denied the story[19] was understandable because guilty people often deny their guilt.[20]

This nonproof is a dangerous fad today, and is spreading from fringe therapy circles and religiously biased advocates into mainstream society. If truth becomes testable only by subjective emotion and personal bias, then anyone can be convicted without evidence. Murder, rape, child torture, and abuse are serious charges to lodge without objective evidence. The innocent as well as the guilty can be condemned by feeling rather than fact.

A case of "nonproof" in Southern California involved two adult daughters who lodged a civil suit against their elderly mother, claiming she and their deceased father had ritually abused them throughout their childhoods as part of their membership in a multi-generational, widespread satanic cult. The sisters had no evidence or corroborating witnesses. The sisters claimed to have repressed all memory of the abuse until they entered therapy with a psychotherapist who diagnosed a significant portion of his clients as suffering from multiple personality disorder (MPD) as a result of repressed trauma from childhood ritual abuse. The therapist, Timothy Maas, admitted in court that he had no scientific or physical evidence of ritual child abuse for *any* of his patients.[21] He explained in testimony that he believed his patients if they were emotional, complained of sympathetic physical symptoms,[22] and "remembered" incidents.

Vigilance in protecting innocent people from abuse is important, but protecting innocent people from unfounded charges is also imperative.

Other than drugs, murder is the crime most often associated with the occult. The dark ritualism of destructive occultism is attractive not only to rebellious adolescents and frustrated adults, but also to some social misfits who engage in almost unspeakably horrible acts. As Lyons notes, "It would not be particularly unusual for a personality so twisted that he would feel the compulsion to molest sexually or kill children to accept the Lord of Evil as his master."[23]

Occult murder is never free of other motives and factors. Most typically, the murder is drug related. Murder during robberies is also common. Sometimes the murder is a hate crime for a particular kind of person singled out on the basis of sexual orientation or race. Sometimes murder results from the threat of a member going to authorities or others to report illegal activities, such as drug use. Occasionally a sociopathic serial killer uses the occult to enhance his killing. Regardless of the complex mixture of motives and factors, occult murder indulges the worst in lawless destruction.

Most murders connected to the occult are performed by individuals or isolated, small groups. There is no evidence to support the urban myth of a national satanic conspiracy sacrificing hundreds or even thousands of victims each year. Sincerely concerned but misguided people who pass on such hysterical rumors inadvertently provide a smokescreen for the twisted individuals who do kill in the name of Satan. If everyone is busy avoiding a conspiracy that doesn't exist, they are less likely to notice the actual evil in their midst.

Statistics cited by credulous individuals show the absurdity of such conspiracy theories. For example, some fearmongers state that anywhere from twenty thousand to two million children are sacrificed in satanic rituals each year. However, there are no statistics available to support any components: the number of children necessary, the number of satanic groups, the number of satanists, or the volume of physical evidence—bones, clothes, ashes, or testable witnesses. Shawn Carlson and Gerald Larue summarize the statistical problem well:

Approximately 240,000 missing child reports are made each year.

More than 120,000 of the missing child reports are closed within several days or weeks because the report turns out to be an error (the child was not missing after all) or because the "runaway" changes his/her mind and returns.

Over 119,900 of the missing child reports turn out to be: abductions of children made by estranged parents or relatives who are involved in a custody dispute with the child's legal guardian, runaways who don't want to return home, or throwaways who are not even welcome at home.

Only 67 of the missing children reports can be attributed to stranger abduction....

A National Child Safety Council spokesperson conservatively estimates that the Council receives more than half of the reports of stranger abductions. Therefore, no more than 140 children are abducted by strangers in the U.S. each year (assuming that 67 abductions is only half of all stranger abductions—a conservative assumption).

About half of the stranger abducted children are eventually recovered—and none of them have ever been recovered from Satanists or Devil-worshipers, or were the confirmed victims of a Devil-worshiping ritual murder.[24]

John Charles Cooper notes, "The reality of satanic crime makes unthinking belief in unsupported claims unnecessary,"[25] and he warns, "One need not propose a 'satanic underground' or 'Satan's mafia'—ideas that scoffers ridicule—to recognize the widespread phenomena of Satanism's several forms across the American landscape....The Satanism above ground, not Satan's underground, should concern us."[26] Tabloid television hysteria obliterates the clear signs of destructive occult enticement luring our vulnerable teenagers.

**Famous Occult Murders.** The Manson Family is the most famous occult group that murdered. Leader Charles Manson and some of his followers were convicted of the murder of movie star Sharon Tate and her friends, and of a couple, the La Biancas, in 1969. Manson and his followers were evil extensions of the complete relativism of the 1960s. Drugs and sex were the food and water of the Family, and murder their relativistic ritual. Forensic psychiatrist Ronald Markman notes,

In addition to drugs and sex, a major part of the Family program planned by Manson was eliminating their fear and resistence to killing. Manson led the Family in 'visualizations' where they imagined they were killing people. Manson told them there was no such thing as bad and no such thing as wrong. Also, [Family member and murderer Charles] Tex [Watson] recounted, "there was no such thing as death, so it was not wrong to kill a fellow human being.'[27]

The kind of destructive occultism the Manson Family embraced was not nearly so clearly defined or organized as the contemporary satanism described in this book. Manson was the god the Family worshiped. Manson took what he liked from older traditions such as Crowley's, the O.T.O, and the Process Church of Final Judgment, but ultimately his satanic system was his own homegrown variety. His followers followed him as though he were God—or the Devil—or both. Satan was not a spiritual entity, the evil one of the Bible. As Tex Watson said to one of his victims just before he brutally stabbed him to death, "I am the Devil, and I am here to do the Devil's Work."[28]

Richard Delmer Boyer was convicted of the robbery and murder of a Southern California couple. Robbery was the primary factor motivating Boyer, also a suspect in at least one other murder, but the occult played a small part: Boyer confessed that he "had committed the murders in a frenzy after watching the movie 'Halloween II.'"[29]

Charges against Hulon Mitchell, Jr. brought a different twist to ritual murder. Calling himself Yahweh ben Yahweh (*God, son of God* in Hebrew), he started his own black sect, built a business empire, and ruled every aspect of his white-robed followers' lives, including when and how they had sex. On November 7, 1990 he was arrested and charged with ordering the killing of fourteen people, including seven "white devils" who were killed ritualistically as part of the initiation rites of the "Brotherhood," the elite subgroup of the main sect.[30] The group's "Temple of Love" served as headquarters in Miami, Florida's mostly black Liberty City area.

The Yahwehs consider themselves the true chosen people, and Yahweh ben Yahweh is their self-appointed leader, who in the past has referred to all whites as devils. Seven white men reportedly were killed by those applying to join the "Brotherhood." Entering the secret group within the sect required a ritual killing, sometimes of a "white devil."[31]

Even cannibalism is not unknown to the world of occult murder. In 1970 Steven Hurd, a self-proclaimed satanist, was arrested for the murder of an Orange County, California schoolteacher. Hurd and his friends killed her, dedicated her body to Satan, and then ate it. Lyons notes the disposition of the case, "After being diagnosed as a paranoid schizophrenic, Hurd was sent to Atascadero State Hospital for the criminally insane, where he claims to be visited by his 'father, Satan,' whom he describes as a 'man wearing a gold helmet, with the skin of a pinecone.'"[32]

During the same time period Stanley Dean Baker murdered a Wyoming social worker, James Schlosser, and ate his heart. Baker and his companion, Harry A. Stroop, drove Schlosser's car to California, where they were stopped by the Highway Patrol on a suspicion of hit-and-run driving. In a search of the two, one of Schlosser's finger bones turned up in Baker's possession. The occult connection shows the attraction satanism has for lonely, psychologically dysfunctional misfits: "Aside from being a cannibal, Baker, who had an IQ of 130, claimed to be a practicing Satanist and to have belonged to a blood-drinking cult in Wyoming. Investigation failed to turn up the cult, however, and the picture that emerged of the Satanic cannibal was that of a psychotic loner, too weird for even the hardened inmates of Deer Lodge Prison, where Baker was sentenced to life. After a few 'werewolf' episodes, during which Baker would crouch in his cell and 'growl like an animal,' he was transferred to a maximum security prison in Illinois."[33]

Teofilo Medina, accused of murdering four convenience store attendants, saw himself as a warlock, a high priest, in collaboration with Satan. Court-appointed psychologist David Pierce said Medina was competent to stand trial, noting, "Violence is one of the ways he responds to stress."[34] Pierce also categorized Medina as "a paranoid schizophrenic who hallucinates and has delusions and problems with stress."[35] Medina had behavior problems over a long period of time. He served seven years in prison for kidnapping and rape, and five years for a barroom shooting. In prison he was caught trying to escape twice and several times was disciplined for violent behavior. In jail awaiting trial on the four murders, Medina was disciplined for crashing a television set on the floor and making death threats against a jail deputy. He also attempted suicide twice. During an interview with another court-appointed psychologist, Medina grew angry and smashed the glass partition separating them. Psychologist Pierce also reported Medina said he had visions of Jesus Christ and St. John in white robes, and heard his dead brother speaking. "He talked about a secret order or a higher power... of having a sixth sense."[36]

One of the more gruesome occult murders occurred when John Lee Fryman, a self-proclaimed satanist, kidnapped and killed a Cincinnati, Ohio waitress with whom he had corresponded while in prison for an armed robbery conviction. After she was dead, Fryman sawed off the victim's legs, so the body would fit into his small car, and dumped them in an Indiana church yard. Butler, Ohio County Prosecutor John Holcomb said, "This is a bizarre business. This [case] is evil business. The evil here shows that this man was making a business out of being evil."[37]

Although most occult murders are done by men, teenager Patricia Hall stabbed an elderly man to death and participated in the rape and whipping of a teenage girl in the Hall of Horrors Wax Museum in New Orleans. Lyons notes, "Hall, described by police as a 'hippie-type with tattoos,' threatened to turn the arresting officers into frogs and claimed to have been baptized by [Anton Szandor LaVey, who] denies that Hall was ever one of his members."[38]

In a Massachusetts murder trial, Superior Court Judge Francis W. Keating carefully warned the jury that the defendant's religious beliefs could not be considered evidence that he killed a young prostitute. "You can believe anything you want to in this country," Judge Keating said. "You [the jury] will not be sidetracked by that issue."[39] The jury convicted Carl Drew of first degree murder for the death of Karen Marsden. Some prosecution witnesses described satanic rites conducted by Drew among Fall River, Massachusetts pimps and prostitutes, and testified that Marsden was killed by Drew and two others in a night ritual because she wanted to leave Drew's satanic cult.

Homosexual rivalries and bad drug deals contributed to the ritual murder of a transient in San Francisco in June 1985. The drifter's body was horribly mutilated, a pentagram was carved into his chest, his body was partially drained of blood, and a candle was set in his right eye and burned. Clifford St. Joseph was convicted three years later of the murder and also of false imprisonment and sodomy of another young man.[40]

John Linley Frazier was into tarot cards and murder. In 1970 he killed Victor Ohta and his family, leaving a note warning "death to all those who defile the environment," and signing it with Tarot card identifications, "the Knight of Wands, the Knight of Cups, the Knight of Swords, and the Knight of Pentacles."[41] During the same time period Herbert Mullin killed nine people, one a priest he kicked to death in a confessional. He said they were killed as sacrifices to appease the Earthquake God, protection for California against "the Big One."[42]

David Berkowitz, the infamous Son of Sam killer, is perhaps one of the most complex occult murderers. Berkowitz was arrested on August 10, 1977, a year after the beginning of a seemingly random series of shootings, most of young women, in greater New York City. The Son of Sam killed six and wounded seven and claimed that the killings were directed by "the Devil's henchmen." His bizarre letters to officials and the press before his capture were heavily overladen with occult symbolic terminology, and numerous occult symbols were found in his apartment and belongings after his arrest. Berkowitz pleaded guilty and consequently was never brought to trial, but immediately sentenced to life in prison. Various researchers, writers, and experts have speculated over the years as to whether or not Berkowitz was insane, a cold-blooded thrill killer, or even part of a sinister occult conspiracy, the theory advanced by Maury Terry in his comprehensive book *The Ultimate Evil.*[43] Terry does a good job of gathering evidence that Berkowitz did not act alone, but his occult conspiracy theory, centered on the Process Church of Final Judgment, is less convincing.[44]

The Night Stalker murderer, Richard Ramirez, appears to be a serious individual satanist. Ramirez was eventually convicted of thirteen counts of murder, thirty other felonies, and eighteen "special circumstances," conditions associated with the murders, enabling the judge to hand down a death sentence. Ramirez bragged to friends and family of his satanic beliefs, checked out books on the occult and satanism from his hometown library, and left satanic symbols at the scenes of some of his murders. During his trial he sometimes flashed the Devil's Horn sign or a pentacle drawn on his palm. Hometown friends described him as a teenager who was "a confused, angry loner who sought refuge in thievery, drugs, the dark side of rock music."[45] Ramirez's comments at his sentencing echo hauntingly the relativism rampant in contemporary occultism: "I am beyond your experience. I am beyond good and evil, legions of the night—night breed—repeat not the errors of the Night Prowler and show not mercy. I will be avenged. Lucifer dwells within us all. That's it."[46]

El Paso, at the western edge of Texas, was Ramirez's hometown. Brownsville, in eastern Texas, is just across the Mexican border from the 1989 site of another occult murder. Fifteen bodies were found at Rancho Santa Elena, outside Matamoros, Mexico. American college student Mark Kilroy was killed by a machete chop to the head. His brain, heart, intestines, and other organs had been removed, as well as his legs. Eight homosexuals were ritually murdered, eviscerated, and thrown into a canal. The brutal murders were done by a drug smuggling ring led by a *palero*, or black magic priest, a homosexual drug dealer named Aldolfo de Jesus Constanzo. Constanzo invented the particulars of his own black magic cult, patterning much of it after West African black sorcery and borrowing some details from the popular movie, *The Believers*. Eventually Constanzo, his high priestess, Sara Aldrete, his male lover, Martin Quintana Rodriguez, and the rest of his cult/smuggling ring were killed and/or captured.[47] The occult aspects of the smuggling ring seemed to serve the triple purposes of 1.) manipulating and controlling the more credulous followers and workers, falsely assuring them of supernatural protection from law enforcement; 2.) providing Constanzo, Aldrete, and the other leaders with thrilling, sadistic diversion; and 3.) protecting the security of their operations with murder and threats.

The incidents related here are only some of the violence, murder, and destruction plaguing our nation. Most crimes have no occult overtones, and most occultists are as law-abiding as typical Americans.

But the dark side of occult relativism and destructive ritual is that some people become instruments of evil, preying on others in their lustful quest for personal power and control. These crimes were committed by adults, but unfortunately some teenagers seem just as committed to destructive occultism and crimes against others.

## TEENAGE OCCULT CRIME

People experience more emotional, physical, and mental growth and change in their teenage years than they do at any other time in their lives. Children become adults through roughly a decade of decisions, impulses, desires, and actions. Most teenagers manage to cope well with these tumultuous years. Some teenagers, however, seem to be on a path to self-destruction, despite the best intentions of their parents, teachers, and loved ones—often despite even their own intentions. For a few of these troubled teenagers, crime mars their lives, and sometimes their deaths.

Drug use plays a central part in almost all teenage occult crime. Law enforcement almost never finds a case involving teenagers and the occult without also finding heavy drug use. While recreational drug use among general teenage populations appears to be dropping slowly, it is almost universal and unchanged among teenagers involved in destructive occultism. Whether a teenager attempts to commit suicide, rob a convenience store, vandalize a cemetery, or kill a neighbor's cat, drugs are involved.

Many teenagers try drugs once or twice, on a dare, as an experiment, or in a social setting where peer pressure becomes too great to resist. Teenagers who are vulnerable to the occult, however, usually lack the necessary skills to leave drugs after one or two experiences. The vulnerable teenager learns almost instantly that drug use provides the power and escapism he or she craves.

One girl described drugs' attraction for her, explaining, "When I'm high nobody can touch me. For the little while I'm high I feel invincible. Reality becomes what I make it." She went on to tell us how hard her recovery was, saying, "Everything in my life is a mess: school, home, my boyfriend, the cops. I have to fight myself every day so I don't just give up and escape again with drugs. Life's so much better when you're high."

Occult ritualism and drugs enhance each other's effects. The more you do drugs, the more the rituals affect you. The more you perform the rituals, the sharper the drug experience. Most teenage satanists see the magic of ritual as the nonmaterial counterpart to the tangible ingredients of a good hit, smoke, or fix.

Marijuana is still the most popular drug among teenage occultists, closely matched by alcohol. Marijuana and alcohol are available around most school campuses, private religious schools as well as public, and almost any place teenagers tend to congregate. Serious drug users usually end up selling enough to pay for their own supplies, so teenagers can always buy from their friends. Almost as popular as marijuana and alcohol are cocaine, speed, crack, prescription pills, and acid (LSD). Sometimes advanced occultists experiment with more exotic toxic plants, such as belladonna and peyote.

Teenagers' drug use is not only illegal itself, but it often incites other criminal behavior. To pay for their drugs, teens often turn to dealing, or steal and fence from friends, family, and neighbors. Paranoia grows and with it suspicion of everyone else. This often leads to assaults against perceived enemies. Sometimes the assault becomes murder.

Ricky Kasso, Jimmy Troiano, and Gary Lauwers were heavy drug users. Ricky was also a committed satanist, Jimmy and Gary kind of following along as Ricky performed rituals and invoked demonic powers. Then Ricky caught Gary stealing drugs from him. Although Gary promised to pay Ricky back, he never got around to it. So Ricky and his buddy Jimmy brutally murdered Gary, who died in a isolated forest clearing crying for his mother as Ricky demanded, "Say you love Satan!" A drug theft had deteriorated into occult murder.[48]

Aside from the almost universal drug use, the most frequent teenage occult crime is suicide. Another American teenager commits suicide every ninety minutes, twenty-four hours a day, seven days a week. Some of those suicides are linked to the occult. Drugs plus destructive occultism too often equals suicide.

Dereck Shaw, a sixteen-year-old Canadian, killed himself after two years of heavy satanic involvement. Shortly before his death he wrote, "There must be some mistake. I didn't mean to let them [demons] take away my soul."[49] The night Dereck killed himself he told his girlfriend, "he had been visited by Satan, appearing in a blue light and demanding his soul."[50] A few minutes later he ended his life with a rifle in his mouth.

On February 9, 1986 Philip Morton, eighteen, hanged himself in his dormitory room at St. John's Military Academy in Delafield, Wisconsin. Philip had been depressed for a long time over what he saw as his parents' unreasonable expectations, and was particularly despondent over a recent breakup with his long-time girlfriend, but he was also an occultist. A skull and lighted red candle, both on top of a red mat, were found beside his body, and his stereo was playing a Pink Floyd tape which contained the song, "Goodbye Cruel World." A note next to his body, perhaps meant for his parents and the school, said, "Hey, you f***ers. Here's your knife in the back."

Michele Kimball, a fifteen-year-old high school sophomore, killed herself in a suicide pact with her boyfriend, who survived. In her suicide note she said she worshiped the devil and knew her parents would never understand. She died on January 6, 1988 in Vermont. The last entry in her journal contained the lyrics to a destructive metal song.[51]

Nineteen-year-old Randy Duncan still wore headphones when he killed himself in October, 1984. He was listening to one of his favorite occult metal musicians, Ozzy Osborne, and his song, "Suicide Solution."[52] Two years later, in 1986, sixteen-year-old Michael Jeffrey Waller committed suicide. The same Osborne song was the last music he listened to. Two years after Waller, seventeen-year-old Harold Hamilton shot himself in the head as "Suicide Solution" played on his tape deck. He died seven hours later.[53] John McCollum also committed suicide and had listened to "Suicide Solution."

Ozzy Osborne protests that his song is actually anti-suicide, carrying the message that anyone who takes drugs is committing suicide. Osborne also says his use of occult symbolism and vocabulary is part of his show—he is not a practicing satanist.[54] The psychiatrist who treated John before his death said, "When a kid is at the breaking point... he is susceptible to other influences, like music or MTV.... Sadomasochism, blood, and violence make big bucks for the producers of rock videos, but such things can push a kid over the edge."[55]

Raymond Belknap and Jay Vance, close friends, occultists, and fans of the metal band Judas Priest, made a suicide pact just before Christmas in 1985. The Nevada teenagers drank beer, smoked pot, and tried to blow their own brains out with shotguns in a churchyard. Belknap succeeded. Vance survived with horrible pain, crippling injuries and horrible disfigurement. He died three years later of a methadone overdose.[56]

Mike Newell was a teenager bent on suicide who had a little help from his friends. He and about thirty other teenagers had their own self-styled Devil-worship group, their favorite ritual being shaking up hamsters in a nail-studded box. Newell, a homosexual, was frustrated because of an unfulfilled love affair. He believed that Satan would give him unbelievable power if he died a violent death. He convinced two other teenagers to help him commit suicide by threatening to murder someone else if they didn't. They cooperated by binding his hands and feet with adhesive tape and pushing him into a sandy wash near his home in Vineland, New Jersey.[57]

David Olive and Philip Gomiser, occult dabblers and metal music fanatics, were ready to end it all when they were only fifteen. So they took their favorite metal band tape, their portable tape player, and a gun out into the woods. There they played their tape, scratched their names and occult symbols on homemade styrofoam tombstones, and one shot the other and then killed himself. David's mother said, "He was so distant, and he just kept getting farther and farther away."[58]

Suicide is a permanent solution to temporary problems. Unfortunately, for the teenagers who succeed, there is no option later to try a different solution. By its very nature destructive occultism, with its relativism and violence, attracts and exploits the most vulnerable teenagers. Their self-control and reasoning abilities further impaired by drugs, it is little wonder that some teenage occultists take their own lives.

Vandalism, especially marking occult symbols on property and desecrating religious sites, is also common among teenage occultists. Four teenagers toppled seventy-six tombstones in a New Brunswick, New Jersey cemetery in December, 1985. Then they arranged small American flags in a pentagram figure on the ground and set them afire with small votive candles. The candles and flags had been stolen from nearby veterans' graves. The teenagers did not appear to have been heavily involved in their own study and practice of satanism, but were copying suggestive lyrics and symbols of their favorite metal bands.[59]

Four teenagers attempted to remove body parts from a grave for use in their homegrown variety of satanic rituals in Myrtle Beach, Florida in 1988.[60]

In Southern California in 1987 at least seven young people, male and female, were arrested for vandalizing a vacant warehouse. The group, wearing satanic symbols and emblems, trashed the warehouse, destroying drinking fountains, light fixtures, toilets, and mirrors, and smashing in walls. After urinating and defecating on the floor, they spray painted occult symbols on the walls.[61]

Occult-dabbling teenagers in the Southern California coastal community of Newport Beach had a favorite deserted little island in Upper Newport Bay. They called it "Death Island," dug a sacrificial pit in the center of it and performed rituals using urns of human ashes stolen from two nearby cemeteries in 1983.[62]

Other Southern California satanic vandalism that same year included teenagers breaking into an elementary shool and scrawling satanic symbols on desks and carpets, and breaking into a church and writing "Satan lives" in gigantic letters on the walls.[63]

Vandalism, robbery, arson, animal torture and killing marked a Denver area teenage satanic group calling themselves the Black Magic Cult. Together the friends took drugs, and worshiped Satan. For their rituals they stole thirteen choir robes from a local church. These rituals included drinking blood from self-inflicted slashes and torturing dogs by burning them with acid.[64]

Lyons notes that satanic activity picked up markedly in the 1980s, especially among teenagers and especially involving vandalism of religious sites and graveyards: "In July 1983, a dozen churches in Portland, Maine, were defaced with Satanic slogans. In that same month, two teenagers were charged in Surrey, British Columbia, with grave robbing and the theft of religious objects from an Anglican church. In January 1984, bodies were snatched from a Tampa, Florida cemetery, apparently for ritual use, and two months later, authorities in Hopkinsville, Kentucky, reported a similar incident, blaming 'Satan-cultists.'"[65]

Teenagers who buy the lies that right and wrong are the same thing, that self-indulgence is the only meaning to life, and that power comes through ritual, commonly end up participating in acts of ritual rebellion such as vandalism and grave desecration. Sometimes that self-indulgent destructiveness turns to murder.

There's a metal song with lyrics all about how great it would feel to kill your mother, the most familiar symbol of authority and the most frequent impediment to a troubled teenager's self-indulgence. Every year a few teenagers try to solve their problems with parents by killing the parents. The teenager may feel driven by years of physical and/or sexual abuse, long-term rebellion against authority, or chronic maladjustment to the family setting. When teenagers involved in destructive occultism turn to murder, their parents are most frequently their victims.

Tommy Sullivan, fourteen, studied satanism on his own, learning from metal music lyrics and library books, and then told a friend that Satan came to him in a vision and told him to kill his family. Tommy stabbed his mother at least twelve times and tried to kill his father and brother by setting his house on fire. He then turned his knife on himself, slit his throat and wrists, and bled to death in a snowbank not far from his home.[66]

"Satanism usually isn't a motive in murder. Rather, murder is a symptom of satanism," explained Orange County, California deputy district attorney Dick Fredrickson.[67] Fredrickson prosecuted a teenage couple who were heavily into satanism and who murdered the girl's mother in her kitchen, stabbing her twice and hitting her more than twelve times with a wrench.

In 1983 sixteen-year-old Ronald Lampasi made a pact with Satan, signed in blood. Then he ambushed and killed his father and wounded his mother. Prosecutor Michael Maguire said Lampasi shot his mother and threw things at her "to see if she would jerk, to see if she was still alive."[68]

Donald Coday couldn't stand his father and thought that praying to God wouldn't help. So in 1985 the sixteen-year-old prayed to Satan and shot his father nine times, killing him.[69]

Jonathan Cantero was nineteen in 1988 when he killed his mother by slitting her throat, stabbing her around forty times, and almost severing her left hand (in satanism, the hand of power). He wrote down the poem he recited over her body: "Lord Satan, thou knowest I have stricken this woman from the earth, I have slain the womb from which I was born. I have ended her reign of desecration of my mind;

she is no longer of me, but only a simple serpent on a lower plane."[70]

Sean Sellers is the best-known teenage satanist to murder his parents. Sean had an unstable home life as a child, although his mother and stepfather genuinely loved him and tried under difficult circumstances to give him a good home. His interest in the occult began before he became a teenager. Fantasy role-playing games such as Dungeons and Dragons were more than games to him—they represented the world of spiritual power and self-fulfilling fantasies. He devoured books on the occult and satanism, studying and practicing to obtain the power he sought so eagerly. As a young teenager in Colorado he instructed his young friends in drug use and the black arts, daring them to greater drug use and more macabre occult rituals, including cutting themselves, drinking their own blood, and sacrificing small animals. Sean's friends soon learned that drugs, sex, and the occult were Sean's tickets to power. Sean's parents didn't know much of what he did, and didn't understand what they did know. In some ways he was a great son, helping with housework, complimenting his mother. But overall he was sullen, uncontrollable, and willful. His mother began seeing signs of serious trouble and occult involvement, but was unable to find the help she needed. Then one night Sean conducted a solitary satanic ritual in his bedroom, moved silently down the hall, and shot his parents to death as they slept in their bed. He spent the rest of the night with a friend and turned up back at the murder scene the next day as the shocked and innocent son, horrified by his parents' brutal deaths. Today he is Oklahoma's youngest Death Row inmate, convicted of his parents' murder as well as the earlier murder of a convenience store clerk who refused to sell him alcohol. Sean has become a Christian, rejected his previous allegiance to the lawlessness of contemporary satanism, and spends his days trying to help the kids who are headed for the same kind of trouble he once had.[71]

Some troubled teenagers choose to murder other people besides their parents. In Carl Junction, Missouri in 1988, teenagers Jim Hardy, Pete Roland, and Ron Clements practiced murdering by torturing and killing small animals, especially cats. They fantasized for months about what it would be like to murder a human, then did it by taking baseball bats to their friend, Steve Newberry.[72]

Philip Gamble killed his brother, Lloyd, as an offering to Satan. It was the first his family knew of his interest in and practice of satanism. Others kids at his high school had been dabbling in the occult, too, but only Philip killed.[73]

## WHAT WENT WRONG?

Exploring the world of occult crime is like descending into a cesspool of decay and devastation. If you feel sick after reviewing this chapter, you should. Moral outrage should be the response against moral decadence. And when the teenager we have loved and nurtured through childhood is trapped in this morass of moral decay and corruption, we should be compelled to risk whatever is necessary to rescue him or her before dabbling becomes death.

Despite our best intentions, our children do not always embrace truth and morality. How do children become servants of Satan? Where does our responsibility for their actions lie? How can we rescue them before it is too late? There are answers to these troubling questions in the following chapters.

# SEVEN

# Did I Go Wrong?

**"I** HATE YOU! I'll make you sorry you ever embarrassed me in front of my friends! You can't stop me from doing what I want!" Heather's voice rose to a screaming crescendo. Her last words struck her mother as hard as if Heather had slapped her. "I hate you! I wish you were dead!"

Heather's mother, Carol, lifted her hand toward the swinging screen door in a half-hearted attempt to stop her daughter's flight. It was a relief, actually, to have her gone after the hour of yelling they'd exchanged. The confrontation over the drugs was only the latest in a seemingly endless cycle of accusations, rebellion, and hysterical threats. Carol remembered back to the first sign of trouble she noticed: Heather's betrayal when she and her friends drank Carol's gallon bottle of wine she used for cooking. Carol still remembered the embarrassment of talking with Heather's homeroom teacher about her school detention for drawing occult symbols on the locker room wall. But that incident paled beside the shame Carol felt when she had signed for custody from the police after Heather and her friends were caught stealing votive candles from the mausoleum. And now today's humiliation. Somehow she had stumbled out some sort of lame explanation to Kathi's mother about the large stash of cash and pills in the purse Heather had left at Kathi's house the night before.

Carol sank to the kitchen floor, covering her face with her hands. "God, oh, God! Did I go wrong? Is it my fault?" She didn't expect God to answer.

Carol and Heather are both out of control. Neither one knows what to do. Neither one is happy with things the way they are. Both of them blame Carol. Heather's sixteen, only a kid. It couldn't be her fault. Carol had always been able to protect and rescue Heather before. Scraped knees, bad dreams, hurt feelings—Mom's warm embrace and cookies and milk had always worked before. What was wrong with Carol that caused Heather to start on a collision course with destruction?

Most parents of kids in crisis blame themselves. Almost always the kids in crisis blame their parents, too. All too often others look at the troubled teen and assume that the parents are to blame, too.

Such simplistic blame-throwing is never wholly right, even in the worst of cases. Teenagers are, in large measure, responsible for their decisions, and their parents are not able to shield them from the many factors influencing their choices. Even if it were possible to pinpoint responsibility for teens' problems wholly and accurately on parents, merely pinning blame is counter-productive and destructive in itself.

Parents don't plan for their teenagers to self-destruct. However, if this does happen, parents need to evaluate the problem constructively and move quickly to life-changing intervention.

If your teen is in trouble, and you're being blamed by yourself, your teen, or others, this chapter will help you understand the problems that can lead to a crisis, and then prepare you to move past the problems and toward solutions.

## FROM CRISIS TO HOPE

"There's no hope. It can't get any worse. I can't see any way out. I'm so scared I can't move. I just know Kevin is going to be killed or kill himself, he's so messed up." Marcia's tear-streaked face, her red-rimmed eyes, and the quaver in her voice revealed the despair she felt for her seventeen-year-old, Kevin, who lay nearby on an emergency room gurney. Kevin's battered and bloody body was a result of the beating he had suffered for a bad drug deal. His emaciated frame, dull hair, and sunken eyes resulted from his almost continual drug use. Kevin was on the road to death, and Marcia felt helpless.

But it's hard for mothers to give up. With her next breath she blurted, "There's got to be a way out! I won't let Kevin die. Things are so bad, there's got to be somebody who can help. I'll do anything for Kevin. I've got to have hope. It's all that's left."

Marcia didn't realize it then, but her refusal to give up was all that stood between Kevin and death. Often parents who don't give up mean the difference between life and death for their children. A commitment to effective intervention and long-term, constructive action is the first step on the road to recovery.

If you are a parent with a crisis teen, don't give up. No matter what has happened, no matter how you try to assign blame, if you have commitment, you can have an impact on your teen's life. There are no magic spells, no secret formulas guaranteed to rescue your teen from destruction. Yet there is hope, and there are proven principles of intervention and restoration that will give your teenager every opportunity to turn his life around. You have already displayed your commitment by reading this book. The problems that accumulated to trap your teen are both short-term and long-term, but none of them place your teen beyond hope or help.

Precipitating problems are short-term difficulties that become the immediate causes of your teen's aberrant behavior. Often they are the most noticeable problems, but rarely are they at the root of a youngster's dysfunctional behavior.

Predisposing problems are the long-term foundational conditions that render children vulnerable to destructive behavior. Predisposing problems have to do with values rather than with statements, with attitudes rather than particular actions. Chapters One and Four discussed the predisposing problems most common to teenagers who end up in serious trouble, and who are often involved in the occult, including extreme alienation, morbid fascination, drug and alcohol use, difficulty working within the system, a sense of powerlessness, a need to control, misdirected intelligence and creativity, an untempered attraction to the mysterious, and other emotional, social, physical, and religious factors.

Here's a simple example of the difference between precipitating problems and predisposing problems. Grace walked into the kitchen just as her five-year-old, Carrie, grabbed a handful of cookies off the counter. Caught in the act, she protested, "It's not my fault, Mommy. Travis told me to get us cookies 'cuz he's not big enough to reach." The precipitating problem is that Carrie stole cookies. The predisposing or underlying problem is that Carrie and Travis have the typical childhood attitude that disobeying is worth it as long as you don't get caught.

As children grow and their worlds expand, they become influenced by many more factors than their parents can control. Their predisposed vulnerabilities become exploited through precipitating problems. A vulnerability to peer pressure is acted out through getting drunk with friends, a weakness for self-control exhibits itself as a violent outburst at school. Following are some of the most common precipitating problems that can indicate serious underlying vulnerabilities that can propel your teenager toward crisis.

**School.** *Has your teenager been given detention increasingly frequently over the last year?* Most teenagers occasionally run afoul of school rules, but the teenager headed for trouble receives detentions at a steadily escalating rate.

*What behavior(s) merited the detentions?* This answer needs to be distinguished carefully from what your teenager *says* is the cause. What is the official justification for the detentions? This answer will be straightforward and fairly simple: "David stole another student's lunch," "Erica didn't have her homework done again," "Matt fell asleep in class."

*What cause did your teenager give for the detentions?* Answering this question will help you to see what your teenager wants you to understand about his or her behavior. Usually, this means shifting the blame to someone or something else— it's never the teenager's fault: "Greg stole my lunch last week," "I didn't think the teacher would ask for our homework," "That teacher is boring enough to put anybody to sleep." Often a teen's explanation reveals his or her own value system, a valuable barometer for future actions. David seems to think it's only wrong to steal from those who never steal. Erica believes responsible behavior is only necessary if it's checked. Matt has decided to learn only if it's entertaining.

*Has your teenager been suspended or expelled from school?* Suspension and expulsion are much more serious than detention and indicate that your teenager has a serious problem conforming to social expectations. The student who risks suspension or expulsion usually fits one of two categories: 1.) what they wanted was worth getting suspended or expelled or 2.) they are unable to control their behavior sufficiently to avoid suspension or expulsion.

The child who calculates the risk and decides "it's worth it" has control. He or she chooses behavior with certain consequences in order to achieve a more important goal. Beating up another student so he doesn't turn you in for drugs on campus is more important than not getting suspended. Earning a "bad" reputation by spray painting pentacles and "Satan Rules" on restroom walls is worth the risk of getting caught. Winning leadership of your "gang" of satanic dabblers by mutilating and killing the mice in the school science lab means more than being expelled. As long as this kind of teenager has clear goals and determination, he will not change his behavior unless the consequences make success not worth the risk.

The child who is unable to control his or her behavior often feels trapped by circumstances or friends. Peer pressure becomes the primary control in life. This teenager doesn't think beating up another student is an action that is deserving of suspension. Even when he is hauled off his victim, he doesn't think about what will happen. When he's sent home, he doesn't think the school is serious about threatening to suspend him. When the suspension notice arrives, he fully expects Mom and Dad to "fix it" somehow. This teenager is much less in touch with reality. As long as this kind of teenager is protected from reality, the consequences of his behavior, and as long as he keeps thinking he can have it both ways, he will have no incentive for getting help to regain control of his life.

*Have your teenager's grades declined drastically?* Kids in trouble are rarely intellectually incapable of achieving average grades. They may have any of a variety of behavior problems, no desire to achieve, drug or alcohol debility, or health deterioration.

There are many types of behavior problems. Three of the most prevalent are submission to peer pressure, rebellion, and apathy. Grades can plummet when a teen changes peer groups from those who value good grades to those who disdain good grades as a sign of submitting to authority. When independence turns into rebellion, one of the easiest, most quantifiable ways a teen can express that rebellion is through deliberately refusing to do homework or study for tests. The at-risk teen experiments with apathy concerning anything connected to authority or to long-range goals. Not caring about homework or grades is an indication of not caring about the future.

Drug or alcohol use makes it extremely difficult for the affected teenager to maintain good grades. Along with the attitude or behavioral problems associated with drug and alcohol use, the physical effects severely impact academic aptitude. The student who comes to school under the influence of drugs or alcohol cannot perform consistently or adequately. Physiological damage from alcohol or drugs continues long after the hangover leaves or the high disappears. Damage related to academic performance includes impaired memory, loss of logical thought processes, inability to concentrate, attention span deficits, and inability to perform repetitive tasks.

As the teen's behavior deteriorates and his or her drug or alcohol use increases, other physiological effects further undermine ability to function in school. Physical deterioration can include slowed wound healing, malnutrition, vitamin and mineral difficiencies, tooth decay, repeated nasal and sinus infections, eye inflammation and infection, and sexual dysfunction (including irregular periods, unplanned pregnancies, sexually transmitted diseases, and impotency). All of these physical factors negatively impact a student's ability to perform in school.

*Has your teenager dropped out of approved extra-curricular activities?* Not all teens are joiners, and your teen may never have been interested in after-school activities. But many teens are active in sports, student government, art, music, drama, or pep squad activities. If a teen who appeared to be fully committed to such activity irresponsibly abandons his or her commitment, there may be more wrong than just changing interests. Such abandonment will be characterized by an "I-don't-care attitude," an unwillingness to go through the necessary channels to resign officially, and a mocking attack against anyone who dares to criticize the teen's irresponsibility.

**Work.** Today most teens in their last two years of high school also have part-time jobs. Teens sliding into trouble are rarely able to keep a good work record and receive approval from their employers. The kind of jobs they do, their performance on the job, and the frequency with which they change jobs can be indicators of trouble.

*Have your teen's work habits changed markedly?* The teen who was always early for work, over the course of time, may become the teen who just doesn't show up, or who shows up seriously late no matter how many threats he or she receives from the employer.

Even parental involvement doesn't help. One mother explained to us,

> Lori was on probation at her fast food job because she missed work twice and showed up an hour late another time. I didn't want her to lose her job, so I made her boss give me a copy of her work schedule. Then I made sure she got up and was ready in plenty of time. It was hard work, and Lori yelled at me for it, but I felt it was worth it. She left for work in plenty of time, but she never showed up. She stopped to see her girlfriend on the way, and they ended up spending all day at the beach. She never bothered to call anyone. How could she do that after everything I did for her?

Often teens in trouble go through a succession of jobs in a short period of time. Remember, a teen in trouble usually blames everything on someone else, it's never his fault. He also can be a master at manipulation and charm—when it suits his purpose. Be wary if your teen keeps getting "laid off," or keeps having bosses that "just don't understand and are mean," or repeatedly "quits" jobs for a variety of reasons that sound too good to be true. Troubled teens usually can turn on the charm long enough to get a new job, but their own troubled situation makes it difficult for them to keep any job for very long.

Sometimes a teen will fabricate an entire employment story for his parents. Without normal verification, his or her parents may never suspect serious problems. A father told us,

> For almost two years I thought my son had a really good job as a document delivery person in our city. He had a nice company car (better than I ever could have given him) and gave me the car phone number so I could call him at work. He sure got a lot more money for the job than they used to pay back when I was a youngster. But times, traffic, and pay scales change.
>
> I was so shocked I thought I was having a heart attack when the police called and said my son had been arrested as part of a major drug ring in town. They said he sold to all the kids at school and had his own territory in town, too. I was such a fool! I protested to the detective on the phone, "You must have the wrong guy. My son delivers documents."

**Family.** Nowhere is the impact of precipitating problems more pronounced than in the family. Part of the reason for this is that the family represents more than one person, and consequently, more than one set of problems and priorities. Family chaos often reigns in the home of an overworked, underpaid single mom, her bored ten-year-old who spends eleven hours a day in day care or school, and her rebellious, undersupervised sixteen-year-old who gets in trouble at school, can't hold a job, and is never home.

Some of the precipitating problems often evident in families with troubled teens include theft, alcohol and/or drug use, lack of control, and physical violence.

*Does your teen have more cash than you expected, or does he or or she buy more than you think he or she can afford?* Troubled teenagers steal from their families for a variety of reasons, the two most common being to support drug or alcohol purchases, and for private use.

*Are items of value, prescription or street drugs, or alcohol missing from your home?* A teen may steal the drugs or alcohol directly from his or her parents, including prescription drugs, cocaine, and marijuana. Many teens say they first tried drugs right at home, using their parents' "stashes." In *The Black Mask* author John Charles Cooper notes, "We are the people our parents warned us against. We, who call *license* 'freedom,' are the sources from which the young and the unbalanced draw the elements to create their individual 'hells.'"[1]

Sometimes parents are unaware their teenagers are stealing drugs and/or alcohol. The missing pills are presumed to have been left absent-mindedly in some restaurant restroom, the gin or vodka bottle looks full so the parent doesn't check to find the bottle has been refilled with water, or the parents think they drank more themselves than they realized.

*Do you find yourself wondering if your teen is using your drugs or alcohol, even if you then quickly dismiss the idea?* Sometimes the parents suspect what's happening, but can't get over the awkwardness of confronting their teens. A mother told us why she waited so long to confront her daughter about her drinking: "For a long time I thought I was drinking more than I should, and I was afraid if I confronted her, she either wouldn't be guilty and I'd be faced with the fact that my own drinking was out of control, or she would say, 'So what? You drink, too.' I didn't have a good argument why it was okay for me, but not for a fourteen-year-old."

A father couldn't accuse his son until he faced the destructiveness of his own drug use:

> I knew Kyle was doing drugs, at least marijuana and probably some cocaine, too. Sometimes he would smell exactly how I would after I smoked weed. He even used the same aroma incense I used. And once at breakfast he looked up at me and it was just like I was staring at myself in the mirror after a night of cocaine—the same tired eyes, reddened nostrils, and haggard face.
>
> But I couldn't talk to him about it for a long time. I tried rehearsing a confrontation in my mind, but for every argument I gave him for not using drugs, I already knew what he would argue back, because they were the same arguments I'd used to justify my twenty years of pot smoking and five years of "recreational" cocaine use.
>
> I finally couldn't take it anymore. I couldn't confront the destructiveness of drug use until I saw it in my own son. I think I was almost as shocked as he was the day I sat him down and told him *I* had a problem with drugs but I was determined to beat it. That was the first step of our joint recovery.

*Has your home been burglarized, perhaps several times, and the police have asked you if your teen could have been involved?* Troubled teens also steal items of value to resell for money to buy what they couldn't otherwise, including drugs, alcohol, occult supplies, and expensive clothes. Sometimes a valuable item such as jewelry may not be missed for months. Sometimes teens will stage a break-in and burglary of their own house and steal electronic equipment, computers, and everything with a good street value.

*Have your relatives or friends lost valuable items after visits you and your teen have made?* Troubled teens frequently steal from neighbors, relatives, and friends. Considering the number of thefts they typically perform, they are rarely caught. Aunt Jane wouldn't think of suspecting her nephew of stealing her diamond bracelet at his last visit, and good neighbor Sally blames the gangs across town, not the teen next door, for stealing the CD player and speakers out of her car.

*Does your teen act nervous or angry when you mention something that has been stolen or is missing?* Sometimes thefts are required by the particular group to which your teenager belongs. A thirteen-year-old, Tamara, was required to steal her father's coin collection as part of her initiation into one occult group. The group made pendants out of the coins for everyone in the group to wear, including Tamara. Her father never recognized his coin hanging from a chain around Tamara's neck. Tamara didn't think she had actually hurt her father, after all, the collection was insured. But she was afraid she eventually would be found out, and wearing the necklace reinforced her fear daily. It effectively bound her to the group and to secrecy.

*Does your teen volunteer that he or she stole something just to make you angry or prove it could be done?* Sometimes theft is an outward sign of inner destructive rebellion. The teen may not need the item, may not even sell it for the money. The act of theft itself reinforces defiance of authority.

*Is your teenager's speech deteriorating to the point that he or she makes little attempt to refrain from swearing, sexually degrading vocabulary, and/or violent images?* A steady diet of metal music, gutter rap lyrics, and friends' examples, combined with unresolved anger and rebelliousness, is dangerous if reflected increasingly over time in your teenager's speech.

*Do you sometimes worry that your teenager may not be able to control anger?* Often the troubled teen is out of control. Sometimes the family initially is unaware of this lack of control because it is exhibited away from home. The teen may trash a fast food restaurant, beat up someone he doesn't like at school, or engage in vandalism in a nearby park. If he or she doesn't get caught, parents are unlikely to know. Sometimes parents subconsciously don't *want* to know.

*Do you ever suspect your teenager might have been involved in an act of violence or vandalism?* Countless parents later regret that they ignored or tried to explain away evidence that their teenager was in trouble until it was too late. They don't want to know where the broken parking meter came from; how their child got glass sliver cuts all over face, hands, and arms; or how close to the street fight was the party that their child was attending. Regretfully, bad behavior doesn't get better if it's ignored or left to go away by itself.

*Does your teenager ever threaten to hurt you physically or destroy something you own (house or car, for example)?* Parent abuse usually occurs after an escalation in verbal fighting and open defiance by teenagers. As the teen's anger increases and self control decreases, the parent may actually flinch at the teen's words as though they were blows. If you have felt ashamed for thinking your child might hit or otherwise hurt you, think more carefully. There may be a genuine basis for your fear. An out-of-control teenager may first wound with words, then with a fist, and, without intervention, perhaps with deadly force. Teenagers involved in the occult who turn to assault or murder usually target parents or other family members.

Each of these precipitating factors is common to teenagers headed for destruction, but nothing is a foolproof test. If you see one or more of these signs in your teenager, consider them seriously and take positive, constructive steps to ensure the best opportunity for your teenager to avoid devastation.

## TESTING FOR PREDISPOSING
## AND PRECIPITATING PROBLEMS

Think honestly about your teenager, his or her friends, interests, activities, and ideas. Then answer "yes" or "no" to the following questions. You may need to check information (like album covers) concerning your child or information contained in this book before you know how to answer some of the questions. Check your score with the risk level listed at the end of the test to get a general idea of the statistical chances of your teenager's serious involvement in destructive behavior, including destructive occultism.

---

____ 1. I don't have much control over my teenager.

____ 2. My teenager rarely obeys me.

____ 3. I don't usually know where my teenager is.

____ 4. I have caught my teenager lying about his or her whereabouts more than three times.

____ 5. My teenager doesn't want me to know his or her friends very well.

____ 6. I don't know where my teenager gets the money for things he or she has.

____ 7. I and my teenager's other parent are not living together or are divorced.

____ 8. My teenager seems unreasonably upset that I cannot or will not pay for everything he or she wants.

____ 9. My teenager listens to metal music continually.

____ 10. My teenager's favorite movies are horror movies.

____ 11. My teenager enjoys books, movies, videos, and songs with lots of violence.

___ 12. Communication between my teenager and me is almost nonexistent.

___ 13. I often smell incense coming from my teenager's room.

___ 14. I don't trust my teenager's friends.

___ 15. My teenager's room has colored candles, unusual figures, symbols, and pictures.

___ 16. My teenager draws strange signs on homework papers, scratch paper, and notebooks.

___ 17. I worry that my teenager may have a drug or alcohol problem.

___ 18. I think I have smelled alcohol or drugs on my teenager.

___ 19. I think I saw my teenager drunk or stoned at least once.

___ 20. It seems like my teenager only wears black clothes.

___ 21. My teenager frequently attends metal music clubs or concerts.

___ 22. My teenager brags that other kids are afraid of him or her.

___ 23. My teenager has been arrested several times.

___ 24. My teenager has been suspended or expelled from school.

___ 25. My teenager's grades are far below what I know he or she is capable of.

___ 26. My teenager frequently misses school.

___ 27. My teenager's school or teacher has recommended professional counseling.

___ 28. A close friend or relative has recommended professional counseling or has asked me what's wrong with my teenager.

___ 29. My teenager has been involved in several car accidents (even if minor or without injuries).

___ 30. I'm embarrassed by the way my teenager treats me or others, and how he or she acts.

___ 31. I'm afraid my teenager may be involved in dangerous activities.

___ 32. My teenager always blames other people for the serious trouble he or she gets in.

___ 33. My teenager always seems tired, even after twelve or more hours of sleep.

___ 34. My teenager consistently exhibits hostility to Christianity and refuses to go to church.

___ 35. My teenager appears to deteriorate physically before my eyes.

___ 36. My teenager doesn't care about personal hygiene.

___ 37. My teenager paints his or her fingernails (or one or two) black.

___ 38. My teenager exhibits and sometimes even acts out hatred toward any authority.

___ 39. I think my teenager frequently lies to me.

___ 40. My teenager sometimes talks about what it would feel like to kill an animal or person.

___ 41. My teenager always seems depressed.

___ 42. My teenager has threatened or attempted suicide.

___ 43. My teenager's behavior is much worse than my friends' teenagers'.

___ 44. Most of my teenager's friends are much older, seem more sophisticated, and are bad influences.

___ 45. My teenager is sexually promiscuous.

___ 46. My teenager's language is full of swearing and sexually derogatory vocabulary.

___ 47. My teenager has engaged in physical violence.

___ 48. I'm sometimes afraid my teenager will hit me or otherwise physically harm me.

___ 49. My teenager says there's no right or wrong, no good or bad, whatever he or she wants becomes right.

___ 50. I've thought of locking my teenager out of the house because he or she is so out of control.

___ 51. I wish somebody else would intervene and stop my teenager before disaster strikes.

___ 52. I've considered calling a psychiatric facility for help with my teenager.

___ 53. I spend a lot of my time worrying about what I did wrong to produce such a dysfunctional teenager.

___ 54. I hate to admit it, but sometimes I think my teenager is becoming evil.

___ 55. My teenager seems to get sick far more than normal, with nonspecific physical deterioration.

___ 56. My teenager has been diagnosed with a sexually transmitted disease.

___ 57. I think my teenager gets medical treatment without my knowledge.

___ 58. One or more of my teenager's friends has attempted or committed suicide.

___ 59. Drugs and/or alcohol have been missing from my house.

___ 60. My teenager has had parties against my orders when I've been gone.

___ 61. My teenager has told me he or she has no reason to live.

___ 62. My teenager seems to repeat certain motions or actions at particular times, almost like secret rituals.

___ 63. My teenager reads magazines and/or comic books with occult themes.

___ 64. I sometimes am afraid my teenager has no conscience, especially when it comes to his or her attitudes about pain and death.

___ 65. My teenager is unable to account for how he or she spends most of his or her time.

___ 66. My teenager's school essays often contain elements of the occult, violence, destruction, or horror.

___ 67. One of my teenager's teachers has expressed concern to me about my teenager's behavior.

___ 68. My teenager has unexplained cuts, bruises, lacerations, or scrapes.

___ 69. I once wondered if my teenager's physical injuries could have been self-inflicted.

___ 70. My teenager exhibits an unnatural fear of one or more "friends."

___ 71. My teenager is afraid God has turned his back on him or her forever.

___ 72. My teenager reads occult books.

___ 73. My teenager won't let me touch some of the things in his room. I think they might be ritual tools.

___ 74. Peer pressure usually affects my teenager's ideas and/or behavior.

___ 75. My teenager seems obssessed with fantasy role-playing games.

___ 76. My teenager won't study for school, but spends hours studying mythology books and occult literature.

___ 77. I think my teenager's diary or journal may be a *Book of Shadows.*

___ 78. My teenager is extremely secretive.

___ 79. My teenager almost never thinks of the consequences or long term effects of his or her actions.

___ 80. My teenager hardly ever sleeps.

___ 81. I think my teenager is malnourished.

___ 82. My teenager's physical condition has deteriorated markedly.

___ 83. My teenager seems to suffer from chronic depression.

___ 84. My teenager has told me, "There's no hope," "I can never escape my problems," "Life isn't worth it."

___ 85. My teenager has talked (even offhandedly) about ways to commit suicide.

___ 86. My teenager has talked about ways to commit murder, torture, or kill animals.

___ 87. I sometimes worry that my teenager won't live through his or her teenage years.

___ 88. I think my teenager may attach unusual importance to certain days, especially his or her birthday and any or all of the occult holidays (see Chapter Four).

___ 89. My teenager has grown only one or a few of his her fingernails extremely long and sharpened them.

___ 90. My teenager appears to be under great stress.

___ 91. My teenager acts violently toward our pets or neighborhood pets.

___ 92. If I were to look at my teenager as the child of a stranger, I would think he or she was unusually troubled.

___ 93. My concern for my teenager has a serious negative effect on my relationship with my other children, my spouse, and/or my close friends.

___ 94. My other children have told me my teenager is heading for crisis.

___ 95. I'm worried that my other children look up to my teenager and may begin to imitate him or her.

___ 96. I worry that it might be too late to rescue my teenager.

___ 97. My teenager has been caught desecrating a cemetery or church.

___ 98. My teenager threatens others with physical violence, death, or evil spells.

___ 99. I'm so concerned I'm willing to do anything to help my teenager.

___ 100. I'm ready to act now.

Calculate the number of "yes" answers you made. Do not change your answers. Review your answers. If none of the more serious or specific questions were answered "yes," and only a few of the less serious or more general questions, then your teenager is probably not at serious risk for destructive crisis. However, if the number and kind of questions you answered "yes" to worries you, then you and your teenager need help. Having come this far in your search for help, now is the time for you to commit yourself to the intervention and long-term actions that can make a permanent, and sometimes life-saving, difference in your teenager. The following chapter provides the concrete information you need to rescue your child from Satan.

# EIGHT

# Rescue Your Child from Satan

K EITH STARED AT THE BLOODY PENTAGRAMS on the school-yard wall. The bodies of the dead birds, whose blood had been used to paint the symbols, lay scattered on the blacktop. Keith also noticed his son, Jared, standing to one side, shifting nervously from one foot to the other, alternately glaring at the vice principal and staring moodily at the ground. He wondered what had happened to his son.

Keith remembered how proud he was when Jared and he had battled the Colorado River rapids through the Grand Canyon the summer before Jared entered high school. Jared had been gangly, but strong, tanned, his closely cropped blond hair gleaming white in the desert sun. His lopsided grin betrayed his youth, but also a hint of coming manhood.

Now, not quite three years later, Jared was almost unrecognizable. His skinny form was lost in his baggy, shredded black clothes. His hair hung in his face and down his back, stringy and dirty. Keith couldn't remember when Jared ever looked anyone in the eye anymore. The backs of his hands were covered with peeling scabs, one long, curved, black fingernail stretched his left index finger. His once expressive mouth now stretched in a continuous wicked leer.

"Mr. Carpenter, you see why we must expel Jared. He needs help, sir. We'd be happy to recommend some places, but he can't come back here. Our parents pay high tuition for us to protect their children from people like him. Get some help. He can't go on like this. Get help!" The vice principal waited only a moment for Keith's reply, then quickly turned on his heel and left the silent father and son.

Keith didn't know what to do. Jared didn't care.

The crisis that slammed into Keith's life is repeated across the country on an almost daily basis, but there is hope and help. You can rescue your child from Satan. Keith could use practical principles of intervention and restoration to regain the son he had lost. If your child is in crisis or headed for crisis, you can make a difference in his or her life. If you have protected your child to this point from the lure of the occult, you can apply the principles in this chapter to equip your child so he or she can grow to maturity and independence without the devastation of occult involvement.

You can't isolate your child from the world forever, but you can prepare him to overcome the pressures of the world as he matures. Violence and destruction *will* affect your child, no matter how careful you are. Today an average of four to five teenagers are killed each day, and three or four teenagers are arrested for murder on a daily basis. Teens are two times more likely to be victims of violent crime than adults, and almost half of them recognize their attacker. Pressure to experiment with cigarettes, alcohol, and drugs ranges from 33 percent to 55 percent among fourth to sixth graders. By the time teens finish high school, 13 percent have experimented with cocaine, 21 percent with inhaled drugs, 50 percent with marijuana, 66 percent with cigarettes, and over 90 percent with alcohol.[1] Suicide is now the second cause of death[2] among adolescents in the United States, three times the rate during the 1950s. Today in the United States another teen commits suicide every ninety minutes.[3]

When you discover your teen is involved in destructive

occultism, you feel overwhelmed with conflicting emotions. You're angry that he or she could do something this bad. You're relieved that your nagging suspicions have now taken tangible form. You're afraid your child will permanently harm himself or someone else. You're terrified your child might die. And you're consumed with guilt because you think you should have been more aware and should have done more.

The situation is further complicated because drug and alcohol use are almost always involved, too. Sexual activity and sexually transmitted diseases are also common. Very likely your present crisis was precipitated by criminal or other out-of-control behavior.

Once you have recognized the crisis or potential for crisis concerning your teen and the occult, you are ready to take steps to rescue your child.

First, you need to be willing to make a commitment to long-term, hard work to successfully rescue and restore your child to emotional, physical, and spiritual health. It would be nice if kids in trouble could be restored with little more than a fix-it drug, a quick deprogramming, or a simple change of locale. But that is a fantasy. You have read in this book how teenagers become vulnerable to the occult. These vulnerabilities developed over a long period of time and involve basic attitudes, experiences, and values. Their effect cannot be erased with a magical spell, but instead must be dealt with realistically with sound principles of Christian maturity. Take a few moments and think about the teen you are concerned for. Think of the problems he or she is experiencing, the values adopted, the attitudes expressed. Honest evaluation will confirm that these problems need long-term, constructive solutions.

Second, find professional and personal support for your lengthy intervention and restoration. The "For Further Reading" section at the end of this book can provide you with needed information and resources. Your local church can help with counseling and prayer support. A carefully chosen, Christian-oriented mental health professional can work with your teenager. Medical professionals can assist in diet and drug rehabilitation. You also need personal support from friends and family who will join you in your commitment for permanent change. In a two-parent household the burden is eased almost immeasurably when both parents agree on the need and pattern for intervention and restoration. A close friend can be invaluable as a trusted confidant when you need to pour out your heart to someone. Relatives can sometimes provide a "cooling off" place where your teenager can safely spend a few days of "R & R" from the battlefield.

Third, study the principles and practical steps to intervention, restoration, and preservation in this chapter. Through almost twenty years of work in this field we have seen hundreds of parents and teenagers in family crisis. Some have rescued their children, some, sadly, have not. But we have learned from each of them and we know the principles presented here can give your teenager a way out of the destruction he or she so blindly chose. In the midst of crisis, most teenagers will respond positively to your involvement, as long as they believe you have something better to offer. There is hope, and you represent that hope to your teenager.

## INTERVENTION

When you intervene in your teenager's life, he or she likely will accuse you of interfering. In a way, they are right. You are interfering with their destructive behavior and the involvements that promoted that behavior. But intervention goes far beyond merely thwarting their desires or plans. Intervention means you care enough about your child's future that you are willing to risk his or her rejection of you to rescue him or her from danger. When you intervene, you "come between" your teenager and danger. Don't confuse interference with intervention, or coming between, your teenager and the occult. The best role model we know of successful, postive intervention is Jesus Christ. Through his birth, life, and sacrifice on the cross, he "came between" all us sinners and the just penalty of our sin, death: "For there is one God and one Mediator between God and men, the Man Christ Jesus, who gave Himself a ransom for all, to be testified in due time...."[4]

Whether your teenager is in jail, juvenile hall, the hospital, a mental health ward, or simply out of control at home, crisis should motivate you to immediate action. As a parent your responsibility is to ensure that in the midst of crisis your teenager is safe, secure, and responsible.

Your teenager needs to be safe from occult activity, his or her own self-destructive actions, and from the ability to hurt someone else.

Perhaps the safest place for your teenager is in a locked mental health facility. Call your county mental health association for advice and criteria for admittance, or call your health insurance carrier or HMO.

Jail or juvenile hall may be the only option law enforcement will allow you to provide for your teenager's safety, and most juvenile authorities attempt to help within a frustrating and often ineffective bureaucracy. But remember that peer pressure is the single greatest influence on most teenagers, and in jail your teenager will be surrounded by peers that are dysfunctional, confused, criminal, angry, and destructive. If you can find another safe place and law enforcement will give you that option, exercise it as soon as possible. One teenager echoed a line we hear all too often from teenagers, law enforcement personnel, and parents. He told us, "All I learned in juvenile hall was a whole lot of other bad things to do and how not to get caught again."

If your teenager has attempted suicide, your insurance may cover hospitalization and intensive therapy. Many HMO facilities have skilled staff trained to deal with suicidal teenagers. Don't abdicate your parental responsibility to these professionals, but do use them for support and to ensure your teenager's safety.

Perhaps circumstances dictate that your teenager's "safe" place is at home. If you choose this option, don't make the all too common mistake of letting the situation slip out of your control because things seem to be back to normal. For your teenager to be safe you need to ensure that he cannot practice destructive occultism, cannot hurt himself, and cannot hurt others. This may mean having family, relatives, and friends rotate shifts to maintain a responsible adult presence in the home at all times. It may mean keeping a responsible adult with your teenager twenty-four hours a day.

Dave, whose son seemed bent on destruction, had more money than willing relatives. He hired a security guard to escort his son to school, counseling appointments, and then home again. When Dave got home at night, the security guard left. A creative mother re-coded her house alarm system and didn't tell her daughter how to disarm it. When she needed to leave for a short time, she "locked" her daughter in with the alarm system. Neighbors knew if they heard the siren to call her immediately. Amanda's daughter was in crisis at the end of the school year. Since Amanda was a teacher and didn't work during the summer, she arranged for her and her daughter to spend two and one-half months at a friend's mountain cabin. Providing a safe place for your teenager is not easy. It demands inconvenience, sometimes expense, embarrassment when you have to tell friends and family, and a lot of time and consistency. But safety is vital for a successful intervention.

Your teenager also needs security. Security enables your teenager to know for sure that your love for him is unconditional and never-ending, even though he is in trouble and you are going to take tough steps to rescue him. Parents are responsible for loving, disciplining, clothing, feeding, and housing their children. Your teenager should feel confident that you will do everything in your power to fulfill your responsibility to him or her, even though discipline means ensuring that your teenager accepts the consequences and responsibility for his or her actions.

When our children were young, we used to teasingly plead, "Will you promise to still love us when you get to be teenagers?" As they approached their teenage years, their behavior became bizarre, our patience wore thin, and they acted as though we were senile. Our refrain changed to, "With the grace of God, we still love you even though you are teenagers!" A teenager in crisis is in a much more serious situation, but he still needs to be assured of your love in spite of his unacceptable behavior. Oddly enough, when your love is expressed through strong intervention, even though he feels persecuted, he will also feel your love in action.

Discipline is not the same thing as yelling, hitting, grounding, or using "Gestapo" tactics. The Bible says that discipline should be without anger[5] and in love.[6] Biblically-based discipline has as its goal the development of mature self-control and responsible decision making. This is impossible without consistency. Inconsistent discipline merely teaches a child that if he waits long enough, the situation will change and he can do what he wants. A good discipliner provides a clearly defined structure within which his child is given age-appropriate freedom to make choices and exercise self-control.

Too often discipline degenerates into one or the other extreme: either dictatorships or anarchy. The dictator parent acts as though the louder he yells, the more he is disciplining; or the more he can force his child to cry, the better the child will act. The dictator's favorite line is "Because I said so!" There is a time and a place for this line, but it's not every time you open your mouth. The anarchist will do anything to please his child. He spends most of his time pleading, bargaining, and crying to persuade his child to do what he wants. The anarchist's favorite line is "Pretty please, for me?"

Biblical, constructive discipline is consistent and encourages responsible behavior, holds the child accountable for bad behavior, and ensures security for your teenager. Several books discuss good parenting techniques, including *Parenting with Love and Limits*,[7] *Choices Are Not Child's Play*,[8] *Your Prodigal Child*,[9] and *The Strong-Willed Child*.[10]

A young man called our office one day and said he was mad at God. He was mad at God because God kept letting him do all kinds of dumb, bad things. God had made him, why didn't God keep him from sinning? Since God didn't keep him from sinning, it was God's fault if he did sin. And if it was God's fault, then he shouldn't get punished! It took a while, but he finally understood that a God who always kept him from sinning or never punished him for disobedience was a robot manufacturer, not the creator of an intelligent, personal, free moral agent.

Our teenagers act like that caller. If we try to punish them for disobedience, they blame us for not stopping them. If we controlled all of their behavior, they would yell even louder that we were denying them freedom.

Good parenting means allowing our children to make decisions within clearly defined limits, and consistently helping them to be responsible for their choices.

In crisis intervention, a parent's first thought is often, "How can I get my child out of this?" That's not always the best thought. We certainly have an absolute obligation before God to rescue them from danger and give them safety and security, but we also have an obligation to help them be responsible for their choices. This sometimes means letting our child be expelled from school as a consequence of his behavior choices rather than trying to wheedle or bully another chance out of the administration. Sometimes teaching responsibility means refusing to buy our teenager new clothes because she spent all of her clothes money on metal CDs and spike jewelry. A teenager who is forced to perform three hundred hours of community service and earn his own money to pay for vandalism of a church learns responsibility for his actions. A teenager who must repeat a semester of school to make up for failures "earned" while he was stoned learns responsibility. A teenager enrolled in a hospital volunteer program in the emergency room will learn responsibility for drinking and driving after he's seen a few drunk driving fatalities and their grieving families.

Crisis intervention involves providing safety, security, and responsibility to your troubled teenager. Don't try this by yourself. Get help from books, public agencies, your church, friends, family, and your spouse. Be committed to intervening for your child before it's too late.

## RESTORATION

Once your teenager is safe, and you are encouraging his sense of security and enforcing his responsibility, then you can begin the lengthy but rewarding process of restoration. If you can remain consistent, firm, and loving, once your child's emotions have stablized after the trauma of immediate crisis, he or she will probably express an interest in restoration. Frankly, a life of destructive occultism is a miserable existence, and if your teenager can be convinced there's something better, he or she will quickly respond.

If your child is headed for crisis, or shows signs of vulnerability to destructive occultism, then you can use these principles to "stand between" your teenager and the potential threat of the occult.

Consistency is the fundamental principle underlying successful restoration. Your teenager will learn to trust you and depend on you if you are consistent. This means sticking to your promises as well as your rules unless there is a compelling reason to change, in which case you explain the change.

If we were consistent with our promises, we would make far fewer promises, but our children could count on us to follow through. Why should we be upset when our children disobey after they have "promised" to obey? After all, how many times have we promised not to yell so much, promised to help with homework, promised to buy a new video game or take the family to the beach, and then using parental prerogative blithely change our minds without ever bothering to inform our children?

When we are consistent with our rules, we expect our children to obey and we take whatever steps are necessary to ensure that behavior. Instead, too often we teach our kids that rules are not enforced if they whine for more than twenty minutes, threaten to run away, or sneak out to do what they want anyway.

Devise a workable plan for restructuring your relationship with your teenager. Solicit advice from trusted friends or other parents who have had problem teenagers. This restructuring plan may include what music you allow your teenager to listen to, and for how long; when you allow him to leave the house and in whose company; when and how you expect him to complete his homework, and so on. The plan also includes your system of discipline. You must be directive, positive, and consistent. Don't devise a penalty you are not willing to enforce. Your teenager is intelligent, clever, and sees himself in the persecuted antagonist role. He will do what he thinks he can get away with and will learn quickly the difference between what you enforce and what you hope for. If you are unwilling to take the time to check his homework every night, then don't tell him you will insist that he work on it until it's right.

Probably the worst trap which you will fall into regarding consistency is that you and other authority figures in your child's life will disagree on how to manage your child. In a two parent household, this conflict is most often between mother and father. When your teen is in crisis, it is vital that he be handled consistently. If you are unable to present a united, consistent front to your teen, you are likely to lose your battle for intervention and restoration. It might be necessary for mother and father to privately agree that one parent will have authority over the child during this short period of crisis as the only workable way to give him the consistency he needs. If you can both act in unison and consistently, that's better. But don't lose your child forever through his practiced ability to divide and conquer because of his parents' differing parenting styles. It becomes a vicious trap when an autocratic parent becomes more autocratic to compensate for the spouse's permissiveness, so the permissive parent becomes more permissive to counter the rising autocracy, so the autocratic parent counters with more force, in a cyclical pattern. In the meantime, you will lose your child.

Consistency is your responsibility. You must transfer that sense of responsibility to your child. The self-centered relativism of destructive occultism naturally encourages an attitude of irresponsibility. The goal is to get what you want with a minimum of risk and responsibility. Why work at a convenience store for minimum wage when you can make more with less effort dealing drugs? As long as you don't get caught, you can ensure your own steady supply and make a relatively limitless income.

Working with your teenager to develop a sense of responsibility takes time, but is absolutely necessary if your teenager is to learn an alternate, acceptable lifestyle. If you have clear guidelines of earned freedoms and disciplined restrictions, you must follow that with making your teenager responsible for his or her own actions. Don't pay for his vandalism. Make him work it off, even if that means the court places him on strict probation. Don't do his homework for him. If he doesn't do it within the guidelines you have established, let him take the consequences at school. Don't commiserate and apply home remedies and aspirin if she gets a hangover. Be loving, but let her suffer the consequences of her behavior.

Responsibility means more than merely accepting the consequences of negative behavior. It also means positive reinforcement. When your teenager's room is finally clean and stripped of objectionable and occult symbols, praise your teenager and give her a related responsibility. Perhaps let her have friends in her room as long as it is clean, or buy her a new bedspread or other bedroom item she has wanted. When your teenager establishes a pattern of regular school attendance, acknowledge that with encouragement and maybe loosen your restriction of his activities enough that he has five or ten minutes after school free with his friends as a reward.

Learning responsibility by negative and positive consequences will help your teenager to make wise and mature choices.

Most of us stumble into life structures. Instead of carefully planning our daily lives, we develop a pattern by default. Our teenager in crisis has stumbled into a destructive life structure often including drugs, criminal activity, and behavior that is paradoxically both self-centered and self-destructive. Parents must help their children in crisis to live with freedom but within a healthy life structure.

Daily routine is at the core of constructive living. This includes amount of sleep, good nutrition, abstinence from drug or alcohol use, personal grooming, and exercise. Your teenager is much more likely to adopt a healthy lifestyle if you participate rather than merely coaching from the sidelines. Get up half an hour early and walk with your teenager five mornings a week. Clear your kitchen cupboards of junk food. Empty your liquor cabinet. Establish one meal a day which you and your teenager eat together without the distraction of television or company. Schedule homework time, and then be available during that time to help, encourage, answer questions, and remind your teenager of the consequences, good and bad, of his homework habits.

Your teenager chose, perhaps through default, the destructiveness from which you are attempting to rescue him. In previous chapters you have read the reasons teenagers choose destructive occultism. Most of those reasons are related to a need to have personal control over one's life and to achieve self-gratification. You intervened in your teenager's life and committed yourself to long term restoration. *Unless you offer your teenager something better, you will fail.* Do not expect your intelligent, creative, willful teenager to change everything about his life just because you say so. If you are not convinced that what you offer is better than what he has, he will recognize it immediately and refuse to participate. You might as well let him be emancipated from your parental authority and do whatever he wants, even if that means self-destruction.

This element of restoration demands introspection on your part. What does your life stand for? What values are actually important to you, not what you say, but what your life pattern reveals? To whom are you accountable for your actions? What is the purpose of your life? What is your ultimate goal for yourself, your family, and particularly your teenager?

Examine your own life. Does your life betray your ultimate commitment to material acquisitions and physical pleasure, even though you may talk about the intangibles of life and service to others? Do you have any ultimate commitment in your life? Do you say you believe in God, but rarely go to church, don't pray unless you're in a jam, don't talk about God except when you hit your thumb with a hammer, and don't read his words, the Bible, because you put all your wedding presents, including that beautiful family Bible, in storage ten years ago? Given your example, can you expect your child to use faith in God to restore his life?

After almost twenty years of work in this field, we are convinced that a biblical, Christian worldview provides the best options for successful, fulfilled living. Whatever the occult or any other false system offers, if it has real value, it can be matched and beaten by what Christianity offers and, more importantly, delivers. Jesus Christ is the only way, the only truth, and the only source of eternal life.[11] We have carefully examined all of the claims of Christianity, and the counter claims of the cults and the occult. Christianity is the truth. God created man in his image, with the ability for personal relationships, reflection, imagination, creativity, intelligence, and the power to make choices. Choices in harmony with God's plan for human fulfillment bring human fulfillment. Choices contrary to his ultimately will end in self-destruction. The peace that comes from God is not the false peace offered by the world.[12] The virtues mankind esteems the highest are those that come from reconciliation with God:

Be anxious for nothing, but in everything by prayer and supplication, with thanksgiving, let your requests be made known to God; and the peace of God, which surpasses all understanding, will guard your hearts and minds through Christ Jesus. Finally, brethren, whatever things are true, whatever things are noble, whatever things are just, whatever things are pure, whatever things are lovely, whatever things of good report, if there is any virtue and if there is anything praiseworthy—meditate on these things. The things which you have learned and received and heard and seen in me—these do, and the God of peace will be with you.[13]

The best restorative your teenager can have is a living faith in God, a vibrant spiritual commitment that can make a difference in how he lives and where he spends eternity. God's plan is not secret and cryptic like the esoteric philosophies of the occult. God's plan is not accomplished by rote obedience to arbitrary law, but by simple but profound reconciliation between sinner and God made possible by Jesus Christ's sacrifice on our behalf. The Apostle Paul reminds us, "For if there had been a law given which could have given life, truly righteousness would have been by the law. But the Scripture has confined all under sin, that the promise by faith in Jesus Christ might be given to those who believe."[14]

It might be easy to see how your teenager has deviated from God's plan. After all, he's the one in trouble who needed intervention and restoration. But if we are honest with ourselves, we recognize that none of us has met God's standards.[15] None of us can fulfill God's plan for our lives on the basis of our own efforts.[16] Spiritual intervention came through Jesus Christ[17] on our behalf[18] and will transform anyone who relinquishes control of his own life to God.[19]

If you have not done so already, make peace with God, surrender your self-centered will to him, and begin living as God intended. Get a good, contemporary translation of the Bible and learn God's plan for your life.[20] There are many books that can help you understand Christian faith. Several that we recommend are: *Loving God* by Charles Colson,[21] *Essential Christianity* by Walter Martin,[22] and two books by J.I. Packer, *Knowing God*[23] and *I Want to Be a Christian*.[24] Talk with the manager of your local Christian bookstore for some good recommendations.

Relativism has so pervaded our American culture that many priests and pastors don't have a strong biblical faith themselves. If you do not know a strong biblical priest or pastor, keep looking until you find one whose life, speech, and values reveal a living, biblical Christian faith. Turn to this spiritual counselor for help in your own Christian faith and to help your teenager come to faith.

No matter what else you do to rescue your child from the occult, Christian commitment for both of you has eternal consequences. Your teenager is unlikely to change his or her life merely to suit you or simply because you say what you have is better. You must be able to fulfill your promise, and that is possible only through strong Christian faith. For the few teenage occultists who have passed from self-indulgent contemporary occultism to the real evil spiritual world, the power of God is the *only* authority spiritually evil persons must obey. Rescue through the power of God in Christ is essential.

Other than peer pressure, role models are the greatest influence on your teenager's lifestyle choices. Look at the role models your teenager has. Are they positive or negative? What values do these role models exhibit? What long term goals do they have? What solutions to life's problems do they offer? Look at yourself. What kind of role model do you represent? What do your actions and commitments reflect about your values and your life goals? If your teenager patterned himself after you, would that be good or bad?

Now make a list of values, lifestyle habits, commitments, and faith you think are positive. Are there role models who reflect these ideas? Where could you go to find an ideal role model? Below are specific, positive steps you can take to evaluate your teenager's role models and to offer new, more positive role models.

*Your Teenager's Role Models*

1. Talk to your teenager about the people he admires or would like to be like.
2. Help your teenager list the characteristics he admires about his role models.

3. Discuss the consequences of the values and commitments made by his role models.
4. Help your teenager distinguish between constructive characteristics and destructive characteristics.
5. Help your teenager to list the values, commitments, and attitudes he would like to see in a role model.
6. Discuss with your teenager how he views you as a role model.
7. Help your teenager list your positive characteristics and your negative characteristics.
8. Make a commitment to him to develop your positive characteristics and overcome or reject your negative characteristics.
9. Discuss with your teenager how he views himself as a role model.
10. Help your teenager to imagine talking to a younger brother or sister, advising him or her about what characteristics in your teenager should be copied and what should be discarded.
11. Listen carefully as your teenager explains what he intends to do about his own life as a role model for others.
12. Agree to help your teenager to improve his personal image through life-changing commitments and values.
13. Over a period of time, help your teenager to find positive role models.
14. If necessary, limit your teenager's continued exposure to negative role models.
15. Reevaluate your commitments periodically with your teenager, soliciting his opinions and advice.

If you really want to see long-term, positive change in your teenager, you have steps to restoration available. Consistency, responsibility, structure, eternal values, and positive role models together provide an environment for positive, long-lasting change.

When we see moral devastation or mental deterioration, we tend to concentrate on the spiritual and intellectual solutions. However, we are not merely spirit and mind, our physical body is essential to our humanness. Often teenagers in crisis, especially those in destructive occultism, need physical restoration as well as spiritual and mental recovery. Schedule a complete physical exam and evaluation by your doctor or local medical clinic.

Ensure that your teenager is getting enough rest. Adolescents use more energy maturing than at any other time in their lives. Good sleep habits are essential to healthy maturation. However, most teenagers who take drugs or alcohol and are on the path to self-destruction have very poor sleep habits. Your teenager may sleep only a few hours a night and suffer the effects of sleep deprivation. Or continuous drug use may cause your teenager to sleep unnaturally long. Most out-of-control teenagers have wildly divergent sleep activities. They may sleep for twenty hours, then party and use drugs for thirty-six hours straight. Each of these aberrant sleep patterns is unhealthy and debilitating. Establish a regular, enforceable sleep schedule, usually with at least eight uninterrupted hours of rest.

Second, evaluate your teenager's diet. Bulimia and anorexia typically afflict girls, but boys sometimes have the same problems of gorging and purging or starving themselves. Teenagers out of control are often malnourished. That is, they eat enough calories, but not the right proportions or amounts of essential nutrients, including vitamins and minerals. Unless you have a tight rein on your teenager, you will not be able to control his or her diet completely, but cleaning junk food out of your own house and committing your family to healthful eating will provide your teenager with a basic healthy diet and reinforce positive role model behavior at the same time.

Insist on cleanliness. Your teenager should keep his or her room clean and livable. Not everyone is neat, but everyone should be clean. Personal health is affected by cleanliness also. Compromise on a haircut that your teenager can live with, but which can be kept clean and neat. If your teenager is unable to keep his or her hair clean and neat, it might be easier if it were shorter. Let him or her choose a preferred hairstyle, but only with the consequent responsibility of keeping it clean and neat. Insist that your teenager keep physically clean and wear clean clothes, even if you don't like the styles.

There is no reason for a teenager to drink alcohol or take drugs, other than medications prescribed and supervised by a medical doctor. A teenager who needs "just a little" drink, joint, or hit is an addict. There are many programs available in most communities for alcohol and drug treatment. Chances are your teenager will end up dead sooner rather than later if drug and alcohol use continue. Life might be much easier around your house, and you would be setting a good example, if you ensure that *all* alcohol and drugs are removed from your home. Is your Saturday afternoon beer too important to give up for your teenager?

Good living habits include sleep, diet and exercise, cleanliness, and especially for people at risk, avoidance of alcohol and drug use. During the restorative process through which you and your teenager struggle, this aspect of recovery can have a marked effect on your progress.

## PREVENTIVE PARENTING

The principles of restoration outlined here are effective even if your teenager is not in crisis. If your children are becoming adolescents, and your desire is to prevent their involvement with destructive lifestyles, including occultism, then you can apply the same principles. This will ensure that your child has the best opportunity possible to develop wholesome, dynamic, positive values and life commitments.

Consistency, responsibility, structure, spiritual values, good role models, and good living habits will equip your children to conquer the chaos of the teenage years.

In addition, you are in a position to take further preventive measures. First, enlist the help of God in preserving your children from destruction. Pray for them. Make Christianity a way of life for you and them instead of a boring Sunday morning detention penalty. Use biblical principles of parenting. Point out biblical examples of good role models. Help your children to turn to the Bible for answers to life's problems. Your trusted Christian priest or pastor can advise you of good youth-oriented materials to help in this area. One study group series we recommend is *Lifelines* by Fran and Jill Sciacca.[25]

Second, teach your children to make wise decisions. Decision-making is a basic tool of maturity. Holt and Ketterman list the needs of adolescents related to decison-making as:

- To explore and to collect information
- Parental confidence and a sounding-board
- A balance of personal freedom and protective parenting
- Time with peers
- Emotional distance from parents
- Criteria by which to distinguish right from wrong
- Increasing opportunities actually to make decisions[26]

Wise parenting gives children the chance to evaluate the options and make decisions within the safety of parental guidelines. For example, parents must intervene to prevent their child from commiting suicide as a solution to depression. But parents should allow their child to explore causes of his depression and a variety of constructive steps toward overcoming depression. Parents should not dictate what music their children listen to, but they can restrict particular artists or songs on the basis of the values and images of the contents. There are musicians and songs in rap, metal, and hard rock that reflect high morals and good values. Listen to your child's favorite music (you don't have to like it), discuss lyrics and singers' lifestyles with him, and help him decide to listen to positive, good messages rather than moral degeneracy. Many Christian bookstores carry music by Christian bands, including rap, metal, and hard rock.

Third, innoculation is one of the most important steps you can take to protect your child from future involvement in destructive occultism. Before he is enticed by promises of power and self-indulgence, explore with him the claims and deficiencies of alternate belief systems. You might choose to go through parts of this book with him, or other books. You might discuss contemporary news stories about occult crime. Your child probably has been exposed to occult ideas through friends at school, a teacher, movies and television, or comic books. Talk about and evaluate with him what he has learned.

Just as a small dose of a germ like measles makes us immune when we are later exposed to the disease, so a brief exposure to the occult can give your child immunity to its false, but powerful, lure. This is even better protection that shielding or isolating him from reality. Em Griffin, in his book on Christian persuasion, *The Mind Changers*, notes the danger of isolating our children from alternative ideas and beliefs:

> This is true with some of our beliefs. They've developed in a "germfree" environment, without question or attack. Such a "hothouse" belief is vulnerable for two reasons. First of all, we may not even realize that there's another way of thinking. When suddenly confronted by a winsome presentation of a new idea, we can easily be swept away by its novelty. Secondly, even if we know there

are opposing opinions, we've never practiced defending against them. We haven't built up an immunity to views which run counter to our original attitudes.[27]

Fourth, individualized parenting can help protect your children from occult and other negative involvement. Children are different, and although the basic principles of good parenting are important for all children, your technique needs to accommodate different children's distinct personalities.

Our three children are alike in some ways: strong-willed, assertive, intelligent, and good critical thinkers.[28] But in many ways they are very different. Our oldest, Mary, has a real talent for making friends, a facility with foreign languages, and adult level skill in fashion, hair, and makeup. Our middle child, Karen, is the most creative, reads and writes voraciously, and doesn't really care about the mundane things of daily living. Our youngest, Paul, is single-minded, believes he can do anything he commits himself to, and can talk himself into or out of any situation. Mary is more susceptible to peer pressure because of her involvement with friends and her appearance. Karen may be more susceptible to the mysterious power of the occult because of her imagination and literary interests. Paul needs to be reminded that he is not invincible and sometimes needs to take orders as well as give them.

A good way to understand the individualized parenting you need to devlop is to sit down and describe your child's positive traits, negative traits, interests, goals, and values. Then review the parenting techniques in this chapter, thinking seriously about how your child's unique personality can best be developed using these techniques and individualized parenting.

Parents are not helpless in the face of occult threats on their teenagers. Through preventive parenting, good living habits, necessary intervention, and principles of restoration, your teenager can be protected from destructive occultism.

During a crisis, the problem seems overwhelming. However, by taking one step at a time, you and your teenager can turn his life around and start him on the road to emotional, physical, and spiritual health and maturity. Yet despite all of your efforts, you cannot live your teen's life for him. He was created by God with the capacity for self-determination. He can make destructive choices with eternal consequences. Using the principles in this book will give your teen every advantage. But ultimately, you are responsible for being the best parent possible. You are not responsible for his ultimate choices. Never give up, but know that finally, the choice is his or hers.

The dangers of the occult are many. Contemporary satanism is the horrible, destructive, but logical consequence of a culture obsessed with self. Your children are in danger, the devil will dare them, but with the help of God and strong parental commitment, they will reject the devil's dare. No responsibility you hold is more important than your children. Do your best, trust in God, and your child will have every advantage necessary to make the right choices.

# NINE

# Answers to Your Questions

**Q: What is demon possession?**

**A:** Many people differ in their explanations of demon possession. Some believe it is an erroneous term used to describe natural mental dysfunction or physical abnormality in spiritual terms. Others believe demon possession is a symbolic term referring to spiritual rebellion and alienation from God. Some religious people, including some pastors and priests, think demon possession is a self-induced condition used as a defense or denial mechanism by people who can't face responsibility for their actions, feelings, or ideas. We believe that demon possession is exactly as it is described in the Bible, that is, an evil spirit entity controlling a person against his will. The Bible distinguishes between demon possession and insanity[1] and disease.[2] From the instances of demon possession described in the Bible,[3] we can know that demon possession is rare, is characterized by abhorrence of Jesus Christ, and that demons are exorcised only by the power and authority of Jesus Christ.

**Q: What are demons?**

**A:** The Bible identifies demons as personal, intelligent spirit entities who can act in this world.[4] They and their leader,

Satan,[5] were created by God as angels,[6] but have been in opposition to God since they chose to sin.[7] Before Satan fell, he was an archangel named Lucifer,[8] or "Light-bearer." Satan is *not* the opposite of God. He is created and limited in power, ability, and knowledge. His ultimate destiny, with the other demons, is eternal separation from God.[9]

**Q: How can a demon be cast out or exorcised?**

**A:** Demonic possession, while rare, is very dangerous, both for the one possessed and for those attempting to help. A genuine case of demon possession (diagnosed by careful and extensive medical, psychiatric, and spiritual testing) should be handled by a pastor or priest who is mature and stable spiritually and emotionally and who has received specific, intensive training and experience in exorcism. Long-term evaluation beforehand and long-term restoration afterward for the person afflicted are essential. Itinerant "deliverance minstries" tend to be irresponsible and ineffective.

**Q: How common is demon possession?**

**A:** Actual demon possession is very rare. The entire Bible records only a few instances of genuine demon possession.

Some Christians think demon possession is very common. There are three common reasons for this mistaken idea. First, some Christians find it hard to believe that people can perform horribly evil acts initiated from their own evil thoughts rather than influenced or controlled by demonic forces. Christians might say, "What spiritual evil! That man must be demon possessed." The non-Christian reveals a similar perspective by saying, "What horrible evil! That man must be insane!" Both comments typically reveal a reluctance to attach personal moral responsibility to acts of unspeakable evil.

Second, some Christians have been misinformed about demon possession and confuse moral failings with demonic control. This is usually the case with the popular itinerant "deliverance ministries." While "deliverance" may be a good cottage industry for producing exciting services and giving people hope for reform, it is not biblical. The demons most commonly identified by "deliverence ministries" are, by contrast, identified as "the works of the flesh" by the Bible: "Now the works of the flesh are evident, which are these: adultery, fornication, uncleanness, licentiousness,[10] idolatry, sorcery, hatred, contention, jealousy, outbursts of wrath, selfish ambition, dissensions, heresies, envy, murders, drunkenness, revelry, and the like...."[11]

Third, demon possession actually could be an attractive diagnosis for some Christians in crisis or their close friends and family. It seems to be easier to hire someone to perform a quick exorcism than to make an enormous investment in time and emotion to repair long-term moral, emotional, and spiritual dysfunction in both the affected individual and his or her family.

**Q: What is a good book on demon possession?**

**A:** Most contemporary Christian literature on demon possession is inaccurate, sensationalistic, and of little value. We conditionally recommend Malachi Martin's *Hostage to the Devil,*[12] a report from a Catholic Christian perspective on five actual cases of demon possession and exorcism. While we may not agree with everything Martin says, his book is less sensational and more well-researched than many others.

**Q: Can a Christian be demon possessed?**

**A:** A Christian, as defined by the Bible, cannot be controlled against his will by Satan or a demon. Whether you call such control possession, or affliction, or influence, or demonization is only a matter of semantics. The Bible defines a Christian as someone who has been redeemed by Christ's atoning death on the cross,[13] has believed the gospel through the power of the Holy Spirit,[14] and who therefore has the Holy Spirit living in him.[15] There is no biblical precedence for Christians to be subject to demon possession, even though some Christians try to argue for it by misunderstanding scripture. In fact, Jesus' parable in Matthew 12:38-45 comparing Israel to a demon possessed man provides positive evidence that Christians *cannot* be possessed. A demon cannot re-enter the "house," or life, of a man whose house is occupied, as is the Christian, by the Holy Spirit.

**Q: Have I committed the unforgivable sin if I sold my soul to Satan?**

**A:** No. Your soul, or eternal destiny, is under God's control, it cannot be bought or sold. The unforgivable sin[16] is utter, complete, and permanent renunciation of Christian faith, or apostasy. If you think you might have committed the unforgivable sin, and it worries you, then you didn't. If you had, you wouldn't care, and the Holy Spirit wouldn't still be drawing you to repentance. If you turn to God, he promises to release you from Satan's power: "Therefore submit to God. Resist the devil and he will flee from you. Draw near to God and he will draw near to you.... Humble yourselves in the sight of the Lord, and He will lift you up."[17]

**Q: How many satanists are there in the United States today?**

**A:** No statistics have been compiled and therefore there is not enough data to give an accurate answer. However, responsible law enforcement personnel and professionals who specialize in adolescent problems agree that the number of formal satanists, like members of the Church of Satan, teenage dabblers, and other self-styled satanists is probably somewhere in the thousands.[18] Reports of hundreds of thousands or millions of satanists is unverified, inaccurate sensationalism.

**Q: How many human sacrifices by satanists take place each year?**

**A:** No one knows. Whatever sensationalistic figure you have heard is undoubtedly wrong. Consult Chapter Six for the best documented evidence available on occult related murder and other occult related crime. Most murders associated with destructive occultism are accomplished for other than merely ritualistic reasons. A person can murder and also be a satanist without his satanism necessarily being the cause or single cause of the murder. John Charles Cooper summarizes the disparity between sensationalism and the facts:

> Nonetheless, we need not become carried away by the many rumors and reports of human sacrifices that students in this field of study encounter, for they generally lack evidence. While it is certainly possible that criminal cults have performed human sacrifices on drifters, hitchhikers, street people (the homeless), and recently born infants whose births are unrecorded, we cannot prove anything from silence....
>
> Some experts on occult behavior hold that criminal Satanists utilize crematoria to destroy all evidence or bury the remains under the casket in a recently dug grave. Though some claim that body parts washed up by the tide are the remains of satanic victims, generally authorities can trace these remains to "ordinary" murders (especially among drug dealers). Probably, therefore, human sacrifice forms little to no part of most satanic rituals. When it does occur, drug-intoxicated self-styled Satanists or criminal occultic groups enact the crime.[19]

**Q: Is there such a thing as multi-generational satanism?**

**A:** It has probably happened and will continue to happen in isolated cases. It is common for younger members of a family to openly and willingly adopt occult practices they have seen their parents or other older relatives practice, such as fortune telling or astrology.

However, the sensationalized, contemporary urban myth of multi-generational conspiratorial satanism and satanic abuse depends on absolutely *no* objective, verified, concrete evidence. Instead, the story is generated, fueled, and inflamed by unsubstantiated, sensationalistic, emotional "testimonies" of people who present themselves as "adult survivors." While we have the greatest compassion for these people who are obviously emotionally distraught and in great pain, empathy is not a test for truth.

**Q: How do you explain the stories of "adult survivors"?**

**A:** At this writing[20] there is not a single verified, documented adult survivor story. In fact, careful research into these stories instead leads us to believe the stories are not true, even when believed by the survivors. There are a variety of alternate logical and psychological explanations.[21] As a general observation, adult survivor stories are not reliable.

**Q: Can a satanist, witch, or occultist practice magic against me and will it have power against me?**

**A:** Not if you are a Christian. God promises that he has power over Satan, not Satan over God or those who belong to God: "You are of God, little children, and have overcome them, because He who is in you is greater than he who is in the world."[22] Destructive occultism has power over those who give it power. If you are afraid you will be harmed by magic or occultists who are angry with you for some reason, take prudent steps to confirm your safety: 1.) ask God's protection and be sure you are a Christian; 2.) talk with a mature Christian you trust, and ask him or her to pray for you; 3.) cut off *all* contact with occultists, occult practices, and occult objects; 4.) if you have been threatened and fear physical retaliation, contact the authorities and be prepared to cooperate for your own safety.

Q: **Is it harmless fun to play with a Ouija Board?**

A: The Ouija Board is a psychic game available in any toy store. Its manufacturers make no claim for its supernatural power, and most people's anecdotes about mysterious supernatural powers are unverifiable and/or self-induced, almost like scaring yourself by telling ghost stories on a dark, rainy night. However, anyone who assents to the occult worldview at the same time rejects the biblical worldview. Therefore, to play with the Ouija Board is compromising truth and flirting with spiritual adultery.

Q: **Are fantasy role-playing games such as Dungeons and Dragons demonic?**

A: There are dozens of fantasy role-playing board and video games, and some are more overtly occult than others. Those who become so absorbed in the game that they confuse reality and fantasy, or who have serious enough personal problems that the game becomes better than real life, can be harmed by their involvement. There is no objective evidence that the game by itself causes anyone to commit suicide, occult crime, or to become a satanist. However, it can be one of many signs or vulnerabilities for someone headed toward crisis. The intentions of the players, the worldviews developed for the characters, and the values the players possess are much more important indicators of occult trouble than the game itself. We must also be careful not to reject all value in using the imagination, story telling, and fiction.[23]

**Q:** Should I forbid my child to watch *The Smurfs, Teenage Mutant Ninja Turtles,* Disney's *Snow White,* or other television shows and movies with magic, eastern meditation, or witchcraft?

**A:** It depends. Magic as a literary motif or a plot device is very different than the occultism discussed in this book. As long as your child understands that what he is watching is "pretend" or "imagination," he or she will be unlikely to be influenced to participate in destructive occultism. Very small children are able to distinguish the difference between fantasy and reality. They don't expect their teddy bears to come alive like the one in the toilet paper commercial. Children have a wonderful ability to enjoy fantasy as fantasy, and reality as reality. Adults have a tendency to commit the either/or fallacy; you can't enjoy fantasy without rejecting reality.

On the other hand, most of the cartoons, television shows, and movies promote objectionable values, tell poor stories, and are bad literature.[24] Rather than focusing on the literary magic, listen to the program's values and evaluate the strength of the story. Hitting to get your own way, rushing frantically to hide disobedience from your parents, laughing at hurting others, and making superhero role models out of self-centered entertainment stars teach our children bad values.

Be discriminating about what and how much television and movies your children digest. An ice cream cone occasionally is fun, but a steady diet of junk food will ruin their physical health. In the same way, a little mediocre entertainment is fun, but a steady diet will ruin their imaginations.

**Q:** What's wrong with good luck charms, rabbit's feet, and other "lucky" items?

**A:** We are created with an appreciation for and attraction to ritual and religious mystery. This enables us to worship

God wholeheartedly, but it also makes us vulnerable to imitations.

The worldview behind "good luck" items or practices is that the world is a psychic machine, and inanimate objects can possess supernatural or paranormal powers by which your daily life can be influenced. This is contrary to the Christian concept of God as the sovereign of the universe, and man created in God's image, with free will, or the ability to make moral choices.

However, most Christians don't assume any literal power in inanimate objects or expressions of good luck. Most people mean "I hope you do well" when they say "Good luck," "Good fortune," or even "Gesundheit." They don't really think they can avert disaster if they "knock on wood" or cross their fingers. These phrases have become meaningless.

The Christian can do more than hope someone does well. The Christian can pray for that person, confident that God works in this world and that prayer is our participation in God's plan.[25]

Superstition is incompatible with a Christian worldview. It is inconsistent for a Christian to think he can't play ball well without his "lucky" hat or to be nervous about taking the elevator to the thirteenth floor of a building.

Q: **Is there any validity to astrology?**

A: No. Numerous scientific studies have proven repeatedly and conclusively that astrology has no validity. Astrology sometimes seems to have validity for several reasons: 1.) the astrological prediction is so general or vague as to be untestable ("Something bad will happen."); 2.) the forecast "predicted" is a safe bet ("You will pay more taxes this year."); 3.) the prediction is common sense ("Don't make rash decisions."); 4.) the recipient makes the prediction self-fulfilling ("Don't leave home today"); and

5.) the prediction is right by chance ("The Dodgers will win the World Series."). Those who trust astrology are not trusting God.

**Q: Is the New Age Movement satanic?**

**A:** The New Age Movement does not fit the kind of satanism discussed in this book. Some basic beliefs of the New Age Movement include: 1.) God is everything and everything is God; 2.) man is God and has unlimited potential; 3.) the world will be transformed and perfected by its inherent divinity, expressed through mankind; and 4.) justice for good and bad actions is based on karma and reincarnation. Many New Agers engage in occult practices such as Ouija Boards, crystal balls, or channeling, but their worldview is different from that of the satanists. The New Age Movement is not compatible with Christianity.

**Q: What is an insightful definition of peer pressure?**

**A:** A common definition of peer pressure is the influence those within your group—for example, age group, or class, or party friends, or coworkers, or those of like interests—have on your ideas and/or behavior. Peer pressure is not invincible. It is possible for teens to be selective as to which peer pressure they choose to follow. Fran and Jill Sciacca note, "Fear is an inner response; it is my reaction to certain circumstances. In the same way, peer pressure is not 'out there,' it's inside you. Only you really make the decisions about whom you will allow to be your influential peers, and to what degree they will make demands on you."[26]

**Q: What are some specific principles for resisting peer pressure?**

**A:** Some principles are outlined in Chapter Eight. The most important principle for your teen to understand is that he or she has the power to say no. If your teenager has a hard time resisting peer pressure, help him or her decide ahead of time how to handle common peer pressure situations. For example, a teenager who doesn't want to stay at a party where there is alcohol and drugs could decide ahead of time that in such a situation she can say, "I need to get home early. I'll see you tomorrow." Kathleen McCoy suggests six principles: 1.) Listen and interact with your child; 2.) Face the fears; 3.) Hold practice sessions; 4.) Promote self-respect; 5.) Appreciate positive peers; and 6.) Intervene with love.[27]

**Q: What are the danger signs of a potential suicide?**
**A:** Most teenagers who attempt suicide leave a number of clues, even though their family and friends didn't anticipate the danger. This is because many of the clues are also common to other problems, some almost universal among adolescents. If you practice open communication, consistent interaction, and unconditional love with your teenager, you will be much more likely to pick up clues indicating the development of a serious problem like suicidal tendencies. Finley Sizemore notes that not all potential suicides exhibit each symptom, but lists these clues as common: 1.) talking about suicide; 2.) talking about "someone else" who's thinking of suicide; 3.) extreme stress; 4.) talking about methods of suicide; 5.) "tying up loose ends;" and 6.) persistent depression.[28]

**Q: What can I say to help my suicidal friend?**
**A:** If your friend is in imminent danger of attempting suicide, words should not substitute for action. Take constructive intervention steps to prevent your friend from attempting suicide long enough that he or she can work past the immediate crisis and be willing to consider other options. Suicide is an ineffective solution with permanent consequences.

If you do not think your friend is at the crisis stage, you can give him constructive advice and encouraging support. Let him know you are aware that he is troubled, and encourage him to talk to you. Recommend professional counseling, perhaps offering to go with him at the beginning. Help your friend to see his problems in the context of his whole life. Work with him on developing constructive, life-saving steps to resolving his problems. If his problem cannot be fixed (for example, the death of a parent or felony charges for drunk driving), then help him to focus on areas of his life he can control. Get his permission to tell someone else close to him so both of you can provide encouragement and support. Hold him accountable for the misery he will cause those who love him if he commits suicide. Suggest he get a thorough physical exam—sometimes depression has a physiological base.[29]

**Q: Do you lose your salvation if you commit suicide?**

**A:** The only unforgivable sin is apostasy, that is, renouncing the Christian faith and rejecting the Holy Spirit's work of regeneration. However, suicide is a sin and although God forgives the Christian who commits suicide, he still holds us accountable for what we do.[30] Suicide is not a solution or an escape. The time of your death is God's prerogative, not yours.[31]

**Q: Can songs suggesting suicide cause people to commit suicide?**

**A:** Lyrics do not have an invincible magic ability to force behavior on listeners. However, songs that promote violence, suicide, murder, rape, and other destructive behavior are not good for emotional and spiritual health. Christians are supposed to bring "every thought into captivity to the obedience of Christ..."[32] When you constantly fill your mind with destructive thoughts, you are much more vulnerable to emotional and spiritual damage. Fran and Jill Sciacca comment,

> One of the most popular and powerful vehicles for promoting suicidal thoughts and minimizing the seriousness of death is contemporary music.
>
> Do you sometimes let your mind dwell on song lyrics or other thoughts that *promote* or *minimize* suicide and death? Although wanting to die can occasionally be a normal thought, it's also a thought that God wants you to conquer. Maybe it's time to unload some of your music or other input (such as television, fantasy role-playing games, magazines, or books) that supports ending your life as a solution.[33]

Q: **Can satanism or other messages be promoted subconsciously or subliminally through backward masking or subliminal messages on records?**

A: Backward masking is laying a track backward under the forward playing music and lyrics of a song. Subliminal messages are placed on a tape or record that cannot be heard normally. No statistical research supports the idea that either practice has any effect on listeners. Careful double blind experimentation has been done with subliminal messages and no effect was produced. Self-fulfillment based on expectations account for the anecdotal stories of people who say it worked for them. Frankly, the explicit lyrics of some metal songs are so offensive and destructive that there is no reason to "sneak" ideas in backward.

Q: **How can anyone be irrational enough to believe in the occult?**

A: Chapters One and Two explained the different factors motivating involvement in destructive occultism. Most are emotional and social factors. There are good, logical reasons disproving both the satanic and the witchcraft worldviews and many reasons for rejecting destructive occultism. However, as Cooper points out, "occultism is essentially irrational, so you won't be likely to rationally argue someone out of belief in it."[34]

**Q: As long as I don't believe in it, why shouldn't I go observe a satanic ritual or pagan rite?**

**A:** The lure of the occult is strong. The factors that attract vulnerable teenagers into the occult are attractive to most people. When you are not around occult influences, you can evaluate them rationally and without peer pressure or emotional and physical lures. Responsible decision making will tell you to stay away. If you surround yourself with the occult, you are much more vulnerable to making decisions with your emotions and your hormones than with your mind. Christians are commanded to avoid evil[35] and avoid entanglement with those who practice the occult.[36]

**Q: Is it true that the president of Proctor and Gamble was on the Phil Donahue Show and said he was a satanist and his profits went to the Church of Satan?**

**A:** No. This false rumor has been spread for years, has cost Proctor and Gamble hundreds of thousands of dollars to counter, and has made Christians who accepted it unquestioningly look foolish. It is also not true that the old Proctor and Gamble trademark of a man in the moon and thirteen stars was a satanic symbol.

**Q: Why isn't satanism against the law?**

**A:** The United States protects the free exercise of religion in this country, as long as criminal behavior is not integral to the religion. The same laws that protect the exercise of Christianity protect the exercise of satanism. Satanists who commit criminal acts are prosecuted for those acts the same as a Baptist criminal would be. If laws were enacted to outlaw satanism, they would threaten Christianity as well.

**Q:** **If contemporary witchcraft is "harmless" by comparison to destructive occultism, then what's wrong with being a witch?**

**A:** Contemporary witchcraft is not characterized by the destructiveness and criminal activity often associated with satanism and many forms of self-styled occultism. Still, there are some self-styled occultists who call themselves witches who actually identify with the satanic worldview more than the witchcraft worldview. However, as the chapter on witchcraft points out, the witchcraft worldview is incompatible with Christianity and encourages a relativism that can allow for a practitioner to justify leaving witchcraft for destructive occultism.

# For Further Reading

Adler, Margot, *Drawing Down the Moon*. Boston: Beacon Press, 1986.

Ashe, Geoffrey, *Do What You Will: A History of Anti-Morality*. London: W.H. Allen, 1974.

Buckland, Raymond, *Buckland's Complete Book of Witchcraft*. St. Paul, MN: Llewellyn Publications, 1990.

Carlson, Shawn and Gerald Larue, *Satanism in America: How the Devil Got Much More than His Due*. El Cerrito, CA: Gaia Press, 1989.

Cavendish, Richard, *The Black Arts*. New York: Capricorn Books, 1968.

Colson, Charles, *Loving God*. Grand Rapids, MI: Zondervan Publishing Company, 1983.

Cooper, John Charles, *The Black Mask*. Old Tappan, NJ: Fleming H. Revell Company, 1990.

Crowley, Aleister, *The Book of the Law*. Pasadena, CA: Church of Thelema, 1926.

Crowley, Aleister, *777*. n.c.: O. T. O., n.d.

Crowley, Aleister, *Gems from the Equinox*. New York: Falcon Press, n.d.

Davis, Wade, *The Serpent and the Rainbow*. New York: Simon and Schuster, 1985.

Dawkins, Vickie L. and Nina Downey Higgins, *Devil Child*. New York: St. Martin's Press, 1989.

Dobson, James, *The Strong-Willed Child*. Wheaton, IL: Tyndale

House Publishers, 1978.

Farrar, Stewart, *What Witches Do: The Modern Coven Revealed.* Custer, WA: Phoenix Publishing Inc., 1983.

Farrar, Stewart and Janet Farrar, *A Witches Bible Compleat.* New York: Magickal Childe Publishing, Inc., 1981, 1984.

Fulce, John, *Seduction of the Innocent Revisited.* Lafayette, LA: Huntington House Publishers, 1990.

Gonzalez-Wippler, Migene, *Santeria, the Religion: A Legacy of Faith, Rites, and Magic.* New York: Harmony Books, 1989.

Grant, Kenneth, *Aleister Crowley and the Hidden God.* New York: Samuel Weiser, 1974.

Griffin, Em, *The Mind Changers.* Wheaton, IL: Tyndale House Publishers, 1976.

Haining, Peter, *The Anatomy of Witchcraft.* London: Souvenir Press Ltd., 1972.

Holt, Pat and Grace Ketterman, *Choices Are Not Child's Play: Helping Your Kids Make Wise Decisions.* Wheaton, IL: Harold Shaw Publishers, 1990.

Hooper, Walter, ed., *C.S. Lewis: On Stories and Other Essays on Literature.* New York: Harcourt Brace Jovanovich, Publishers, 1982.

Institoris, Heinrich, *Malleus Maleficarum.* New York: B. Blom, 1970.

Kahaner, Larry, *Cults that Kill.* New York: Warner Books, 1988.

Kennedy, D. James, *Your Prodigal Child.* Nashville, TN: Thomas Nelson Publishers, 1988.

King, Francis, *Modern Ritual Magic: The Rise of Western Occultism.* Dorset, England: Prism Press, 1989.

Kraig, Donald Michael, *Modern Magick.* St. Paul, MN: Llewellyn Publications, 1989.

LaVey, Anton Szandor, *The Satanic Bible.* New York: Avon Books, 1969.

LaVey, Anton Szandor, *The Satanic Rituals.* New York: Avon Books, 1972.

Linedecker, Clifford L., *Night Stalker.* New York: St. Martin's Press, 1991.

Luhrmann, T. M., *Persuasions of the Witch's Craft.* Oxford,

England: Basil Blackwell, Ltd., 1989.

Lyons, Arthur, *Satan Wants You*. New York: Warner Books, 1988.

Markman, Ronald and Dominick Bosco, *Alone with the Devil*. New York: Bantam Books, 1989.

Martin, Malachi, *Hostage to the Devil*. New York: Bantam Books, 1976.

Martin, Walter R., *Essential Christianity*. Ventura, CA: Gospel Light Publications, 1980.

Narramore, Bruce, *Parenting with Love and Limits*. Grand Rapids, MI: Zondervan Publishing Company, 1979.

Packer, J.I., *Knowing God*. Downers Grove, IL: InterVarsity Press, 1973.

Packer, J.I., *I Want to Be a Christian*. Wheaton, IL: Tyndale House Publishers, 1977.

Rhodes, Henry Taylor Fowkes, *The Satanic Mass*. Secaucus, NJ: Citadel Press, 1974.

Rose, Elliot, *Razor for a Goat*. Toronto: University of Toronto Press, 1962.

Ryken, Leland, *Reading Between the Lines*. Westchester, IL: Crossway Books, 1990.

St. Clair, David, *Say You Love Satan*. New York: Dell Publishing Company, 1987.

Schutze, Jim, *Cauldron of Blood: The Matamoros Cult Killings*. New York: Avon Books, 1989.

Sciacca, Fran and Jill, *Lifelines: Getting a Hold on Life*. Minneapolis, MN: World Wide Publications, 1987 (series).

Sellers, Sean, *Web of Darkness*. Tulsa, OK: Victory House Publishers, 1990.

Sizemore, Finley H., *Suicide: The Signs and Solutions*. Wheaton, IL: Victor Books, 1988.

Smith, Michelle and Lawrence Pazder, *Michelle Remembers*. New York: Congdon & Lattes, Inc., 1980.

Spence, Lewis, *An Encyclopaedia of Occultism*. Secaucus, NJ: Citadel Press, 1960.

Starhawk, *Dreaming in the Dark: Magic, Sex, and Politics*. Boston: Beacon Press, 1982.

Starhawk, *The Spiral Dance: A Rebirth of the Ancient Religion of the*

*Great Goddess.* San Francisco: Harper & Row, 1979.

Stratford, Lauren, *Satan's Underground.* Eugene, OR: Harvest House Publishers, 1988.

Stratford, Lauren, *I Know You're Hurting.* Eugene, OR: Harvest House Publishers, 1989.

Symonds, John and Kenneth Grant, eds., *The Magical Record of the Beast 666: The Diaries of Aleister Crowley (1914-1920).* Quebec, Canada: Next Step Publications, 1972.

Terry, Maury, *The Ultimate Evil.* New York: Bantam Books, 1987.

Wilson, Elizabeth, *Books Children Love: A Guide to the Best Children's Literature.* Westchester, IL: Crossway Books, 1987.

# For Further Help

Bob and Gretchen Passantino
*Answers in Action*
P.O. Box 2067
Costa Mesa, CA 92628
(714) 646-9042

Jon Trott
*Cornerstone Magazine*
939 W. Wilson
Chicago, IL 60640
(312) 989-2080

Dan Korem
P.O. Box 1587
Richardson, TX 75080
(214) 234-2395

Dr. Paul Martin
*Wellspring Counseling and Retreat Center*
P.O. Box 67
Albany, OH 45710
(614) 698-6277

*Christian Research Institute*
P.O. Box 500
San Juan Capistrano, CA 92693
(714) 855-9926

# Notes

## ONE
### *Satan Wants Your Child*

1. Larry Kahaner, *Cults that Kill* (New York: Warner Books, 1988), 90.
2. John Charles Cooper, *The Black Mask: Satanism in America Today* (Old Tappan, NJ: Fleming H. Revell Company, 1990), 77.
3. We use the term "destructive occultism" and its equivalents to differentiate between the blatantly destructive activities and those that are promoted as "good," "white," or "positive." We do *not* mean to imply that there is such a thing as *constructive* occultism, or that we agree with any form of occult belief or practice.
4. Arthur Lyons, *Satan Wants You* (New York: Mysterious Press, 1988), 11.
5. These vignettes represent accurate descriptions of people in different situations. They are not meant to be identifiable and are presented as illustrations of the principles discussed, not historical documentation.
6. In this book, *witch* and *pagan* and *neo-pagan* are used almost interchangeably to refer to a contemporary practitioner of ritual, polytheistic nature religion. *Witch* is our preferred term for practitioners of other centuries. The use of the term *witch* in a contemporary context is not meant to be prejudicial or to evoke images of *The Wizard of Oz*'s Wicked Witch of the West.
7. This list is not meant to be exhaustive, and a teenager's life could reflect several of these factors without him or her being involved in destructive occultism. Most other lists prepared by experts are similar, for example, the list used by Detective Bill Wickersham of the Denver Police Department: "loner, above average IQ, underachiever, strives for control or power, takes drugs, preoccupation with death, pornographic material, secretive" (Kahaner, p. 93). These factors should be taken into consideration in an attempt to help a troubled teenager, even if he is not actively involved in destructive occultism.
8. Lyons, 115-116.

9. David St. Clair, *Say You Love Satan* (New York: Dell Publishing Company, 1987), 221-222.
10. Vickie L. Dawkins and Nina Downey Higgins, *Devil Child* (New York: St. Martin's Press, 1989), 58.
11. Slayer, "Spill the Blood," from the album *South of Heaven.*
12. Information compiled from the annual survey conducted by the University of Michigan's Institute for Social Research, funded by the National Institute on Drug Abuse, as reported in *The Los Angeles Times,* January 25, 1991.
13. Some public satanic groups forbid drug use within the organization, and most witchcraft or pagan groups do also. (In fact, some pagan groups strictly forbid and talk against even private drug use.) However, drug use is a common indicator among most self-styled satanists and many solitary witches/pagans. Some of the same factors that make occult study and practice attractive, also make drug use attractive to some people.
14. Many contemporary ritualists distinguish their practices from sleight of hand or stage magic by calling them magic*k.*
15. See, for example, the stories of Ricky Kasso and Jimmy Troiano, who murdered a friend over a bad drug deal and who were heavily into satanism, chronicled in *Say You Love Satan* by David St. Clair.
16. St. Clair, 57.
17. Ronald Markman and Dominick Bosco, *Alone with the Devil* (New York: Bantam Books, 1989), 285.
18. Dawkins and Higgins, 164.
19. Kahaner, 90.
20. Kahaner, 85.
21. Lyons, 116.
22. Richard Cavendish, *The Black Arts* (New York: Capricorn Books, 1968), 1.
23. Anton Szandor LaVey, *The Satanic Bible* (New York: Avon Books, 1969), 33.
24. LaVey, 45.
25. Margot Adler, *Drawing Down the Moon* (Boston: Beacon Press, 1986), 399.
26. Adler, ,449.
27. T.M. Luhrmann, *Persuasions of the Witch's Craft* (Oxford, England: Basil Blackwell, Ltd., 1989), 103.
28. Lyons, 10.
29. Luhrmann, 337.
30. Cooper, 60-61.

TWO

*Satanism*

1. Cooper, 11-12.
2. Duncan Strauss, "Rock Singer Is Raising the Devil," *The Los Angeles Times,* August 14, 1986.

3. Quoted by Cooper, p. 13, from Jeff Lilley, "Evil in the Land," *Moody Monthly,* 89:7, 14-16.
4. Tom Strong, "Satanism Linked to Son Killing Mother and Himself," *The Detroit News,* January 13, 1988.
5. Isaiah 14:12; Luke 10:18.
6. Jude 6; 2 Peter 2:4.
7. Luke 10:18. Other names reflect his character, such as "accuser" (Revelation 12:10), "adversary" (1 Peter 5:8), "murderer" (John 8:44), "ruler of darkness" (Ephesians 6:12), and "wicked one" (Matthew 13:19).
8. Revelation 19:6.
9. Isaiah 57:15.
10. Matthew 25:41-46.
11. Sorcery (Exodus 7:12; 22:18), Witchcraft (Deuteronomy 18:10), Spiritism and Necromancy (Deuteronomy 18:11), Divination (Deuteronomy 18:14), Astrology (Isaiah 47:12-13).
12. Acts 19:18-20.
13. John 8:44.
14. Cavendish, 291.
15. Zoroastrianism was one of the most prominent, and through the teachings of the prophet Zoroaster ethical dualism spread to most of the known world by the early Middle Ages (Lyons, 20-21).
16. Lyons, 34.
17. Aleister Crowley's motto is an expanded version, "Do what thou Wilt shall be the whole of the Law; Love is the Law, Love under Will."
18. Quoted from Rabelais by Geoffrey Ashe, *Do What You Will: A History of Anti-Morality* (London: W.H. Allen, 1974), 20.
19. Ashe, 48.
20. For further information on the history of satanism, see Ashe's book and Lyons (pp. 16-83).
21. Lyons, 9.
22. Kahaner, 63.
23. LaVey, 25.
24. Cavendish, 338.
25. Cooper, 22.
26. Isaiah 5:20-21.
27. Cavendish, 289-290.
28. Shawn Carlson and Gerald Larue, *Satanism in America: How the Devil Got Much More than His Due* (El Cerrito, CA: Gaia Press, 1989), 16.
29. Lisa Levitt Ryckmana, "Troubled Youth Turn toward Satan, away from Life," *The Orange County Register,* February 28, 1988.
30. Cooper, 64.
31. Lyons, 61.
32. Lyons, 61.
33. LaVey, 110.
34. LaVey, 111.
35. Kenneth Grant, *Aleister Crowley and the Hidden God* (New York: Samuel Weiser, 1974), 5.

36. Lewis Spence, *An Encyclopaedia of Occultism* (Secaucus, NJ: Citadel Press, 1960), 377.
37. Dawkins and Higgins, 157.
38. Romans 12:1.
39. Cooper, 107-108.
40. LaVey, 87.
41. The Matamoros killings near Brownsville, Texas, were not done by the kind of occultists discussed in this book, and drug dealing was an integral part of the group and its activities.
42. Cooper, 109.
43. Lyons, 177.

THREE

## Witchcraft

1. Dick Roraback, "Pomona College Witch Studying Wicca Ways" in *The Los Angeles Times,* July 9, 1986.
2. As we stated in Chapter One, we use the terms *witch* and *pagan* or *neo-pagan* rather interchangeably to refer to a contemporary practitioner of ritual, polytheistic nature religion. The use of witch in a contemporary sense is not meant to be prejudicial.
3. A good introduction to the various ways "witchcraft" is used is contained in the *Encyclopaedia Britannica* (Chicago: William Benton, Publisher, 1978) 19:895-900.
4. Hosea 4:12.
5. R. Laird Harris, Gleason L. Archer, Jr., and Bruce K. Waltke, eds. *Theological Wordbook of the Old Testament* (Chicago: Moody Press, 1980) II:2044. Also Lawrence O. Richards, *Expository Dictionary of Bible Words* (Grand Rapids, MI: Zondervan Publishing House, 1985), 232.
6. Deuteronomy 18:9-14.
7. Genesis 41:8; Ezekiel 13:6-7. For further language information on the Hebrew and Greek equivalents for *magic,* see Richards, pp. 424-426; Harrison, Archer, and Waltke I:1051 and II:685; and Johannes P. Louw and Eugene A. Nida, eds. *Greek-English Lexicon of the New Testament* (New York: United Bible Societies, 1988) 1:545, 760.
8. Isaiah 2:6.
9. Deuteronomy 13:1-3; 18:9-14; 18:20-22; Jeremiah 14:14; Micah 5:12; and Galatians 5:20.
10. Galatians 5:20 cf. Acts 19:18-20. See Richards, pp. 424-426 and W.E. Vine, *Expository Dictionary of New Testament Words* (Old Tappan, NJ: Fleming H. Revell Company, 1940) IV:51-52.
11. Acts 17:24-31.
12. *Encyclopaedia Britannica,* 19:898.
13. Raymond Buckland, *Buckland's Complete Book of Witchcraft* (St. Paul, MN: Llewellyn Publications, 1990), 5.
14. *Encyclopaedia Britannica,* 19:899. Raymond Buckland, the "father" of contemporary American witchcraft, adds, "Wicca was by no means as far-reaching and widespread as Murray suggested (nor was there proof of a direct, unbroken line of descent from the cavepeople), but

there can be no doubt that it did exist as an indubitable religious cult, if sporadic as to time and place." Buckland, 6.

15. Roraback.

16. Peter Haining, *The Anatomy of Witchcraft* (London: Souvenir Press Ltd., 1972), 9.

17. *What Is Wicca?* (Blue Mounds, WI: Our Lady of the Woods, n.d.).

18. For discussion of four inadequate definitions of the term *witch*, see Elliot Rose, *Razor for a Goat* (Toronto: University of Toronto Press, 1962), 8-16.

19. Adler, ix.

20. Adler, vii.

21. Adler, viii.

22. Animism sees a divine life force within all living things.

23. Adler, 4.

24. There are hundreds of independent groups and traditions of witches or pagans, including Alexandrian Wicca, American Celtic Wicca, Church of the Crescent Moon, Frosts' Wicca, Gardnerian Wicca, The Aquarian Tabernacle Church, Arachne, Church of the Eternal Source, The Council of Isis Community, The Feminist Spiritual Community, Grove of the Unicorn, Pagan/Occult/Witchcraft Special Interest Group of Mensa, Pagans for Peace, and Women in Constant Creative Action. Expanded listings and descriptions are in Buckland, 229-232 and Adler, 510-544.

25. Adopted by the Council of American Witches. *Principles of Wiccan Belief* (Ukiah, CA: Green Egg, 1974).

26. *Principles of Wiccan Belief.*

27. Buckland, 13.

28. They usually also borrow terminology and sometimes practices from other occult disciplines, including satanism, and use it in their own peculiar ways.

29. This is discussed at more length in Chapter Eight, "Rescue Your Child from Satan."

30. "Common Themes of Neo-Pagan Religious Orientation" in *Green Egg,* IV:43.

31. Ephesians 5:23-32.

32. Isaiah 43:10 is one of many verses expressing that there is only one true God.

33. John 14:6.

34. Ephesians 5:25.

35. Genesis 1:28; 2:15-25.

36. John 3:16.

37. *Principles,* number 8.

38. Ecclesiastes 12:9-10.

## FOUR

### *Is Your Child Involved in the Occult?*

1. Kahaner, 184-185.

2. Markman and Bosco, 161-196.

3. Lyons, 111.
4. Lyons, 172.
5. Cooper, 91.
6. Cooper, 89.
7. Cooper, 54.
8. LaVey, 34.
9. LaVey, 149.
10. LaVey, 30.
11. LaVey, 30.
12. LaVey, 94.
13. LaVey, 25.
14. LaVey, 51.
15. Kahaner, 136.
16. LaVey, 25.
17. LaVey, 33.
18. Hebrews 10:30.
19. LaVey, 20.
20. LaVey, 21.
21. Some ancient manuscripts of the passage read "616" instead of "666."
22. LaVey, 25.
23. Anton Szandor LaVey, *The Satanic Rituals* (New York: Avon Books, 1972).
24. Heinrich Institoris, *Malleus Maleficarum* (New York: B. Blom, 1970).
25. Aleister Crowley, *777.* n.c.: O.T.O., n.d.
26. Aleister Crowley, *Gems from the Equinox* (New York: Falcon Press, n.d.).
27. John Symonds and Kenneth Grant, eds., *The Magical Record of the Beast 666: The Diaries of Aleister Crowley (1914-1920)* (Quebec, Canada: Next Step Publications, 1972).
28. Aleister Crowley, *The Book of the Law* (Pasadena, CA: Church of Thelema, 1926).
29. Cavendish.
30. Henry Taylor Fowkes Rhodes, *The Satanic Mass* (Secaucus, NJ: Citadel Press, 1974).
31. Kahaner, 185.
32. Lyons, 101-102.
33. LaVey, *The Satanic Bible*, 96.
34. Isaiah 44:24; Colossians 1:15-17; Hebrews 3:4.
35. "Common Themes of Neo-Pagan Religious Orientation," *Green Egg*, IV:43 (November 1, 1971).
36. "Common Themes of Neo-Pagan Religious Orientation."
37. "Common Themes of Neo-Pagan Religious Orientation."
38. "Common Themes of Neo-Pagan Religious Orientation."
39. "Common Themes of Neo-Pagan Religious Orientation."
40. "Common Themes of Neo-Pagan Religious Orientation."
41. Spence, 240.
42. Starhawk, *The Spiral Dance: A Rebirth of the Ancient Religion of the Great Goddess* (San Francisco: Harper & Row, 1979).

43. Starhawk, *Dreaming in the Dark: Magic, Sex, and Politics* (Boston: Beacon Press, 1982).
44. Adler.
45. Donald Michael Kraig, *Modern Magick: Eleven Lessons in the High Magickal Arts* (St. Paul, MN: Llewellyn Publications, 1989).
46. Stewart Farrar, *What Witches Do: The Modern Coven Revealed* (New York: Coward, McCann & Geoghegan, 1971).
47. Stewart and Janet Farrar, *A Witches Bible Compleat* (New York: Magickal Childe Publishing, Inc., 1981, 1984).
48. Francis King, *Modern Ritual Magic: The Rise of Western Occultism* (Dorset, England: Prism Press, 1989).
49. Buckland.
50. Zephr Starwater, "Witchcraft," *What Are Paganism and Witchcraft?* (San Jose, CA: Pagan Occult Special Interest Group of Mensa, n.d.), 2.

## FIVE
### The Media Connection

1. Clifford Linedecker, *Night Stalker* (New York: St. Martin's Press, 1991), 274-276.
2. "Metal" music includes heavy metal, thrash metal, death metal, and other variations. To avoid confusion we refer to all of these varieties by the single generic term "metal."
3. Cooper, 91.
4. Cooper, 60-61.
5. Alice Cooper interviewed in *The Decline of Western Civilization Part II: The Metal Years* video, New Line Cinema Corporation, 1988.
6. Ozzy Osbourne.
7. The band is named Helloween, not Halloween.
8. The band is Megadeth, not Megadeath.
9. A demon having sex with a woman.
10. A demon having sex with a man.
11. Sexual activity with the dead.
12. Member of a band's road crew.
13. Patrick Goldstein, "Bytches Producer Has a Labeling Problem," *The Los Angeles Times*, March 24, 1991.
14. Katherine Ludwig, "Suicidal Tendencies' Mike Muir: Sometimes You Fight with Your Mind," *Metal Maniacs*, June 1991, 17.
15. Alice Cooper.
16. Alice Cooper.
17. Alice Cooper.
18. An Oliver Stone film, *The Doors*. Starring Val Kilmer and Meg Ryan. Mario Kassar presents a Sasha Harrari/Bill Graham Films/Imagine Entertainment production of an Oliver Stone Film, a Tri-Star release, 1991.
19. Alice Cooper.
20. Katherine Ludwig, "Megadeth: Just Plain, Old, Nice Dave," *Metal*

*Maniacs,* June 1991, 25.

21. Katherine Ludwig, "Iron Maiden: An Amsterdam Experience," *Metal Maniacs,* June 1991, 33.

22. LaVey, *The Satanic Bible,* 33.

23. Katherine Ludwig, "Sepultura: Arise in the Studio," *Metal Maniacs,* June 1991, 11.

24. Lyons, 172.

25. Cooper, 83.

26. Lyons, 170.

27. *Magill's Survey of Cinema,* on-line computer search service, 1991.

28. Romans 1:18-32.

29. Associated Press, Boston, November 21, 1987.

30. Steve Eddy. "Crimes Rooted in Devil Worship Rising in County." *The Orange County Register,* September 28, 1986.

31. Co-produced by Ron Howard, an independent movie released by Universal Pictures.

32. A Caribbean amalgamation of Roman Catholics and Nigerian Yoruba tribe religion.

33. Somewhat similar to Santeria, but more purely African society, used primarily for destructive purposes in this country and the Caribbean.

34. Michael Medved, "Tarnished Images on the Silver Screen," *The Orange County Register,* March 24, 1991.

35. Medved.

36. Medved.

37. Cooper, 83.

38. John Fulce, *Seduction of the Innocent Revisited* (Lafayette, LA: Huntington House Publishers, 1990), 47.

## SIX
## *Occult Crime*

1. Cooper, 79-80.

2. Wade Davis' *The Serpent and the Rainbow* (New York, Simon and Schuster, 1985) deals extensively with voodun, and Migene Gonzalez-Wippler's *Santeria, the Religion: A Legacy of Faith, Rites, and Magic* (New York: Harmony Books, 1989) comprehensively examines santeria.

3. LaVey, 51.

4. Myrna Oliver, "Father Gets Custody of Girl Living in House of 'Witches,'" *The Los Angeles Times,* October 30, 1982.

5. Oliver.

6. This case has been discussed in various books and reports, including Cooper, 117-121, and Lyons, 141-143, 153, 148. At the date of this writing there is no comprehensive, responsible book dealing with the case.

7. Lyons, 151.

8. Lyons, 152.

9. Lyons, 4, and Linedecker, 96-97.

10. Michelle Smith and Lawrence Pazder, *Michelle Remembers* (New York: Congdon & Lattes, Inc., 1980).

11. Lauren Stratford, *Satan's Underground* (Eugene, OR: Harvest House Publishers, 1988).

12. Cooper, 89.

13. Cooper, 91.

14. Lyons, 87.

15. "Sex Slave Keeper Receives 104 Years." Associated Press, November 23, 1985.

16. Lyons, 144.

17. Gretchen and Bob Passantino and Jon Trott, "Satan's Sideshow," *Cornerstone,* December 1989, 18:90.

18. Including *The Wall Street Journal, Christianity Today,* and *The Orange County Register.* Our article won a journalism award from the Free Press Association and first place in reporting from the Evangelical Press Association.

19. Our conclusions were based on independent evidence, not family testimonies.

20. Of course, innocent people deny guilt, also.

21. Sonni Efron, "Witness Denies Defense Allegation in Cult Case," *The Los Angeles Times,* April 2, 1991.

22. Such as headache, sore throat, itchy palms, and queasiness. Testifying against Maas, Greg, ex-husband of one sister, said that Maas suggested Greg had been sexually abused because he was sniffling during a therapy session. "I told him I had a cold," Greg testified (Pat Brennan, "OC Mother Denies Pair's Satanic-Abuse Claims," *The Los Angeles Times,* April 4, 1991).

23. Lyons, 159.

24. Carlson and Larue, 96-97. Carlson and Larue go on to discuss the other statistical absurdities of the common satanic conspiracy theory, 98-101.

25. Cooper, 119-120.

26. Cooper, 19.

27. Markman and Bosco, 205.

28. Markman and Bosco, 216.

29. "Boyer Retrial," *The Los Angeles Times,* February 11, 1991.

30. "Black Sect Leader Charged with Directing 14 Slayings," *The Los Angeles Times,* November 8, 1990.

31. "Black Sect Leader Charged with Directing 14 Slayings."

32. Lyons, 96.

33. Lyons, 97.

34. Jerry Hicks, "Psychologist Says Murder Suspect Fit for Trial, Though Schizophrenic," *The Los Angeles Times,* July 18, 1986.

35. Hicks.

36. Hicks.

37. "Man Convicted in Severed Legs Murder Case," *Associated Press,* September 20, 1987.

38. Lyons, 96.
39. "Jury Convicts Cultist of Satanic Murder," *The Atlanta Journal-Constitution*, March 14, 1981.
40. Robert Popp, "Ex-Waiter Found Guilty in Satanic S.F. Murder," *San Francisco Chronicle*, March 15, 1988.
41. Lyons, 95-96.
42. Lyons, 96.
43. Maury Terry, *The Ultimate Evil* (New York: Bantam Books, 1987).
44. Arthur Lyons critiques Terry's theory in *Satan Wants You*, 92-94.
45. Linedecker, 141-142.
46. Linedecker, 287.
47. Jim Schutze, *Cauldron of Blood: The Matamoros Cult Killings* (New York: Avon Books, 1989).
48. The most complete story of this tragedy is recounted in *Say You Love Satan* by David St. Clair.
49. Chris Wood, "Suicide and Satanism," *Maclean's Magazine*, March 30, 1987.
50. Wood.
51. Lisa Levitt Ryckmana, "Troubled Youths Turn toward Satan, away from Life," *The Orange County Register*, February 28, 1988.
52. Linedecker, 97.
53. Linedecker, 100.
54. Lyons, 162-163.
55. Lyons, 171.
56. Linedecker, 98.
57. Lyons, 98.
58. Cooper (quoting the *Miami Herald*, February 10, 1989), 84.
59. Forrest S. Clark, "Officials: Cemetery Vandals Influenced by 'Heavy Metal,'" *The Courier-News*, Sommerville, New Jersey, December 7, 1985.
60. Robert D. Hicks, "Police Pursuit of Crime," *Skeptical Inquirer*, 14:277.
61. Andrew Sheridan, "Devil Worshippers Go on Rampage in Building," *The Los Angeles Tribune*, June 21, 1987.
62. Steve Eddy, "Crimes Rooted in Devil Worship Rising in County," *The Orange County Register*, September 28, 1986.
63. Eddy.
64. Ryckman, also Lyons, 11-12.
65. Lyons, 101.
66. Tom Strong, "Satanism Linked to Son Killing Mother and Himself," *The Detroit News*, January 13, 1988.
67. Eddy.
68. Eddy.
69. Eddy.
70. Cooper, 11-12.
71. Sellers' case has been discussed in numerous books and articles. The most complete treatment is by Vickie L. Dawkins and Nina Downey Higgins, *Devil Child*. Sean gives his new Christian perspective on the evils of teenage involvement in contemporary satanism in his own

book, *Web of Darkness* (Tulsa, OK: Victory House Publishers, 1990).

72. Tamara Jones, "Dead Pets to a Human Sacrifice," *The Los Angeles Times*, October 19, 1988 and "Fun Killers' Now Paying Devil's Dues," October 20, 1988.

73. Kahaner, 184-185.

### SEVEN
### *Did I Go Wrong?*

1. Cooper, 53.

### EIGHT
### *Rescue Your Child from Satan*

1. Statistics reported in *Choices Are Not Child's Play: Helping Your Kids Make Wise Decisions* by Pat Holt and Grace Ketterman (Wheaton, IL: Harold Shaw Publishers, 1990), 9-11.

2. after accidents.

3. Statistics from *Suicide: The Signs and Solutions* by Finley H. Sizemore (Wheaton, IL: Victor Books, 1988), 8-9.

4. 1 Timothy 2:5-6.

5. Ephesians 6:4.

6. Hebrews 12:5-7.

7. Bruce Narramore, *Parenting with Love and Limits* (Grand Rapids, MI: Zondervan Publishing Company, 1979).

8. Holt and Ketterman.

9. D. James Kennedy, *Your Prodigal Child* (Nashville, TN: Thomas Nelson Publishers, 1988).

10. James Dobson, *The Strong-Willed Child* (Wheaton, IL: Tyndale House Publishers, 1978).

11. John 14:6.

12. John 14:27.

13. Philippians 4:6-9.

14. Galatians 3:21b-22.

15. Romans 3:23.

16. Romans 7:24.

17. 1 Timothy 2:5.

18. Acts 20:28.

19. Romans 3:21-23.

20. Some of the better contemporary translations include the New International Version, the New American Standard Version, and the Jerusalem Bible. The Living Bible is not a translation, but a paraphrase (a person's simple interpretation), and so is not as accurate, but it is particularly helpful for those who have no previous understanding of the Bible. These Bibles are available in any Christian bookstore and often in secular bookstores as well.

21. Charles Colson, *Loving God* (Grand Rapids, MI: Zondervan Publishing Company, 1983).

22. Walter Martin, *Essential Christianity* (Ventura, CA: Gospel Light Publications, 1980).
23. J.I. Packer, *Knowing God* (Downers Grove, IL: InterVarsity Press, 1973).
24. J.I. Packer, *I Want to Be a Christian* (Wheaton, IL: Tyndale House Publishers, 1977).
25. Fran and Jill Sciacca, *Lifelines: Getting a Hold on Life* (Minneapolis, MN: World Wide Publications, 1987). This is a topical series of booklets designed specifically for teens. A few of the titles include *Desperately Seeking Perfect Family, Caution: Contents under Pressure, Some Things Are Never Discounted,* and *Does Anyone Else Feel This Way?*
26. Holt and Ketterman, 30.
27. Em Griffin, *The Mind Changers* (Wheaton, IL: Tyndale House Publishers, 1976), 170.
28. As parents we have the prerogative of revealing only their good points in print.

## NINE
### Answers to Questions

1. Matthew 4:24.
2. Mark 1:32.
3. Matthew 8:28-34; 9:32-33; Matthew 12:22-26; Matthew 15:22-28; Matthew 17:14-21; Mark 1:23-26; and Mark 16:9.
4. Luke 10:17-19.
5. Matthew 12:24-30.
6. Ezekiel 1:15.
7. John 8:44; 1 John 3:8; etc.
8. Isaiah 14:15; Luke 10:18.
9. Matthew 8:28-29; Matthew 25:41; Revelation 20:10.
10. "lawlessness"
11. Galatians 5:19-21.
12. Malachi Martin, *Hostage to the Devil* (New York: Bantam Books, 1976).
13. Romans 5:9-11.
14. Romans 10:9-10.
15. Romans 8:9.
16. Matthew 12:31, 32; John 8:24.
17. James 4:7-8, 10.
18. Arthur Lyons' opinion is that "discounting distortions due to hype and hysteria, and a tradition by neo-Satanic churches of inflating membership figures for publicity purposes, I would estimate the total number of Satanists of all types, worldwide, to be no more than five thousand." *Satan Wants You,* 14.
19. Cooper, 109.
20. Spring, 1991.
21. See, for example, our "Satan's Sideshow" (*Cornerstone,* December 1988) or "Satanic Cult 'Survivor' Stories" by Jeffrey S. Victor (*Skeptical Inquirer,* 15:3:274-280).

22. 1 John 4:4.
23. The dynamics of reconciling the reality of Christianity with the fantasy of fiction is a good subject for discussion and involves both theology and literary criticism. C.S. Lewis discusses this at length in several essays [see, for example, Leland Ryken, *Reading between the Lines* (Westchester, IL: Crossway Books, 1990), or Walter Hooper, ed., *C.S. Lewis: On Stories and Other Essays on Literature* (New York: Harcourt Brace Jovanovich, Publishers, 1982).
24. For suggestions of good children's literature, consult Elizabeth Wilson's *Books Children Love: A Guide to the Best Children's Literature* (Westchester, IL: Crossway Books, 1987).
25. James 5:16.
26. Frank and Jill Sciacca, *Cliques and Clones: A Bible Study for Young Adults on Peer Pressure* (Minneapolis, MN: World Wide Publications, 1987), 15.
27. Kathleen McCoy, "Help Your Child Beat Peer Pressure," *Reader's Digest*, May 1991, 67-70.
28. Summarized from Finley Sizemore, 82-86.
29. Good suggestions are in Fran and Jill Sciacca's, *Does Anyone Else Feel This Way?* (Minneapolis, MN: World Wide Publications, 1987), 55.
30. 1 Corinthians 3:11-15.
31. Acts 17:26.
32. 2 Corinthians 10:5.
33. Sciacca, 46.
34. Cooper, 135.
35. 1 Thessalonians 5:21-22.
36. Isaiah 8:19-22.

# Glossary of Common Terms
*(See chapter four for occult symbols and tools)*

**666**
"The Mark of the Beast" mentioned in the cryptic book of Revelation (Revelation 13:18). Used symbolically by satanists as identification with the worst in anti-Christianity.

**adept**
One skilled in the practice of magic.

**adult survivor**
Commonly used to refer to someone who claims to have been ritually abused as a child (sometimes into adulthood) and who is now adult. Most adult survivors come to their belief that they were ritually abused through therapy aimed at recovering "repressed memories." Many adult survivors claim to be suffering from Multiple Personality Disorder (MPD).

**Aganyú**
A Santería god, associated with the volcano, the father of the most popular Santería god, Changó.

**agogó**
In Santería, a bell used in ritual.

**air dagger**
Used primarily in witchcraft, refers to a short dagger or knife used to make magical motions in the air, especially to open or close a magic circle.

**alchemy**
The precursor of chemistry, focused on working with the elements and minerals, especially in an attempt to change base metals into gold. Used figuratively to mean personal enlightenment.

**Alafin**
Alternate name of the most popular Santería god, Changó.

**All Hallow's Eve**
Halloween, the day (evening) before "All Saints' Day" (November 1), which corresponds to the pagan holiday of Samhain, the "day of the dead" midway between the Fall Equinox and Winter Solstice.

**All Saints' Day**
November 1, in the Christian calendar, a celebration remembering all those Christians who suffered and died for their faith (martyrs), or who were specially honored for their service in the name of Christ. All Saints' Day is celebrated on the pagan holiday of the dead (see All Hallow's Eve).

**altar**
Any flat surface used for religious rites and for any arrangement of ritual tools or other items.

**amulet**
Any object said to possess power to bring good luck or to ward against bad luck.

**animism**
The belief that all things (animate or inanimate) have spirits or souls within them.

**ankh**
An Egyptian heiroglyphic representing life, fertility, or immortality.

**anti-morality**
Can refer to a particular popular diversion among some upper class men in Europe and the British Isles at various times during the seventeenth and eighteenth centuries. The movement was characterized by a disdain for authority, indulgence in sex, alcohol, gambling, and gluttony, and a rejection of Christianity.

**antichrist**
1 John in the Bible describes an "antichrist" as anyone who denies that Jesus is the Christ, in other words, anyone who denies the Christian faith. From other allusions to similar figures in other Scriptures, some biblical interpreters say there will be one great Anti-Christ immediately before the Second Coming who will epitomize anti-Christianity and enforce his blasphemy throughout the world.

**Anton Szandor LaVey**
The founder of the Church of Satan.

**apocalyptic**
A specialized kind of literature (such as Daniel or Revelation) concerned with revelations of unknown future events.

**arcane**
Pertaining to what is secret, esoteric, or mysterious.

**Association for Research and Enlightenment**
Cult founded by Edgar Cayce, precursor to the New Age cults, conducts "research" supportive of reincarnation and "spiritual" healing.

**Astarte**
Popular in goddess worship, the Phoenician goddess of love, transformed in the kabalah as the male demon Ashtorath.

**astral**
Of or pertaining to the immaterial world or alternate reality in which magic takes place or is practiced.

**astral projection**
"Soul travel," or the supposed ability to extend one's person or consciousness past the limits of the physical body.

**astrology**
Divination or foretelling based on a belief in the deterministic relation between earthly events and the heavens (stars and planets).

**athamé**
In witchcraft or magic, the consecrated ceremonial knife used in rituals.

**August Eve**
July 31, called Lughnasadh, one of the four great festivals celebrated by witches.

**aura**
A alleged biomagnetic field said to surround each living thing.

**babalawo**
A high priest of Santería.

**babalocha**
A Santería santero who has initiated other santeros.

**backward masking**
In the recording industry, the practice of laying one track of a record or CD backward. Usually done as a promotional gimmick; said by some to be a method of passing evil or harmful ideas to innocent listeners through their subconscious.

**Baphomet**
The goat-headed god of sexual indulgence and physical gratification; the trump card in the Tarot deck; common symbol of satanism.

**Beltane**
One of the major Celtic festivals celebrated on May Day (May 1), occurring between the Spring Equinox and the Summer Solstice, named after the sun god of flocks and the underworld. The day before is called Walpurgisnacht and is said to be when the underworld and the world of the living can communicate freely.

**bind**
In magic, to restrain through the use of magic.

**black book**
In witchcraft, a witch's personal workbook, also called the Book of Shadows.

**black magic**
Destructive magic, or that magic directed against someone else. While

some people try to distinguish qualitatively between black magic and white magic, there is no qualitative difference. Both attempt to shape reality through the power of the will, usually through manipulation of supposed "psychic" powers.

### Black Mass
A reversal and profaning of the Roman Catholic mass, the Black Mass was once a popular feature of satanism and anti-morality, but is less popular now since so many people are unfamiliar with Christian ritual.

### blasphemer
Someone who curses, denounces, or profanes God.

### blood ritual
A ritual involving sacrifice; typically satanic, not witchcraft (although some self-styled occultists may do blood rituals and call themselves witches).

### Book of Shadows
The "black book" of a witch, the collection of spells, rituals, and journaled experiences, unique to each witch, usually including traditions received from other witches.

### botánica
Santería religious supply store.

### brujeria
In Santería; witchcraft, the casting of spells.

### Candomblé
The Brazilian version of Santería.

### cantrip
In magic, a palindromic spell or charm (it reads the same forward or backward).

### cartomancy
Divination through the use of cards, especially the Tarot deck.

### Cernunnos
The ancient Celtic version of the "horned god," equal to the collective spirit of the animal world.

### Changó
The most popular deity of Santería, associated with fire, thunder, and lightning.

### chalice
A sacred ceremonial cup, used in witchcraft to symbolize the element of water, and in satanism for the desecrated communion drink.

### channeling
Mediumship, or "channeling" the supposed spirit of a higher life form, someone who has died, or a spiritual master.

**charm**
Magical words or an object associated with magical power.

**Church of Satan**
Founded by Anton Szandor LaVey in San Francisco (1966), the archetype of the contemporary public satanism. LaVey does not believe in a personal devil or in religious power as such, but believes that worship of the self is the highest human goal.

**cingulum**
In witchcraft, the magical cord or belt used in ritual for binding, measuring, or counting.

**cone of power**
In witchcraft, the collective psychic energy of the ritual group, generated in ritual and used to accomplish magic outside the ritual circle.

**coven**
Common term to describe a group of witches who share a common witchcraft tradition, work magic and worship ritually together. Usually the group numbers thirteen or less.

**coven sword**
The ritual sword used symbolically in a particular coven's rituals.

**Craft, the**
Common designation of contemporary witchcraft.

**Crowley, Aleister**
Forerunner of much of contemporary magical thought, especially of witchcraft and satanism. He articulated the most comprehensive system of ceremonial magic before or since. Crowley (1875-1947) called himself "the Great Beast (666)" and promoted a magical system of drug and sexual indulgence, and enjoyed being called "the wickedest man in the world."

**cryptic**
Coded, symbolic, or hidden communication.

**crystal ball**
Often used in magic as a method of divination.

**cuchillo**
In Santería, the sacrificial knife used in sacrifice rituals.

**curse**
The use of magic to harm someone or something.

**deity statue**
Often used in witchcraft, the statue representing the main god of the individual witch or coven's tradition, usually kept on the consecrated altar.

**demon**
Evil spirits, created as angels by God but who fell through their personal sin.

**demon possession**
Or demonization, or to be demonized: to be controlled against one's will by a demon.

**demonology**
Study concerning demons.

**devil**
Comes from the Sanskrit meaning "little god," and used in a Christian context to refer to a demon or, as in "the Devil," to Satan.

**Diana**
The most widely worshiped deity of contemporary witchcraft, the Roman goddess of the moon and the hunt.

**divination**
Discerning of hidden, past, or future knowledge or events through magic.

**drawing down the moon**
In witchcraft, the ritual of invoking the moon goddess, one of the most important ceremonies for those groups dedicated to the moon goddess. Also the name of a definitive work on contemporary witchcraft by Margot Adler.

**druid**
An ancient Celtic priest, now used to refer to any witch worshiping in a reconstructed magical tradition associated with ancient druidism.

**Dungeons and Dragons**
A fantasy role-playing game using characters patterned after a myriad of gods, goddesses, and mythological figures; the game requires careful study, intelligence, and a dedication to the game. The game and others like it have been accused of compelling teenagers to suicide or other violence. While such a connection has not been proven, the destructive, magical orientation of the game appeals to teenagers vulnerable in that area of their lives.

**elegun Changó**
A priest of the most popular Santería god, Changó.

**epe**
A Santería curse.

**equinox, fall**
The autumn date when the amounts of light and darkness in one twenty-four hour period are approximately the same (caused by the sun crossing the celestial equator). Important holiday in both witchcraft and satanism.

**equinox, spring**
The spring date when the amounts of light and darkness in one twenty-

four hour period are approximately the same (caused by the sun crossing the celestial equator. Important holiday in both witchcraft and satanism.

**esbat**
A full-moon meeting of a witches' coven.

**evocation**
The magic rite of calling something out from within.

**exorcism**
The Christian ritual of releasing a demonized person from demonic control.

**familiar**
An animal with whom the magical practitioner feels a psychic affinity.

**fantasy role-playing game**
Any number of games, most patterned after Dungeons and Dragons, with an elaborate mythological and/or supernatural world, a heavy dependence on magic and ritual, and requiring intelligence, commitment, and study to play successfully.

**FFF**
Coded form of the number of "the Beast" of Revelation 13 (666). F is the sixth letter of the alphabet.

**fortune teller**
One who practices divination on behalf of a client for a fee, donation, or reward.

**Gaea**
The Greek goddess of the earth, "Mother Earth." In contemporary witchcraft, this term refers to the living planet, our biosphere, as a totality of physical, emotional, and spiritual being. Gaea is the primary deity of most neo-pagans.

**Gaia**
Alternate spelling of Gaea.

**Gardner, Gerald**
The "father" of contemporary witchcraft (1884-1964), whose book *Witchcraft Today* introduced the ideas and practices of contemporary witchcraft to the world. Gardnerian Wicca, the form of witchcraft he popularized, is still one of the most popular forms of witchcraft.

**Goat of Mendes**
Also called Baphomet, the goat-headed god of witchcraft and satanism, originated by the Knights Templar. Described and used differently in witchcraft than in satanism.

**God**
In witchcraft, the male aspect of divine or spiritual reality; the male aspect of life; usually the consort of the goddess in ritual worship. In satanism, Satan, as a being to be worshiped; the Christian God, as a being

to be blasphemed. In Christianity, the God of the Bible, eternal, omnipotent, triune, etc.

### Goddess
In witchcraft, the feminine aspect of divine or spiritual reality; the feminine aspect of life; the object of worship; called by various names according to the particular witchcraft tradition.

### Great Rite
In witchcraft, ritual sex within the magic circle; carefully stylized and representative of eternal life, fertility, and the union between male and female.

### grimoire
A collection of one's spells, traditions, rituals, and thoughts; also called "the black book" or the Book of Shadows.

### Halloween
All Hallow's Eve, the day before All Saints' Day. Corresponds to the pagan holiday of Samhain, the "day of the dead" midway between the Fall Equinox and Winter Solstice.

### head banging
A common practice among some metal music fans, consisting of banging one's head against the wall, floor, stage, or speaker in time to the music.

### heavy metal
A form of rock music characterized by discordant, high decibel, innovative, and chaotic music with lyrics celebrating decadence, sexual indulgence, drug use, and self gratification.

### heresy
Literally, a teaching or belief that contradicts what is accepted. A heresy against Christianity, for example, would be a teaching or belief that contradicts the clear teaching of the Bible, sustained by the Christian Church through the centuries.

### Hoodoo
A black southern American form of voodoo.

### horoscope
A chart of the positions of the planets and stars of the zodiac, relative to a particular time and place, especially of a person's birth. The horoscope assumes a spiritual or psychic link between the heavens and earthly life as well as a physical link.

### I Ching
A Chinese form of divination using magical sticks.

### idols
According to Christianity, any physical representation of a false god. No physical representation is possible of the Christian God, who is infinite and omnipresent.

**incantation**
A rhyming or repetitive chant used for the purpose of casting a magical spell.

**incubus**
A spirit having intercourse with a woman.

**invoke**
To magically call something in (usually to the ritual circle) from without.

**Isis**
The chief Egyptian goddess, a popular deity in contemporary witchcraft; represents the "Queen of Heaven."

**kabalah**
An ancient occult mystical system of interpretation with medieval Jewish roots; widely used in witchcraft, satanism, and other forms of occultism.

**knot magic**
A form of magic using the cord or cingulum for tying and untying knots; representing binding, loosing, and measuring; especially for "storing" magical power.

**Lammas Day**
A witchcraft and satanic summer holiday corresponding to Lughnasadh.

**Left-Hand Path**
Destructive occultism, satanism, a distinction made by "white magic" practitioners, who practice magic only for healing or help rather than for cursing or hurting.

**Lucifer**
Literally, "light-bearer," Satan's name before he fell through personal sin. Used sometimes by witches and more often by satanists to refer to the "enlightenment" possible through throwing off the oppressive, narrow-minded, closed world view of Christianity.

**Lucumi**
The designation of the Yoruba people after they had been taken to Cuba in slavery.

**Lughnasadh**
August 1, a "Grand Sabbat," one of the four great feast days in witchcraft.

**Macumba**
A Brazilian spiritism.

**magic**
Often spelled "magick" by its practitioners to distinguish it from stage magic or sleight of hand; the supposed ability to use rituals, spells, thoughts, and spiritual power to affect the material world.

**magick**
Alternate spelling of magic; used by some occultists to distinguish it from stage magic, or sleight of hand.

**magic circle**
In witchcraft, the psychic circle corresponding in plane dimensions to the circle drawn on the ground or floor; used as a focus of power to allow communication or passage through different dimensions.

**matricide**
The murder of one's mother.

**May Eve**
In witchcraft, the day immediately preceding May Day, or Beltane.

**medium**
One who claims the ability to act as a physical go-between for communication or visitation from the pyschic or spiritual realm, usually by entering a trance and allowing another "entity" to use the medium's body (called trance channeling in New Age thought).

**monotheism**
Belief in only one true God. Judaism, Islam, and Christianity are the three major monotheistic world religions.

**MPD**
Multiple Personality Disorder.

**multiple personality disorder**
A psychiatric designation referring to the rare and controversial phenomenon wherein an individual copes with a traumatic event or experience by "splitting" or "fragmenting" corresponding "personalities" (or parts of personalities) while the "core" personality represses the traumatic memory.

**myth**
A traditional story (whether true or not) that appeals to the values or worldview of a group by embodying its cultural ideals, deep emotions, and convictions.

**necromancy**
Divination associated with the dead; supposed communication with the dead.

**necrophilia**
Having sexual intercourse with a corpse.

**Nema Natas**
"Satan Amen" backward. Writing backward is one magical tool of satanism, as well as an elementary code.

**neo-pagan**
A worshipper of a pantheistic folk religion who does not descend culturally or ethnically from that religion's source, but who identifies his or her own worship of nature or Gaea with that particular tradition.

**New Age Movement**
A broad term covering a variety of individuals, groups, beliefs, and prac-

tices associated with commonly held ideas, usually including 1.) a coming New Age of peace and harmony accomplished by human spiritual development; 2.) karma and reincarnation; 3.) a magical worldview; 4.) a spiritual humanism, that is, man's potential is limitless because he is divine.

**nganga**
In Palo, the palero's cauldron.

**occult**
Literally, hidden or secret knowledge; usually refers to any of a number of magical, ritualized practices commonly associated with psychic phenomena and in opposition to historic Christianity and biblical revelation.

**Odin**
In witchcraft, popular male deity from the Norse tradition; popular patron deity of shamans and wizards.

**Oloddumare**
The Yoruba name of God.

**orisha**
A Yoruba deity syncretized with a Catholic saint in the religion of Santería.

**Ormelc, Feast of**
Also spelled Oimelc; in witchcraft, one of the eight annual festivals, celebrated on February 1 or 2; also called Candlemas.

**Ouija board**
Produced as a game by Parker Brothers, taken from a nineteenth-century form of ancient divination using an alphabet board and a "pointer" supposedly manipulated by psychic power to spell out psychic messages.

**pagan**
Originally used in a Christian context to refer to any religious person who is not Christian; more specifically refers to any pantheistic or polytheistic folk religion or people; currently used by contemporary witches as a descriptive way of explaining their worship of nature, and commitment to the sacredness of life.

**palero**
A Palo priest.

**Palo Mayombe**
A sect of Palo, based on the beliefs of the Kongo African tribe.

**Pan**
Greek god of untamed nature; popular among contemporary witches; often confused with the goat head symbol of satanism.

**pantheism**
Literally, "all is God;" the religious world view that sees all of reality (material or immaterial) as divine: God is everything, everything is God.

**patricide**
The murder of one's father.

**pentacle**
The five pointed star surrounded by a circle or ring.

**pentagram**
The five pointed star, a common symbol of witchcraft (with one point at the top) and satanism (with the one point at the bottom).

**phallic symbol**
A symbol of the penis, common in magic and ritual.

**polytheism**
Belief in more than one god or many gods.

**potion**
Any liquid herbal concoction used for healing or harming in conjunction with the practice of magic.

**precognition**
The supposed ability to "see" the future.

**psychic**
Broad term used to refer to anyone who claims psychic powers, or the ability to affect reality by non-physical means.

**Quimbanda**
Black magic in Macumba.

**reincarnation**
A belief assuming that one's life force, life principle, consciousness, or some other non-material part passess through a succession of lives, in conjunction with the working out of one's karma, or the debt of one's negative actions; usually reincarnation refers to a succession of human lives, while transmigration can include animal or even inanimate existences.

**rune**
Any magical alphabet and/or words or writings using such alphabets.

**sabbat**
One of the eight annual festivals of witchcraft and satanism; four correspond to the solstices and equinoxes; four (called Grand Sabbats) occur midway between the solstices and equinoxes.

**sado-masochism**
A complex of behavior between individuals who receive sexual pleasure or release either through giving or receiving pain.

**Samhain**
The most important witchcraft and satanist holiday, corresponding to the Christian All Saints' Day (November 1); the Celtic festival of the dead.

**Santería**
Cuban religion combining African Yoruba religion with Roman Catho-

licism. The polytheism of Yoruba religion is syncretized with the worship of Roman Catholic saints, a distortion of Catholic teaching on the saints.

**santero, santera**
Priest and priestess of Santería.

**Satan**
Hebrew for "Adversary," the angel Lucifer who rebelled against God and became the chief of the demons (other angels who sinned).

**satanism**
Any religious system incorporating the worship of Satan, whatever Satan is conceived to be (the self, self-indulgence, evil, evil principles, myth, demon, or deity).

**scrying**
Divination by gazing into a reflective or transparent surface such as a bowl of water, a mirror, or a crystal.

**Seal of Solomon**
The Star of David, two interlocking equilateral triangles, used in witchcraft and satanism, symbol of the Order of the Golden Dawn.

**seance**
A psychic experience in which a group attempts to talk with someone who has died through the use of a medium.

**Set, Temple of**
One of the public satanic churches, founded by Michael Aquino, who used to be an important member of the Church of Satan.

**sky clad**
Nudity for the purpose of a special witchcraft ritual.

**solstice, summer**
One of the eight great witchcraft and satanism festivals, occurs on June 21, corresponds to the Christian celebration of St. John's Day.

**solstice, winter**
One of the eight great witchcraft and satanism festivals, occurs on December 21, corresponds to the Christian celebration of Christmas.

**sorcery**
The manipulation of non-physical forces to affect the physical world or other people.

**spell**
The particular combination of magical practices and words to accomplish a specific work of magic.

**spiritism**
The practice of communicating with the dead, usually through the use of a "medium" or human go-between (in the New Age called a "channeler").

**subliminal message**
A visual or audio message indiscernible to the conscious mind, incorporated into a visible or audible message.

**succubus**
A spirit having intercourse with a man.

**superstition**
Used to refer either to a religious or magical belief held in the face of contrary evidence; or to a belief contrary to what is accepted within the group.

**talisman**
Like a charm or amulet, but manufactured, said to embody magical power, especially for good luck or protection.

**tarot**
The source of our modern playing cards, the Tarot Deck contains 78 cards illustrated with magical arcane symbolism. There are as many interpretations of the tarot as there are tarot readers. The cards are representative of the sum of all occult knowledge and are used in divination.

**thaumaturge**
The use of magic on people, places, or events outside the magician himself or herself.

**Theosophy**
An occult mystical religious sytem founded by Helena Blavatsky in the late 1800s by combining western occultism with Hindu or Sanskrit esotericism; fountainhead of ideas preceding the currently popular New Age Movement; headquartered in Wheaton, Illinois.

**trance channeling**
The New Age Movement form of mediumship.

**Tree of Life, The**
In the kabalic system, one of the most common interpretive forms of the magical kabalistic pattern of circles and lines; also used in witchcraft as the symbolic representation of the evolution of life forms.

**Umbanda**
The "white magic" aspect of Macumba.

**unholy kiss**
In satanism the kiss of allegience to Satan, usually done by kissing the buttocks of the figure representing Satan.

**urban myth**
A contemporary story in general circulation with the following characteristics: 1.) the story teller usually claims to have personal knowledge of the event ("It happened to my mother," "It happened in the town where my cousin lives," etc.); 2.) the story appears to be true, although incredible; 3.) the story validates a commonly held, but unverifiable belief; and 4). no evidence or documentation can be adduced to prove the belief.

**vampire**
In the occult genre, a dead person who comes in spirit or magical form to destroy living persons by drinking their blood.

**visualization**
The psychic process coupling mental images with magical power to manipulate reality.

**voodoo**
Properly called "voodun," the religion indigenous to Haiti, based on parts of several African tribes, including the Fon, Arada, and Yoruba. Voodun is inextricably entwined with magic.

**Walpurgisnacht**
A holiday in witchcraft and satanism, also called Beltane, the spring equinox (May Day).

**warlock**
Originally used to refer to a witch who betrayed fellow witches to the ecclesiastical authorities; erroneously used to refer to male witches (sometimes self-styled witches use the term themselves).

**white magic**
Constructive magic, or that magic directed in healing or helping. While some people try to distinguish qualitatively between black magic and white magic, there is no qualitative difference. Both attempt to shape reality through the power of the will, usually through manipulation of supposed "psychic" powers.

**Wicca**
The umbrella grouping of the majority of contemporary witches and witchcraft groups; "wicca" is said to mean "the Craft;" the most common traditions within Wicca are Gardnerians, Georgians, Alexandrians, Dianics, and smaller groups following Welsh, Druid, Norse, Celtic, etc. persuasions.

**Wiccan Rede**
The "motto" or "Golden Rule" of witchcraft; "An' it harm none, do what thou wilt."

**witch**
In contemporary usage, a person, male or female, a trained (sometimes self-taught) practitioner of magic who has a pantheistic worldview, coupled with polytheistic or animistic ritualism.

**witchcraft**
In contemporary usage, the practice of magic or shamanism from a European cultural context; a subgroup of paganism.

**wortcunning**
Herbal magical tradition or lore.

**yag-dirk**
In witchcraft, one of the ceremonial knives.

**yin and yang**
In Chinese Taoism, the divine dualism of existence.

**yoga**
In Hinduism, the exercise leading toward spiritual fulfillment; only some yogas involve physical exercise.

**Yoruba**
The seventeenth- and eighteenth-century African people from the area of present day Nigeria whose beliefs were incorporated into Santería, Candomblé, and Shango.

**zodiac**
The complex elliptical plane of the twelve astrological constellations through which pass the sun, moon, and planets as observed from the earth; said to exert a spiritual as well as a physical force on earthly events.

**Zoroastrianism**
The dualistic religion founded by Zoroaster out of ancient Persian polytheism; the zoroastrian sacred writings are used by many occultists today.

# Index